PENGUIN BOOKS

Round the Bend

Jeremy Clarkson began his writing career on the *Rotherham Advertiser*. Since then he has written for the *Sun*, the *Sunday Times*, the *Rochdale Observer*, the *Wolverhampton Express & Star*, all of the Associated Kent Newspapers and *Lincolnshire Life*. Today he is the tallest person working in British television.

Round the Bend

JEREMY CLARKSON

PENGUIN BOOKS

PENGUIN BOOKS

Published by the Penguin Group
Penguin Books Ltd, 80 Strand, London WC2R 0RL, England
Penguin Group (USA) Inc., 375 Hudson Street, New York, New York 10014, USA
Penguin Group (Canada), 90 Eglinton Avenue East, Suite 700, Toronto, Ontario, Canada M4P 2Y3
(a division of Pearson Penguin Canada Inc.)
Penguin Ireland, 25 St Stephen's Green, Dublin 2, Ireland
(a division of Penguin Books Ltd)
Penguin Group (Australia), 250 Camberwell Road,
Camberwell, Victoria 3124, Australia (a division of Pearson Australia Group Pty Ltd)
Penguin Books India Pvt Ltd, 11 Community Centre,
Panchsheel Park, New Delhi – 110 017, India
Penguin Group (NZ), 67 Apollo Drive, Rosedale, Auckland 0632, New Zealand
(a division of Pearson New Zealand Ltd)
Penguin Books (South Africa) (Pty) Ltd, Block D, Rosebank Office Park,
181 Jan Smuts Avenue, Parktown North, Gauteng 2193, South Africa

Penguin Books Ltd, Registered Offices: 80 Strand, London WC2R 0RL, England

www.penguin.com

First published by Michael Joseph 2011
Published in Penguin Books 2012
006

Typeset by Jouve (UK), Milton Keynes
Printed in England by Clays Ltd, St Ives plc

ISBN: 978–0–241–95695–3

www.greenpenguin.co.uk

ALWAYS LEARNING   **PEARSON**

For my children

The contents of this book first appeared in Jeremy Clarkson's *Sunday Times* column. Read more about the world according to Clarkson every week in the *Sunday Times*.

Contents

Just a couple of tweaks and it's an iPhone on wheels

Daihatsu Materia

By now, you will have heard all about the new Apple iPhone. You will have been told its battery has the life expectancy of a veal calf, and that if you want to take a photograph, you'd be better off setting up an easel and breaking out the oils.

What's more, you'll have been told – by people who haven't got one – that it works only on O_2, that it can't receive pictures via the text service and that it jams a lot.

There's something else as well. It is able to deliver the weather forecast from San Diego and clips from YouTube of young Asian men falling off motorcycles, because it can be connected to the internet. This, however, is not easy. Certainly, you won't be able to do it. So you're going to need a 'little man'.

It used to be that wealthy families in rural idylls would have a 'little man' in the village who could be called upon to come round at a moment's notice and remove dead pigeons from the chimney pot. Or start the car. Or free the satellite dish from the clematis.

He was the most vital cog in the community. But not any more. Because today he's been surpassed by someone far more important. The 'little man' who will come round to fix your broken laptop.

Unfortunately, my little man, who is called Hugo, recently met with some success and is now busy installing vast intranets on industrial estates. So asking him to come round to unblock a stubborn wireless network is a bit like asking Led Zeppelin to come round and be the turn at your four-year-old's birthday party.

This is a disaster because Hugo is the only man alive who knows how my house works. He knows the systems that prevent reporters from sitting in the road outside and reading my e-mails. He knows the codes that allow my daughter's laptop to speak to my phone. He knows the DNA of every socket and every inch of cable. And now he is gone.

So when my iPhone asks for an APN and a username and a password before it can hook up to something called the Edge, I have no idea what it's on about. Nor do I know if I want the VPN on or off because I don't know what a VPN is. Or data roaming. And then I have to tell it whether I am WEP, WPA or WPA2.

And, of course, my new little man can't help either because all the information is locked in the mind of my old little man.

The upshot is that I can't access the internet when I'm out and about, and do you know what? That is not the end of the world, because when I'm on location I rarely have the time or the inclination to think, 'What I'd like to do now is watch a Korean explode, and then maybe I'll watch a plump lady in Houston playing with herself.'

Nor can I access my e-mails, which is also a good thing because nothing has ever been said in an e-mail that needed to be said at all.

And anyway, even without these facilities, the iPhone sits in the pantheon of great inventions alongside the wheel, fire and Sky+. It's one of those things that come into your life and you think, 'How in the name of God did I ever manage without it?'

Sure, the camera, as has been suggested, can't take pictures if it's too dark, too bright or something in between, but everything else is brilliant. You type out texts on a proper qwerty keyboard, and even if you make a mistake it uses witchcraft to correct the error. And then there's the telephone, which comes with big, special-needs numbers that you can't miss even if you have fingers like burst sausages. And on top of this, it's an iPod.

Problems? Honestly, there aren't any. I've had mine hacked so it works on Vodafone, and I'm sorry, but the battery is fine. It lasts for four days. Though this might have something to do with the fact that I'm a man, and therefore only think to use a phone when I'm on a cliff, clinging to a branch, in a howling gale. And only then as a last resort.

This brings me on to an interesting idea. Why doesn't Apple make a car?

The fact of the matter is that the established car makers are timid and afraid of change. They think the mini MPV is a revolution and that the Smart car can be mentioned in the same breath as penicillin. This means they never think outside the box.

Why, for instance, does a car have a steering wheel? Or pedals? Or a dashboard? No, really. As anyone under the age of fifteen will tell you, the handset for a PlayStation can be used to steer, accelerate and brake a car. And there are still spare buttons on the handset that can be used to fire machine guns.

And, of course, without a steering wheel or a dashboard, there'd be a lot more space in the cabin, and no need for expensive, weighty airbags. And that's just me, thinking off the top of my head.

I feel fairly sure that if Apple were asked to make a car, it would come up with an automotive iPod, and within weeks we'd view the current alternatives in the same way that we now view the cassette tape, the LP and the 8-track. Until then, however, we will have to make do with the Daihatsu Materia.

In essence, this is a small, five-door hatchback that you can buy for £10,995. But as you can see from the pictures, it doesn't look like a small five-door hatchback. It looks like the Johnny Cab Arnold Schwarzenegger used when he was on Mars.

You may not care for the styling very much, in the same way that you may think an iPod is no match for the gloss and the joy of an album cover. But there is one big advantage. And I do mean big. Inside, the Materia is absolutely vast.

On the outside, then, you have a car that is as easy to park as a small Volkswagen. But inside, five adults can luxuriate.

It's a nice place to be, too. The dashboard doesn't look like it was designed to a price – which, because they've put the instruments in the middle so they don't have to be changed for left-hand-drive markets, it was. However, precisely because the instruments are in the middle, it looks like it's all been styled by someone with a vision, and a polo-neck jumper.

The Materia is well equipped, too. You get a CD changer – wow – air-conditioning, rear parking sensors, electric bits and bobs and, if you fork out £800 more, an automatic gearbox.

Under the bonnet there's a 1.5-litre engine that produces – just – enough get-up-and-go to mean the Materia can be used on a motorway. It's not like today's Euro-smalls that have too much weight and too little oomph to get out of the inside lane.

To drive? Well, it's fairly terrible, if I'm honest. Any attempt to make it dance is resisted with lots of bouncing around, and because the front seats are so utterly lacking in side support you tend to fall out of them if you are even remotely spirited.

It doesn't matter, though. Criticizing the little Daihatsu for not being sporty is a bit like criticizing Postman Pat's van for not being any good at making mashed potatoes.

The only thing I will criticize is the fuel consumption. Maybe because the body has the aerodynamic properties of a warehouse, or maybe because the engine's bigger than is normal, it isn't the pound stretcher you might imagine: around 35mpg will be the norm.

This will add a few pounds to your annual motoring bill but I think it's worth it. I liked this car very much. You will, too, whether you're a school-run mum, an old lady or a surfer dude who wants a boxy replacement for your recently expired VW Microbus.

However, there is a long way to go. Daihatsu has wandered off the well-worn path with this one, and come up with what the motor industry would call radical and daring. But imagine what might be possible if the Materia were now handed over to the computer industry. We'd get a properly amazing car. And little men everywhere would be in work for the rest of time.

6 January 2008

It's far too cool for you, Mr Footballer

Mazda MX-5 Roadster Coupé 2.0i

As the reputation of all the most exquisite cars continues to be embrowned by the nation's footballers, those who try to combine extreme wealth with a splash of discretion and good taste find themselves in a bit of a quandary.

In the olden days, if you were to turn up at a party in a Ferrari or a Maserati, women might imagine that you were the Aga Khan. Today, however, they will cower in a cupboard all night, fearful that if they come out they will be roasted in front of a jeering mob who'll record the event on their mobile phones and, in the morning, upload it all to the internet. 'I have a Ferrari,' is code for 'I am a rapist.' Or, worse, 'I am Kerry Katona.'

The solution, then, for wealthy people who are not rapists or Kerry Katona is to buy a car that simply isn't on a footballer's radar. A car that manages to be expensive and comfortable, and possibly even quite fast, without shouting, 'Look at me.' A fatboy car.

The Bristol Blenheim is a fatboy car. So is the Mercedes SL. Then you have the Rolls-Royce Phantom, the Bentley Continental Flying Spur, the Jaguar XJR, the Range Rover – but emphatically not the Sport – the BMW 7-series, and the car I was given for Christmas. A thirty-seven-year-old Mercedes 600 Grosser.

Launched in 1963, it was by far and away the most

expensive car in the world, with a price tag, in America, of $20,000. In its eighteen-year production run only 2,677 were made and almost all were bought by people who did not play football. Idi Amin, Louis Winthorpe from the film *Trading Places* and Leonid Brezhnev. Mao Tse-tung was said to be very fond of his, and it's easy to see why.

Today we marvel at the power-operated boot lids on cars such as the Lexus LS 600h but the Mercedes Grosser had this feature forty-five years ago. And yes, while it does without such luxuries as a heated rear window, and the dim/dip light switch is on the floor, it does have power-operated seats, windows, sunroof and even doors. And the power does not come from a fickle electric motor either. Oh no. Everything that moves on the Grosser is powered by hydraulics. Small wonder it weighs three tons.

It's not a car you can just get into and drive, either, because hydraulics also operate the suspension. So after starting the engine you must do a crossword while the body rises to the correct height.

Still, you can then make up lost time because it has a 6.3-litre engine. The first production V8 Mercedes ever made, it develops 300bhp, thanks to fuel injection. In other words, in terms of luxury and power this was quite literally forty years ahead of its time. In terms of style, however, it was bang-on, pure, 100 per cent 1963. This was a time when designers were allowed to fit a car with ornaments, and the Grosser is fitted with so many it could almost be twinned with Elton John's head.

The double bumpers, the enormous grille, the chromed wheel arches: it is a festival of brightwork and I'm only surprised it isn't followed everywhere by a flock of magpies.

It's the same story inside, where it's fitted with nothing so vulgar as tinted glass. Instead you get curtains, along with interior glass wind deflectors should you feel the need to drive along with the windows down, waving serenely at the *Untermenschen.*

The only thing that it didn't come with as standard – but that I shall be adding as soon as I've designed them – are two flags on the front wings. This is the only sound you want to hear as you cruise along. The fluttering of two pennants.

Or, rather, this is the sound I imagine you'd like to hear. I can't say for sure because I've had the car for a week now and so far I haven't actually driven it. This is because most of the time it won't start.

Sometimes it turns over with a decreasing level of enthusiasm for ten minutes before the titanic battery gives up the ghost. And sometimes it doesn't turn over at all. Occasionally it coughs a little burp of hope and I prod the throttle, trying like a man marooned on a desert island to breathe a little life into the sliver of flame. But never quite succeeding.

So then I plug it into a trickle charger, and after two hours have been spent pumping some fresh enthusiasm into the battery, the engine bursts into an uneven V8 strum. The sound of joy. Followed by the groan of despair as I realize that, this being Christmastime, I've passed the time as the battery charged with my face in a bucket of red wine. And now I'm too drunk to go anywhere.

And so we must now leave the olden days when cars worked only if there was some warmth in the month, and look at the complete opposite of the 600 Grosser. The Mazda MX-5.

When I first encountered the new version of this modern classic, I reported that it was a better-looking, more practical version of something we all loved anyway and that you should all have one. And you all responded by buying something else.

No, really. The new MX-5 is like the new Ford Mondeo and the Subaru Legacy Outback. It is one of those cars that's absolutely brilliant . . . and nobody buys it. You never see one on the road.

Fearful, therefore, that I'd missed some crucial aspect of the car – a spike in the driver's seat, perhaps, or a snake in the glove box – I decided to have another look. And there's nothing; not even a preposterous price tag. The new soft-top Mazda starts at just £15,730.

So what's the problem? I've given the matter some serious thought and I've decided what the car missed most of all was the mark. I liked the way the old car had few luxuries, because that made it light. For the same reason it had a canvas roof you raised and lowered by hand, and I liked that too. But actually, the fact is most of us would prefer some creature comforts and a roof that moved about using electricity. We may have been drawn to the idea of an MX-5 but actually we all went out and bought a convertible Vauxhall Astra instead.

Well, Mazda has obviously realized this too because the new 2-litre Roadster Coupé I tried has a superfast electric metal roof, a surround sound Bose stereo, and a button on the dash that says 'Media'. God knows what it did.

All of this must be terribly galling for the engineers who struggled to make the new car only 22lb heavier than the old one. To find the marketing department adding stuff is probably enough to have them all disembowelling themselves but the fact is this: it doesn't make a jot of difference.

The engine still feels unsullied by cotton wool damping and active exhaust tuning. The gearbox still snicks. The handling is still deliciously front-engined and rear-drive. You still feel hemmed in behind the wheel and the plastics appear, correctly in a car of this type, to have been fitted to shroud various wires and rough edges. Not as a surface you feel inspired to lick and caress.

The MX-5, then, still feels simple and sprightly and lively. It still feels basic and honest and wonderful. It's still a bacon sandwich made with good bread, good butter and good meat. Only now it has a splash of HP sauce.

It is an epic car, this. A car for fatboys who are still thin.

13 January 2008

Tailor-made for the hard of thinking

Subaru Impreza WRX STi

There are many ways to tell if someone is a bit thick. You can sit them in a room and ask them to push various bits of plastic into a wooden box. Or you can ask them to describe a cloud. Or you can carefully measure the distance between their eyes, the height of their forehead or the length of their arms.

But there's another, easier way of establishing whether someone is two spanners short of a tool box. Just ask them this simple question, 'Are you wearing a Subaru rally jacket?' Because if they are, you will need to speak more slowly.

I'll let you into a little secret. Each week, when *Top Gear* is on air, we prepare two scripts. One is a polysyllabic orgy of complex thoughts on the meaning of human happiness. And the other is full of words such as 'tits' and 'arse'. Choosing which one eventually gets used depends on how many audience members turn up in Subaru Imprezas.

No, really. If the audience is largely in tweed and Viyella, you can make them laugh with oblique references to Dickens and the iniquities of colonialism in nineteenth-century Calcutta. If it's a forest of Subaru baseball caps out there, we stick to genitals and spend the day skidding around the studio on banana skins.

Of course, there are intelligent Subaru drivers, but for the

majority of them, there are only eight letters in the alphabet.
WRX STIR and B.

I think the problem may be this. A Subaru Impreza is seen
by the rallying fraternity as the golden-wheeled wonder boy.
It was a Subaru that took Richard Burns to his world championship, and a Subaru with which Colin McRae became
synonymous. Subarus are to rallying, then, what Ferrari is to
Formula One.

And rallying, I'm afraid, is a sport for the terminally gormless. You stand there, on a frozen Welsh hillside, not knowing
whether to drink the soup you've made or pour it into your
wellingtons. And the evening is enlivened only when a pair
of extremely noisy headlights whiz by, hurling a million bits
of gravel into your face. The only good news about this is
that your face is so chuffing cold you can't feel the blood
tricking out of all the open wounds.

What's more, you do not know what sort of car the headlights were attached to. You do not know who was driving.
And you do not know whether they were travelling faster
than the previous set of headlights that spewed stones into
your iced-up cheeks.

Rallying is the only sport on God's earth where you watch
the event live but do not know who's won until long after
you've got home and had a bath to remove all the mud that
became stuck to you when you fell over in a Welsh wood at
three in the morning.

The only possible reason for being there is to see someone called Stig Stigsson crash. Except you won't, of course,
because the rally is thousands of miles long and the chance
of there being a prang right where you're standing is remote.
And even if you are lucky, you won't actually see the impact

because you'll have been blinded by grit thrown into your eyes by Stig Magnesstig's Citroën.

Of course, there is another way of going rallying, and that's to take part. This is very simple. You buy a car that costs thousands of pounds. You then have that car tweaked and prepared, which costs even more. And then you drive it at incredibly high speed into a tree.

Show me someone who has a Subaru, then, and I'll show you someone who thinks rallying is fun. And that means we're almost certainly talking about a person who breathes through his mouth and has short legs, no forehead and one, possibly lacerated, eye.

Strangely, however, Subaru Imprezas have always been rather intelligent cars. They were so much quieter and more refined than alternatives from Ford and Mitsubishi. You got the impression that an Impreza would know how to hold a knife and fork. And whether to have its cheese before its pudding.

Whereas an Evo, you suspected, would goose your wife, eat with its mouth open and vomit into the sugar bowl during the coffee and mints. A Ford Escort Cosworth, meanwhile, would stab you just to get an electric ankle bracelet and an Asbo.

And now into the mix comes the new Subaru Impreza. I drove the WRX model recently and was terribly underwhelmed. It was too ugly, too soft, equipped like an Eskimo's khazi and about as exciting as Tuesday. The car you see in the picture this morning, however, is what we've really all been waiting for. The STi version. The one with the flared wheel arches, four exhausts and almost 300 horsepowers.

First things first. The looks. And I'm sorry but I'm still not sold. The standard car looks like a lightly melted Rover 25.

With its flared aches, this looks like a lightly melted Rover 25 with bingo wings.

Then there's the interior. As is customary, the STi badge on the dash is pink and I'm afraid it really doesn't go with the orange dials or the green indicator lights. It's like a four-year-old has been let loose in there with a box of felt-tip pens.

Still, the vibrant colouring does at least take your mind off the fact that this is a £25,000 car that comes with fewer toys than an Ethiopian birthday boy. You know if a car maker is in trouble when, in its own brochure, it says the car is fitted as standard with locking wheel nuts and pneumatic bonnet struts. This is code for saying, 'Sat nav's extra.'

But of course the most important question is how the STi drives. And the answer is: provided you are the sort of person who can set the timer on a 1989 video recorder . . . it depends.

You see, down by your left elbow there's a small panel featuring a number of buttons and acronyms that you won't find in any other car. First of all, you choose what sort of throttle response you'd like. Then you choose from six settings how much power you'd like to go to the front wheels and how much to the back.

Or you can go for the auto setting, which unlocks the centre differential, sending most of the torque to the rear, or the Auto +, which sends it to the front. And now we get to the three-way vehicle dynamics control system, which turns the traction control system on, off or very off.

I have no doubt that on a track, when nothing is coming the other way and you can go beyond the limits, you will be able to spend many happy hours fiddling about, choosing exactly how you'd like to hit a tree. But you know what? On the road, even if you drive quite quickly, you can do whatever you like with any of these settings and it makes not a blind bit of difference.

I suspect the control panel is primarily designed as a talking point at Subaru owners' club meetings. In the same way that the button that turns the traction control off in your car is something you mention to colleagues when giving them a lift. But you'd never actually use it.

Honestly? The only time I ever deactivate a car's traction control is when I'm driving past a camera on *Top Gear*. On the road? Never. And so it goes with the STi. I pushed and prodded all the various buttons and, having realized they weren't making much difference, put everything in auto and left them alone.

In this mode, the STi is demonstrably better than the WRX. Harder, more taut and noticeably faster. There's still understeer, in any setting, which was always a tiresome characteristic of the old car. But there is something new. The flat-four strum is gone. The new 2.5-litre engine just sounds boring and I must therefore recommend you opt for the Prodrive sports exhaust to liven it up a bit.

So even though Subarus are probably the most reliable cars made – they make Hondas look like South American dictatorships – the new STi doesn't look or sound good, it isn't equipped very well and it doesn't excite like its bingo wings and four tailpipes suggest it will. Put simply, I did not enjoy driving it.

I think, therefore, you may have to be a bit dim to buy one. If you're a Subaru fan with a full range of Subaru clothing in your wardrobe, you'll probably love it.

20 January 2008

Clarkson on road safety

I'm criticized by some Scottish chief constable one day for encouraging people to drive fast and then lambasted by Welsh assembly members for saying public transport is for poor people. Which it is. My crime is simple. I like cars.

As I drove down the M20 into Kent last Monday, I noticed that most of the speed cameras had been burnt out by vandals. This is disgusting. It is ridiculous, criminal and stupid that the person who savaged these life-saving devices should target the M20 . . . and then stop. Why did you not keep right on going? I can think of six cameras on my way home that would be immeasurably improved with a spot of petrol and a match.

With 6,000 speed cameras nestling in every bush and parked van, they will not stop until they've got the accident rate down to zero. Which will be never.

Lycra Nazis have already taken over a third of the roads with their green tarmac cycle lanes, now they want to take over the whole lot.

A third of all those injured and killed on the roads are young men, aged in a startlingly narrow band from seventeen to nineteen. Drowning in testosterone, and filled with a youthful sense of immortality, being seventeen is dangerous. It always has been. The fact is, you simply can't make a seventeen-year-old see sense.

In London, drivers do 42 million kilometres each year while lost, and that's the same as driving from New York to Los Angeles 9,200 times. Needlessly.

There are many rules for the elderly in the *Highway Code*. I have one, too. And here it is. Get a bloody move on.

It's this obsession everyone has got with speed now that speed kills – it doesn't. Suddenly becoming stationary, that's what gets you.

A general rule of thumb. If a car has less than 100 horse-power, it is never safe to pull into the outside lane if there is a car in sight . . . even if it's three miles away. If a car has less than 60 horsepower, it is never safe to pull into the outside lane at all.

27 January 2008

The rubbish, brilliant saviour of Jaguar

Jaguar XF SV8

There are so many questions about the new Jaguar XF. How much is it? Who will own the company tomorrow? And how did Tony Blair manage to get one before it goes on sale? But the biggest question of the lot is this: how in the name of all that's holy is Jaguar still with us?

The problems began in the mid-1970s, when Jaguar was part of the Communist party. Back then, everyone at British Leyland was so enamoured of the Soviets, they came within an ace of renaming it the Large Car Division. I'm surprised they didn't settle on Zil.

Eventually Jaguar was sold off to Ford, which never really understood what Jaguar was all about. The people at Ford managed Aston Martin well, and Land Rover too, but Jaguar stumped them. They couldn't even say it properly.

And so, in the past few years, we got the new XJ, which looks like a fatter version of the old XJ. We got the X-type, which was an expensive way of buying a Mondeo, and we got the S-type. Which was a Lincoln dressed in Mallory's tweed suit. And fitted with Danniella Westbrook's idiotic nose.

Of course we also got the new XK, which is a brilliant car. However, buying one is the same as standing on top of a very tall building with a megaphone, telling everyone that you can't afford an Aston Martin.

Then, of course, Ford lost all its money. And then it lost all of everyone else's money, and so, while the boffins and the stylists were beavering away on the new XF, Jaguar was put up for sale. 'Wanted: someone to buy a car company that no one understands. Has made little or no profit for twenty years or more. Offers in excess of £1 billion. Willing to p/ex Land Rover as well.'

Weirdly, it seems an Indian company called Tata, which makes horrid cars for people who are fed up with falling off their motor scooters, is said to be interested. God, I bet Gandhi is laughing his socks off. And I bet you're very sad that this once great British manufacturer has been allowed to sink to such depths. The thing is, though: should you be sad? Was Jaguar ever really that great?

Oh I'm sure people in chunky jumpers will be choking on their pipes at this outrageous proposition. They'll point out that in 1948 the XK 120 was the fastest production car in the world and that the D-type married monocoque thinking with aeronautical design. And that with Lofty England at the helm it won Le Mans in 1956.

This is all true. But claiming that Jaguar is great today because of something it did in the 1950s is like claiming Egypt is a world power because of the pharaohs. The fact is that in my lifetime Jaguar's forages into the realm of brilliance have been few and far between.

Oh sure, people go all dewy-eyed about the Mk 2, but as we know from the historical document that is *The Sweeney*, if it were ever chased by a Granada Ghia, it would immediately crash into a pile of cardboard boxes.

Then along came Arthur Daley, whose comic genius overshadowed anything achieved at Le Mans by Lofty England.

As a result, Jaguars became vodka-and-tonic cars for the sheepskin classes. A car you drove when your taxi was at the menders.

There was an attempt to get back on track with the XJ220 but that all went horribly wrong. Customers put down a deposit on what they'd been told was a four-wheel-drive V12 supercar and were understandably miffed when they found the actual car was two-wheel drive and had the engine from a Metro. Some resorted to the law to try to get their money back.

Then there was the XJR-15, which crashed a lot, and the much publicized foray into Formula One, which blew up, didn't start or cruised around quite slowly at the back.

We like to think, then, that Jaguar's history is as rich and as lustrous as a maharajah's bathrobe, but the truth is, it's a mish-mash of strikes, unreliability, sheepskin, failure, vodka, tonic and public humiliation. In fact, I would venture to suggest that the company's reputation among the vast majority these days hangs solely on one car: the E-type – Jaguar's 1966 classic.

That's why we care where Jags are made. That's why we care about who owns them. That's why we care about the new XF. So here goes . . .

First, there's the styling. Jaguar says it looks like the stunning concept car we saw a couple of years ago but I'm not so sure. Some of the exquisite detailing on the concept – the guardsman-sharp creases on the bonnet and razor-thin headlamps – have not made it onto the production car.

And I'm sorry, but arguing that the two have the same proportions and stance is like saying I have the same proportions and stance as Brad Pitt. I do. But I'm never asked for his autograph.

Had there been no concept car, I would never have known

how good the XF could look. But there was, so I'm sorry, but as a styling exercise the finished product just doesn't float my boat.

In fact, when I came home to find it sitting in my drive I thought it was a Mondeo and ignored it for two days. When I finally took it for a drive the disappointments kept on coming. The dipped headlamps are not bright enough, the light switch is on the indicator stalk – a hallmark of cost-cutting – the cruise control wasn't working, the throttle felt slack, the sat nav screen was unreadable thanks to too many reflections, and the windows don't work when the ignition is off.

Then there's the starting procedure. To earn extra points from the Euro NCAP safety people, Jag, like everyone else, has replaced the traditional ignition key, which can damage your kneecap in a frontal crash, with a starter button. But unlike in everyone else's cars, sometimes the starter button doesn't actually start the engine. I don't know why.

But I do know that by the time I'd got out, remembered the window was down, got back in and spent God knows how long trying to coax some life back into the ignition system, I was purple with righteous indignation.

And then there's the gearbox. It's a normal auto but you can override it with paddles behind the wheel. Lovely. But if you change down into, say, fourth it won't, after a while, go back into drive. Not unless you put the circular lever into 'Sport' and then back into 'D' again. This is wearisome and indicates that the whole car was built on a bit of a shoestring. There isn't that much rear legroom either.

Strangely, however, despite all of this, I enjoyed my time with the XF enormously. I'd have one over an equivalent BMW, Audi or Lexus any day. First of all, the interior is such a joyous place to sit. The high centre console makes you feel hemmed in, cocooned, safe. The materials used are modern, such as you would find at Zurich airport. The leather is hand-stitched with contrasting cotton and the blue lighting is brilliant. It doesn't feel remotely like a Jag in there. And is that a bad thing?

It doesn't feel like a Jag to drive either. It's quite noisy, for a kick-off, and it rides with a firmness that would shake the pile out of Arthur Daley's car coat. The firmness is never uncomfortable, as it is in an Audi. It's not a jiggliness that annoys. It's a feeling that the suspension is sorted and that if you put your foot down, all will be well.

It is. It may have the same engine as Noah used in his ark but as a car for covering ground, on A roads, my God. You can forget your BMWs. This is fanbleedingtastic. Balanced. Meaty. Pretty soon you'll not give a damn that the light switch is on the indicator stalk and you won't worry about the poor dipped-beam lighting either. The beam from your smile will illuminate the road ahead well enough.

This, then, is a car that's flawed and fantastic, irritating and rewarding, mad and bad. But when all is said and done – and this is the nonsensical joy of cars – I liked it. I looked forward to driving it. I'm sad it's not here any more.

Because of this I have a sneaking suspicion that Jag, after forty years of misery, is about to have the most delightful Indian summer.

10 February 2008

David Dimbleby made me wet myself

Mercedes-Benz CLK Black Series

I've been in a 1950s Russian plane that had spent most of its life with the Angolan air force before some hopeless Cuban drug addict in a soiled baseball cap flew it, and me, into one of the most savage tropical thunderstorms the world has ever seen.

I've also raced a drag snowmobile, rolled an F-15 fighter, spun a Koenigsegg and been in a helicopter gunship, over Basra, when someone stepped into his garden 500 feet below and fired a heat-seeking missile at it. So I understand the concept of fear.

But there is nothing quite so buttock-clenchingly terrifying as the moment when David Dimbleby turns to you on *Question Time* and asks for your opinion on something about which you know absolutely nothing.

There you are, in front of an audience, with the television cameras rolling, and you have to summon up a cohesive thought, immediately. You can't joke because jokes aren't allowed in the serious world of political debate. You can't mumble. You can't even look at your shoes and, in the best traditions of the school bad boy, mumble, 'Don't know, sir.'

The best person I ever saw on the panel was Enoch Powell. When asked for his thoughts on, oh I can't remember what it was now, some frightfully important issue that mattered then but doesn't now – homophobia in the fishing industry, probably – he didn't bluster and talk about how he has an understanding of the trawlerman's way of life because he once spent a lovely holiday in Lowestoft, which is the sort of thing Patricia Hewitt or Margaret Beckett might do.

He didn't thump his tub either, making platitudinous noises to whip up a frenzy of applause. He said simply, 'I have no knowledge of this subject.'

I was reminded of old Enoch's honesty last year when I telephoned a chap at Mercedes-Benz and asked if I could borrow a quasi-racing, hard-topped version of the AMG SLK. It was called the Black and it all sounded very exciting.

Now, there are a number of excuses the public relations executive can use when he doesn't want to lend a demonstrator to someone. He can say, 'It's been crashed.' Or, 'It's being used by the motoring correspondent of the *Welsh Pig Breeders' Gazette* at the moment.' Or he can say, 'I'll get back to you on that,' and not do so.

But the chap at Mercedes said straight away, 'Ooh, the SLK Black. No. I don't think you'd like it very much.' And put the phone down.

This means, of course, that when he rang the other day and offered me a drive in the Black edition of the CLK, I figured that since he was such an honest chap, I was going to like it. The thing is, though, I had absolutely no idea how much.

The standard CLK is not the most exciting car in the Mercedes range. It sits in the mix like Peter sits in the Fonda family. Or that other bloke who wasn't Paul Weller and Bruce Foxton in the Jam.

It's based on the old C-class saloon, which means it's not as nice to drive as the current C-class saloon. And to make it even less appealing, it has fewer doors, less space inside and is considerably more expensive. This wouldn't be so bad if it were a looker, but it's a bit like the girl next door's plump sister.

On paper, the Black looks like even more of a cock-up. Because they've removed most of the luxury trimmings and the rear seats found in the normal 63 AMG version, and this has somehow made the car heavier. And then they've added a whopping £34,000 to the standard car's already eye-watering list price of £66,000.

So, the car you are looking at in the pictures this morning is priced to take on a Ferrari F430 and the Porsche Turbo. I know, I know. It sounds like a German idea of a joke. But I promise you this: it is not a joke at all. Like everything to come out of the Fatherland since it was formed in 1871, it is utterly and deadly serious.

The reason why this car has gained weight over the standard version, despite the absence of electric seats and sat nav and so on, is because, underneath, it has been radically altered with a chunky limited slip differential, a new wider axle and lots of other Brunelian strengthening beams.

They've had a fiddle under the bonnet, too, completely redesigning the intake and exhaust systems and fitting a new management system so that now, the 6.2-litre V8 churns out a thunderous 507bhp. Couple this to the beefed-up undersides and the results are remarkable.

Imagine drinking a pint of hemlock, setting yourself on fire and then jumping out of a plane when it's directly overhead a combine harvester. You don't know what's going to kill you: only that you are going through the Pearly Gates at great speed very soon.

That's what the Black feels like. Exciting beyond words. Terrifyingly exciting. White-knuckle, eyes-on-stalks, sweaty-armpit and tensed-buttocks exciting. David Dimbleby exciting.

Initially, you don't drive this car: you just cling on for dear life. For the first few miles, I genuinely thought it was actively trying to kill me. But then I became used to the way the back skips and settles and started to enjoy it. Then the enjoyment turned into sheer, unparalleled joy. Then I started to think that I might have actually wet myself a bit.

It does not drive like any other car, this one. It doesn't feel planted like a Porsche Turbo, or alive, like a Ferrari 430. It feels skittish, as though it's balancing all the time on a knife edge; that razor-thin sliver that separates absolute joy from certain death.

And what makes it all the more extraordinary is that you don't feel like you're in a hunkered-down racer. You have an automatic gearbox. You have a hands-free telephone, and air-conditioning, and a ride that is not exactly soft. But it's not killer hard either.

It's the same story with the noise. When you accelerate, it sounds much like I imagine a burning dinosaur might sound. But on the motorway, you can still hear Terry Wogan, even when he is muttering.

Sadly, all is not sweetness and light. The front bucket seats are stunning but only Jon Bon Jovi has snaky enough hips to sit in them and do the seatbelt up. And then there's the back. Because the rear seats have been taken out, you end up with half a square mile of carpeted but inaccessible uselessness.

Technically, it's possible to put them back in again – and it's not like the extra weight will make much of a dint on an engine that produces more than 460 torques – but sadly, the European Union rule makers say that's not allowed because it would cause the rear axle to snap, and the headlamps to point at Mars.

And then there's the styling. All those Mr Universe bulges

are absolutely necessary to shroud the wider axles, and cool the carbon brakes. I know this. And I don't doubt it would look great at Silverstone. But would it look right on a wet Wednesday in Tamworth? Or would you just look like the most terrible show-off?

You might think, then, that if it's a look-at-me head turner, you may as well go the whole hog and buy a Ferrari instead.

I'm not so sure. Quite apart from the fact that the Merc is likely to be more reliable and comes with a proper boot, and all the iPod 'n' sat nav tinsel that you really need these days, the simple fact of the matter is this: for sheer excitement, the CLK Black is a match for the 430.

For sheer excitement, the CLK Black is a match for absolutely anything. Since it went back to Mercedes, I have been thinking about it a lot. Because I'm not sure that anyone's life is quite complete unless they have one.

24 February 2008

Look, you traffic wombles, I've had enough

Renaultsport Clio 197 Cup

Recently, a mother of three appeared in court charged with 'knowingly causing the deposit of controlled waste on land which did not have a waste management licence'.

So what do you suppose she'd done? Emptied a sack of polonium into a school playground? Urinated in Alistair Darling's finger bowl? Secreted 6,000 burning tyres in Bourton-on-the-Water? Nope. The 'controlled waste' was an apple core that she had allegedly tossed out of her car window.

Shortly afterwards, two young men appeared in another court, accused of 'interfering with a dolphin'. It turns out they'd been hitching a ride on it, in much the same way that tourists do on exotic holidays throughout the world. Then, the following day, the government announced that from now on Gordon Brown would be listening to every single telephone call you make.

Small wonder the Archbishop of Canterbury announced, just twenty-four hours later, that he wants sharia law in Britain. He was mocked, of course, but come on: Muslimism lets you throw apple cores onto the grass verge and swim with the dolphins and make telephone calls without having a Scottish man grunting and moaning in the background. Plus, we'd have the added benefit of being able to dismember shoplifters.

Also, though I have only a scant acquaintance with the

Koran, I'm fairly certain it contains no call for motorists to be fleeced, hounded, mocked and, worst of all, held up on purpose by a swarm of power-crazed traffic wombles.

No one seems to have noticed this sinister new development. But think. In the olden days, when policemen had to have two O-levels, a moustache and a burning desire to join the Freemasons, you never really heard of a motorway being closed.

Then, however, the state introduced a new breed of Diet One-Cal policeman called highway officers. We were told they'd race to the scene of an incident and clear up the mess as quickly as possible, thus allowing the real police to concentrate on more important things, like filling in forms and arresting people for interfering with dolphins.

It sounded a brilliant idea but, sadly, these new highwaymen have plainly been told that the most important thing, when attending the scene of a crash, is their own safety. Which means that their first reaction, always, no matter how trivial the accident, is to close the road.

Just listen to the Radio 2 traffic reports. One day last week the M40, the M5, the A34 and the M4 were all shut. Single-handedly, these mollycoddled imbeciles were bringing the whole country to a standstill.

That night, it got worse. A small hatchback had broken down in the middle lane of the A40, going into London. Now, in the not-too-distant past, other motorists would have got out of their cars and pushed the blockage to the side of the road. Not any more. Now, the traffic wombles come and cone off two lanes. And then they sit in their big 4x4, eating Mars bars, until the government-approved, safety-qualified removal-truck driver arrives.

When my wife crawled past at 6.30, they were just sitting

there. When I drove past an hour later, having been stuck in a five-mile queue, they were still sitting there, and I'm afraid that, for the first time in twelve years, I lost my temper. They say a Dutch bargee can swear for two minutes without repetition or hesitation. I beat that easily.

I'd had enough. I'd had enough of people being charged for throwing apples out of their car windows, and speed cameras, and bus lanes, and those villages that have plant pots in the middle of the road. I'd had enough of bendy buses and the congestion charge, and sanctimonious beardies in Toyota Priuses getting away with it. I'd had enough of petrol at £1 a litre, and idiots saying that if we build more roads, people will only end up using them. I'd had enough of exhaust emission tables, and Al Gore and being asked to let the bus go first. I'd had enough of mobile CCTV cameras and Gordon Brown's smile and photographs of polar bears on icebergs. And I took it all out on those fat, power-crazed wombles who'd shut two lanes of one of the busiest roads in the world because they were too obsessed with health and safety to get off their fat arses and push a broken-down hatchback out of the way.

There is some hope, however, in this broken and useless world and it comes in the shape of Renault's Clio 197 Cup.

I've always liked hot hatchbacks and they make even more sense now than they did at the peak of their popularity twenty years ago. Back then, when you could smoke indoors and smack your children and the police were allowed to punch burglars in the face, they were a great way of enjoying what would turn out to be freedom's last gasp.

Now, however, they do something even more important. In an over-controlled, deliberately jammed world, they make going slowly fun.

Sure, a mid-engined car with 600 brake horsepower is always going to be a riot in the Yorkshire Dales, but you don't live in the Yorkshire Dales. You live in Coalville and on your dismal crawl to work every morning all that power and finesse is, frankly, a complete waste of time and effort. You'd be better off putting your money in the dishwasher.

This is where the Clio Cup comes in. Its engine produces 197bhp, which is an awful lot from a normal-aspirated 2-litre, but in a world of M5s, it's a dribble; it's less than half what AMG thinks is necessary to have a good time.

AMG is wrong. The people at Renault say the Clio Cup will accelerate from rest to 62mph in 6.9sec and that flat out in sixth it'll sound and feel like you're outrunning a Saturn V rocket. They also say it has Formula One-style aerodynamic aids and a compromise-free chassis designed to make every left at the lights feel like the Eau Rouge at Spa at 180.

If I may be permitted to liken the world of performance cars to Battersea dogs' home, this is the eager little terrier, an ice-white scamp that whizzes about chasing its tail. Sure, it's slower than a greyhound but, in theory, it should be a lot more fun.

The trouble is: it isn't. While the engine is amazingly powerful for something the size of a toaster, it doesn't translate into much in the way of fizz. What I want in a car like this is a rev counter that zooms up to the red line if you even so much as breathe on the throttle pedal. But in the Renault it feels like you're trying to push a piano up a hill.

I like a hot hatch to deceive. I like to hurtle round a corner with blood spurting from my ears, and the engine doing 16 million revolutions a minute, imagining that I'm doing 5,000mph. Whereas in fact I'm doing about six.

That doesn't happen in the Renault. It's not stodgy. It's not an overcooked cauliflower, but neither is it a freshly picked radish. It just isn't as exciting as the rear diffuser and preposterous roof-mounted spoiler would have you believe. And as a further droplet of wee in the soup, it has electric power steering, which is cheap to engineer but not quite as feelsome and lively as it should be.

Then there's the interior. It's not terrible. It's not built with that usual French soggy dishcloth integrity. But really, it should have air-conditioning as standard.

I'm not saying the Clio Cup is a waste of wiring and metal. I like the way it looks and I like the seats a lot. I especially like the fact it costs less than £15,000. But it's one of those cars that gives off the distinct impression it could be a little bit better.

I'd trade some of the power for a bit more whizz. Which, funnily enough, is what I'd do with the traffic wombles as well.

2 March 2008

No, princess, you may not have my Fiat

Fiat 500 1.2 Pop

If you are a northern businessman whose solutions-system company has just been bought for thirty-thirteen million pounds, there are any number of people on hand with advice on how best to spend all your newly acquired loot. I find, however, that the best person to consult on these matters is the former mustachioed pop star Peter Sarstedt.

Today, Peter fills his time writing songs about global warming, which is rather wearisome, but back in 1969 he wrote the definitive guide on how life should be led if Mammon were suddenly to vomit untold riches into your bank account. It was a song called 'Where Do You Go to My Lovely?'

In it, he explains who should make your clothes, what you should wear in your hair, whose records you should buy, what sort of brandy you should drink and even what you should do if the Aga Khan were to send you a racehorse for Christmas: 'keep it, just for fun, for a laugh. Aha-haha'.

Left to your own devices, you may choose to go on your summer vacation somewhere terrible, such as Greece. But if you listen to the wise words of old Pete, you know it should be Juan-les-Pins. Similarly, if you were to buy a bolt-hole in Paris, as somewhere to keep your old Rolling Stones records, you might go for an apartment on the rue Saint-Honoré. Pah. Peter says you should be on the Boulevard Saint-Michel. And he's right.

He even has some sensible advice on where you should be when the snow falls. The travel agent will tell you all about the sheer size of Val d'Isère or the wide-open China Bowl in Vail. He'll talk about the ski-in, ski-out facilities at the Park Hyatt in Beaver Creek or maybe tempt you with the joys of somewhere small and friendly, such as La Clusaz. Nonsense. You should go, as Peter suggests, with 'the others of the jet set' to St Moritz.

St Moritz is the most bonkers town in all of the world. Superficially, it looks like any other ski resort, which means it resembles the outskirts of Warsaw in 1956, but the people: wow. I have never seen so much expensive hair in all my life. Sure, the Russians have more oil in their barnets than you'd find in a Kazakhstan well. And their wives are as orange as the interior of the average Lamborghini. But mostly, the whole place is crammed with people so bewitchingly beautiful that even Keira Knightley would feel like a zoo animal.

Then there are the titles. One chap introduced me to his companion and I'd nearly died of old age by the time he'd finished. 'This is Princess di Contessa, di Sant' Agata, de Baroness, Dowager de Luxembourg, Principessa . . . it went on for about a week. Until he said, 'And this is Jeremy Clarkson,' and for the first time in my life I felt about six inches tall.

Mind you, if you set foot in any of the shops, you are made to feel smaller still because it is immediately apparent you are not Bill Gates, which means it's immediately apparent you cannot afford to buy a single thing they have on offer. It's all Hermès and Armani. God knows where the locals buy a box of Winalot or some bog roll.

Of course, you can buy a watch. Some even cost as little as £32,000. Mostly, though, they are much more than that because they all have 16 dials, a Swiss midget in the back winding all the cogs, 400 Kohinoors in the bezel, a device that summons an SAS extraction team if you get kidnapped and a facility for converting dollars into euros, which, at the touch of a button, can also convert your business rivals into pig food. Usually, they are bigger than a ride-on lawnmower.

Strangely, however, for what is certainly the watch capital of the world, nobody gets anywhere on time. When someone says they'll be there at eight, what they mean is, 'I will be there either at two in the morning or, more likely, not at all.' Probably, this is because the jet set has no real concept of time. They don't have to catch a plane because they have their own and it'll wait. They don't have to be at a meeting in the City at four because they don't have jobs. They don't even have to boil an egg, because they have an egg manager. I even met one who employed his own projectionist. And you know what? I loved it. I've always been fascinated by the jet set and if I had the chance to come back as anyone, at any time in history, I wouldn't want to be Warren Beatty on the set of *Shampoo* in 1975 or even a hippie on the corner of Haight and Ashbury in 1967. Nope. I'd want to be Gianni Agnelli on a Riva speedboat in Juan-les-Pins in 1959.

Back then, easy travel had just become an option for the super-rich, which meant they could breakfast in Turin, lunch in St Tropez, fit in a cocktail in St Moritz and be at the opera in Milan by 10pm. They were making it up as they went along, sorting out the rules that were then enshrined by Peter Sarstedt. But strangely, they never really sorted out what sort of car you should drive. You see the problem in St Moritz today. It's a mess. One chap turned up in a brand-new Rolls-Royce Phantom drophead in white, and, oh dear – that didn't work at all. He'd driven it all the way from England and teamed his paintwork with the mountain backdrop. But it looked, I'm afraid, ridiculous.

I had a Mercedes M-class. It had the AMG 6.2-litre V8 under the bonnet, four exhausts and a restrained but good-looking body. I like this car very much but in St Moritz it was wrong as well. Certainly, the four-wheel-drive system was superfluous because this is Switzerland and any snow that falls on the road is immediately arrested.

I noticed that the Russians were partial to the Range Rover in the same way they are partial to onyx television cabinets and that most of the old guard, the ones with Scrabble high-score titles, had normal Vogues. But this struck me as a cop-out. Something they'd done because they couldn't think of what else to buy.

Every one of the big hotels, the Kulm, the Palace and the Carlton, had an Audi R8 parked outside, among the May-bachs and Phantoms that they use as taxis, but nobody was looking. And that's because everyone's attention had been grabbed by a car that fitted into the place more perfectly than even Princess Caroline. The new Fiat 500. They were every-where and everyone wanted one. There's been a trend in recent years for bringing back old designs. VW started it when it reintroduced the Beetle; then Ford gave us the new GT, BMW relaunched the Mini and now it's Fiat's turn with this homage to its little people's car from fifty years ago. It's the most successful comeback of them all.

First of all, it's cheap. Really cheap. The base, 1.2-litre model I drove when I came home is just £7,900. And that makes it a staggering £3,700 less than the cheapest Mini. It is bigger inside than a Mini too and, best of all, it looks better. It looks fantastic.

The looks are so wonderful, in fact, that you probably

won't care about the drawbacks. But there are a few. The headlights are hopeless, you really can't see what's coming from the left at oblique junctions, the engine is defeated by hills, and the ride, thanks to the short wheelbase, is awfully bouncy. Intolerably so, occasionally. This was the genius of the Mini. BMW gave it chic, want-one looks but underneath it was, and is, a proper car. One you can use everywhere, every day. The Fiat, on the other hand, is only an A to B car, and only then if B isn't too far away.

But, my God, you come away from an experience behind the wheel absolutely loving it. It's cheeky and non-threatening without being pathetic. It's practical without being boring. It's well priced as well. And there's something else.

It was born in the backstreets of Naples and, thanks to a burning ambition, it's shaken off its lowly born tags. Now it's mixing it with the others of the jet set in St Moritz. Ring any bells?

9 March 2008

A mainstay of the car-washing classes

Renault Laguna Sport Tourer Dynamique 2.0

Last weekend, I was driving through one of those junior-executive, Tory-stronghold housing estates – the sort where they have wife-swapping parties every Thursday at No 22 and everyone has baggy-knicker curtains. And I was staggered because just about every single man was out on his drive washing the car.

What a meaningless way of passing the time. You don't wash your vacuum cleaner or your television set, you have a machine to wash the dishes and you employ a man to clean your windows. So how much do you have to hate the sight of your wife and children before you think, 'I'd rather go outside into the cold and spend a couple of hours burnishing my wheel nuts'?

I am aware, of course, that many men do hate the sight of their wife and children. Doctors even have a name for these people: 'anglers'. But even the concept of sitting in the drizzle by a canal for six hours and then throwing everything you catch back into the water is not as daft as washing a car.

First of all, it's very hard work. You have to do all the exercises favoured by homosexuals in gyms. Bending over, stretching, rubbing. But at least when homosexuals finish, they have glistening, toned bodies that make them look good. You? You're just going to put your back out. And the more you clean, the more you'll notice is dirty. If you're not careful you'll end up polishing the inside of the tyre valves and then not wanting to use your car if it's raining.

This behaviour is called 'being a concours enthusiast' and it's very dangerous. Many 'concours enthusiasts' go on to be murderers.

And have you ever actually tried those cleaning products that are available in supermarkets? There are any number of sprays, creams, waxes, shampoos. It's like being in Richard Hammond's bathroom cabinet. Except, so far as I can tell, they don't actually do anything. 'Simply spray onto the glass,' it says on the tin, 'then, after two minutes, wipe down with a clean cloth.' Rubbish. You can never trust any instruction that begins with the word 'simply'.

I'll give you a little hint here. When your windscreen is completely covered in dead flies, the best way of seeing where you are going is to buy a new car.

Why are you washing the car in the first place? A car will not get smelly armpits or a cheesy groin. Bathing it will not increase its life expectancy or decrease the chances of a breakdown. All it does really is demonstrate to others that you have a tiny mind and an empty life. I want you to think carefully about this. Can you picture in your mind George Clooney washing a car? Quite.

The Germans have realized that it rots the mind and that's why it is illegal in most towns to wash your car on a Sunday. There is simply no place for such useless nonsense in an industrial powerhouse.

Oh, and here's another thing. Washing a car is the only time you ever get up close and personal with all of its panels. Which means you will find a million depressing little dings and scratches that you would never have spotted had you left it caked in grime.

Mind you, cleaning out the interior is even more silly because I can absolutely guarantee you will remove something that next week you will need. Everything I have ever bought is in my car. People say it's a skip and disgusting, and refuse to get in there. That's one advantage. Another is that last week, I needed a headache pill and it was simply a case of rummaging under the seat until I found one. Because it's so full of junk, I always have everything I could conceivably need. A Biro, a refreshing drink, lots of loose change, all sorts of maps, an iron lung, and so on. I kid you not. There's even a wetsuit in there.

Finally, we must discuss the chamois leather. And here, I have two more tips. Number one: if it is imitation chamois or a leather made from another sort of animal, it will not work. And number two: if it is a real chamois hide that has been crafted by walnut-faced men of the mountains, it will not work either.

You have to feel very sorry for the goat antelopes whose skin is used to make these things. No, really. Had they been native to Africa, they'd have been eaten by lions. Had they been horses or cows, they'd have been turned into burgers. And had they been native to Spain, the locals would have dreamt up some bizarre torture that would have involved them being flung off a tower by a man in pink satin trousers.

But no. They had everything going for them. They were cute and tasteless and they lived in Alpine meadows with nothing to disturb them except nuns singing. They even had a kindly Swiss man who came into their field once a day to play with their tits. Life was blissful. And then, one day, the world got it into its head that their skin could be used to clean cars. And that was it for Johnny Chamois. Now, and for no reason, the poor buggers are on the endangered list in some places.

Only the other day, I set off in my car on one of those crisp winter mornings when the sun is low in the sky and, because I never wash my car, I really and truly could not see where I was going. The inside of the windscreen was caked in gunk and, for reasons I couldn't fully understand, iced over just as thoroughly as the outside.

So, breaking with the tradition of a lifetime, I went to a petrol station and bought a scraper. Sadly, because it had been made in China, it was about as good at getting ice off a windscreen as the back of a dog. So, having made the situation much worse, I bought a chamois leather. What this did was remove all the moisture, mix it with the dirt . . . and put it back again. Honestly, I may as well have tried to clean the windscreen with a muddy stone.

I'm running out of space so I'd better move on to the car I've been driving this past week. It is a mainstay of the car-washing classes. A Tory-stronghold car. A car designed for the Barratt junior executive who dreams one day of going on his own. 'The bank's with me. John's with me . . .' In my mind, everyone who has a Renault Laguna is a wife swapper.

I liked the old model very much for reasons that are now lost in the mists of time and I wish I could say the same of the new one. I tried the hatch version a few months ago, and honestly, when I sat down to write the road test I couldn't remember anything about it. Except, perhaps, that it might have been brown. Fearing that you might need more information than this, I've just tried the Sport Tourer estate and that was definitely brown, and quite ugly.

Ooh. I've just remembered why I liked the old one. It was

the first car ever to be awarded a Euro NCAP five-star safety rating, and of course the new model is similarly blessed. But most cars are, these days. That's no reason for choosing the Renault over anything else.

In fact, I struggle to think why you might even want to buy a five-seat estate like this. For the same money every month you could have an Audi or a BMW. Or, if you are mad, you could have one of the smaller four-wheel-drive cars. The list of other things that would be better is long and includes rickets.

If, however, you are determined to have something boring and brown, buy a Vauxhall Zafira or a Ford S-Max. At least that way, you get two extra seats thrown into the mix. But if you absolutely insist on a boring brown car with only five seats, I'd go for the Ford Mondeo. It's more spacious and though I doubt you'll care, nicer to drive. Certainly, I found the new Laguna's steering a bit clattery. I also felt the trim was rubbish and that some of the softness I usually like in French cars had been replaced by an unnecessary German firmness.

To conclude, then, this is a car I'd rather wash than drive. And it doesn't get worse than that.

16 March 2008

Lovely to drive, awful to live with

Porsche Cayenne GTS

If you were to find yourself on the fearsome Nürburgring with a pressing reason to complete a lap in about nine minutes, the new Porsche Cayenne GTS would do nicely. It really is extremely fast. Similarly, if you were to become involved in a life or death battle with fifty tons of fire-breathing Challenger tank on the Bovington proving ground, I feel certain that this, the biggest Porsche of them all, would handle the punishment without falling into a million pieces.

However, if – and this seems more likely – you live in London and you want a car that can take five people in comfort, then the GTS is completely hopeless. No, really. It doesn't work and on top of that, it isn't welcome.

In the olden days, when I lived in London, many of the more idiotic boroughs erected signs explaining that you were entering a nuclear-free zone. I never knew why this was necessary because, so far as I could tell, these boroughs were also free from dinosaurs and spacemen. So why single out the absence of atom bombs?

Of course, today, dizzy anti-nuclear campaigners have become eco-mentalists and so, for the most part, the anti-nuke signs have been replaced with a million new ones which explain that you are entering a low-emission zone. Plainly, this isn't true. The Yorkshire Dales are a low-emission zone. So is the middle of the Sahara desert. But London? I think not.

Quite apart from the shops and businesses, you have all the low-emission signs that had to be mined, smelted, fashioned, painted and then distributed on every road in every suburb by an army of council vans. Compared with the emissions generated by this huge undertaking, a Porsche Cayenne simply isn't a problem at all.

But that's by the by. The city doesn't want it, you're going to be made to pay £1,000 a year in road tax and £125 a week if you drive into London, and even if you get there there'll be the biggest problem of them all. It's just too big.

Honestly, I took the Cayenne to Wandsworth the other night and it was the most miserable drive of my life. Frankly, I'd rather have gone there on my hands and knees.

The streets, with cars parked on either side, are just about wide enough for two small cars to pass. But there are no small cars in Wandsworth. For reasons that are unclear, everyone has a Volvo XC90. This meant I spent half the evening backing up, looking for a parking space in which I could wait while the lady with lovely hair coming the other way squeezed by.

But there are no parking spaces. You hear stories of people not using their cars because they know that when they come home again, they will be unable to park. I can believe it.

Fifteen years ago, I lived in Wandsworth, very briefly, and things were bad. Sometimes I'd have to park in the next street. But now that even more of the already titchy houses have been converted into flats, bringing more people and more cars, and even more people have turned their front lawns into car lots and everyone has an SUV, the situation is simply impossible. Often the nearest parking space is in Oslo.

Eventually, after an hour of reversing out of everyone's way and being jolted out of my seat by an endless series of speed humps that are completely pointless when nobody ever exceeds 2mph, I did find a spot that was handily located just 16 miles from the party I was attending. But unfortunately, it was exactly 4 inches smaller than the Cayenne. This meant I had to phone my hosts and explain that I'd try to get there for the coffee and mints.

This must happen to Wandsworthites all the time. And I'm sorry, but anyone who buys a huge car knowing it will never fit into a space is certifiably mad. Think how much life you're wasting by driving round and round the block. Think of all the other things you could be doing instead. And while you're doing that, we'll have a think about what can be done.

I've always argued that market forces dictate behaviour. That there's no need for congestion charges and so on because people will take only so much hassle before they'll leave the car at home and use an alternative. Not the bus obviously; that would be ridiculous. But a scooter, perhaps, or a sedan chair carried by four greased Egyptians.

Strangely, however, it seems I'm wrong. Wandsworth went past bursting point years ago but the people there are still buying idiotic cars that won't fit. I guess image down there is important and that if you don't have the right hair and the right accent you will be sent to Coventry. Or Tooting, as it's known in those parts.

You can be a convicted fraudster in Wandsworth and still engage with your social group. But you cannot have a Ford Fiesta.

Some might suggest the government should act, but really it is not the job of a state to decide who drives what sort of car. That's just meddlesome nonsense. I therefore propose that Wandsworth and Clapham Commons should be paved and turned into car parks.

One of two things will happen as a result. Either the plan

will go ahead and in a stroke the parking problem will be solved. Or there will be such an outcry that everyone will switch to a smaller car, which will make the scheme unnecessary.

If it works there, it could be extended to Hyde and Regent's Parks and then, in the fullness of time, to every green space in every town and city in the land. You tell the people of Harrogate that the Stray is to be turned into a car park and see how long it takes for everyone to change their Volvo XC90 into a Toyota Aygo.

But anyway, back to the GTS. We've established that it works on the Nürburgring and on a tank proving ground. We also know that it's useless in a big and busy city. But what about elsewhere?

In many ways, this car is a bit odd. I mean, the Cayenne was built to be a big, tall off-road car. You pay a premium for that height. And now along comes a version which is £17,000 more than the base model, precisely because it's not quite so tall.

The one I drove sat on air suspension rather than conventional steel springs. This is an option and not necessarily a good one, because air is simply not as good at the job as metal. Try this simple experiment if you don't believe me.

First of all, jump out of your bedroom window onto a well-sprung mattress. Okay? Good. And now try jumping out of the same window with no mattress at all. Will the air cushion your fall? No. Exactly.

Nevertheless, I massively enjoyed pushing this heavyweight hard. The heaviness of the controls makes you feel like a man, like you could take on the England front row and win. It is a car you drive with your chest pushed out and your tummy sucked in.

What's more, it doesn't handle well for an off-roader. It

handles well full stop. And it shifts, too. The 4.8-litre V8, especially with the sport mode engaged, goes like stink and sounds much as I would imagine Brian Blessed might sound if he fell into a vat of boiling oil. It is the sound of glorious, unabated, wanton consumption. It is the sound of pure, unbridled hedonism. Some have said they can't see the point of such a car. Why have an off-roader that handles this well, they say. It's like buying an iron in the hope it can make toast as well. Hmmm. I suspect they might change their minds if they had to make a sudden swerve on the motorway at 70mph.

I'm afraid, however, that while I respect the engineering of the GTS – it's by far the best of the Cayennes – and I loved driving it, I could never actually buy one because of the way it looks. This really is a car that drowned in Lake Ugly. And to make it even worse, my test car was finished in exactly the same colour as a diseased placenta.

So I still think the Range Rover is a better bet. It doesn't work half so well on the Nürburgring, it's just as hopeless in London and I bet it wouldn't last half as long on a tank proving ground. But at least it doesn't make you feel sick every time you see it.

23 March 2008

The aristo ruined by the devil's brew

Subaru Legacy Outback TD RE

Each of the summer's social occasions has its own code of conduct and everyone makes much effort to ensure they turn up in the correct clothes. At Royal Ascot, for instance, it is important to demonstrate that you started with nothing and have become very rich. And so you must go to www.russian brides.com and rent yourself a 6-foot hooker whom you then make taller still by kitting her out in a hat made from tinsel and old tractor tyres.

At Wimbledon you must develop phlebitis and a set of bingo wings bigger than most hang-gliders. At the Goodwood Revival you will need David Niven's moustache. And at Glyndebourne your black tie should be aubergine.

At Silverstone it's a gold-buttoned blazer teamed with pleated-front chinos and topped off with the branded-badge-and-tie combo. Henley requires that your Russian 'wife' wears some clothes for once, and at the Chelsea Flower Show, for reasons that are entirely unclear, you must wear a suit and a straw hat.

Of course, all of this requires a wardrobe that stretches from here to the Philippines, but at least a century of tradition means you won't ever commit the mortal English sin of turning up at the wrong place in the wrong clobber. I mean, can you imagine going to Glyndebourne with bingo wings? It'd be social suicide.

Unfortunately, while the sartorial rules are clear, first impressions are actually made in the car park. And here, because there are no rules at all, it is desperately easy to make a complete tit of yourself.

A couple of years ago someone arrived at my local prep school's sports day in a pink stretch Hummer. At first, I thought they were being ironic. But the gazebo they then built in the car park suggested they weren't. Honestly, they couldn't have got it more wrong if they'd turned up in split-crotch scuba suits.

The first thing you have to remember is that at any of the summer events you will be parking in a field, which means you can forget any dreams you may have had of arriving in a Ferrari Scaglietti. You absolutely have to have four-wheel drive.

Once there, you will be having a picnic, which means the boot must be big enough to serve as a hole for the dogs, a kitchen, a pantry and a boot store. A drop-down flap on which aged guests can perch is also a good idea. And the car should be grey or silver. Not red. Never red. Red cars are for Lebanese teenagers on Park Lane at two in the morning.

Above all this, though – above every other consideration – your car should be good in a traffic jam. Because that, no matter where you're going, is how you'll spend most of the day.

A social event in what *Tatler* calls 'the season' is invariably held in a part of the world that was designed for the ox, not half a million people in hats the size of the moon, with a boot full of vodka and bouillon.

Obviously, the Range Rover is your best bet. It is the little black dress of cars, a one-size-fits-all solution to every social and practical requirement. It works in fields, there's enough headroom for the most preposterous of hats, the tailgate splits in two and it's just as happy in a field as it is when the B4746 is jammed up all the way from Nethercombe Bottom to Piddlecomb End. But it is very expensive: filling it with fuel costs £111, the road tax will soon cost more than a beachfront villa in Miami and few cars made today depreciate with such vim.

That's why, when I was invited for lunch at the Cheltenham Festival recently, I chose to go in the smart man's Range Rover. The Subaru Legacy Outback.

Now, I have written about this excellent car before, twice actually, but I have an excuse for reviewing it again because it's now available with the world's first flat four diesel engine.

In a flat four, there are two cylinders on each side of a central crankcase, and the pistons move towards one another. Imagine two men boxing and you'll see why these engines are known as boxers.

Petrol-fuelled boxers have been used before, in quirky cars such as the Citroën GS, the Alfasud, the Beetle and several Porsches. There are some notable advantages. A boxer engine is well balanced, it is easy to cool, it takes up little space in the engine bay and, because it's flat, it can be mounted low down, giving a lower centre of gravity.

The disadvantage is that it's expensive to make. It was for this reason that Sir Alec Issigonis abandoned his plans for a flat four in the Morris Minor and it is why most car makers today have followed suit. But not Subaru. It continues to use a boxer in the Impreza and has now built one that runs on the fuel of Lucifer.

Quite why, I don't know, because the flat four's main advantages – you can have a sleek front end and good handling – are largely irrelevant in a car that sounds like a canal boat and goes with the vigour of a Norfolk Broad. And they are especially irrelevant in an estate car that was designed for muddy car parks.

No matter. I set off for Cheltenham in convoy with some friends in a Range Rover. And possibly because of the fuel they'd use if they spent all morning sitting with half of Ireland in a jam, the route they chose seemed, as far as I could tell, to be made up of roads that were 'unsuitable for motorists'.

We went through villages that were lost to a strange mist 400 years ago. We saw signs telling us that 'there be witches'. We saw people in smocks. We went through Henry Dent-Brocklehurst's kitchen. We drove over twigs, logs and a field full of turnips and we forded rivers that don't even feature on Royal Geographical Society surveys. And the Subaru laughed at it all, clinging onto the Range Rover's tail like an eager puppy out for the first time with its mum.

Of course, the Range Rover has more ground clearance and a computer program that allows it to cross the Sahara, and do a rainforest before lunch. The Subaru has no such wizardry. Just a straightforward four-wheel-drive system, and that, trust me, could take everything that Gloucestershire placed in its way.

Inside, it has five seats, a dashboard, some leather and a sat nav screen that works well. Except at night, when it stares out of the dash like a second-world-war searchlight. Oh yes, and either I've grown or the car's shrunk since I last tried it out, because I can report that life for the taller driver is cramped.

Outside, it's just very good-looking in a Chelsea Flower Show suit sort of way.

In the car park at Cheltenham, it looked like it belonged. And not only because there must have been a thousand others, all slightly bent, dirty and blue-blooded. This is the car of the aristocrat. The person who uses money to buy time. Not things. It really should come as standard with a black lab in the boot.

And . . . I'm repeating myself. You probably already know that I am a huge fan of the Legacy. And what you want to know is: the new engine. Any good?

No. It's crap. Normally, diesels are happiest at low revs in a high gear. Not the Legacy. It has the torque of a pencil sharpener, the life and soul of a corpse. You need to be in first until the whole engine has revved itself clean off its mountings, and even then when you go for second it judders and shivers in protest.

I don't care if it uses only a gallon of fuel every 6 million miles; it is just not worth the bother. And to make matters worse it's not available with an automatic gearbox.

The Legacy with a petrol engine? Yes. Definitely. It has bingo wings, a great suit, the right moustache and a silly hat in the shape of a mad sunroof. If it could talk, you know it would sound like Edward Fox. It's a brilliant all-rounder. But the diesel? Not in a million years.

30 March 2008

A beauty cursed by travel sickness

Callaway Corvette C6

Today, if you want something to be a commercial success, it must be designed from day one with a passport and legs. Whether a beefburger, a plastic Doctor Who toy, a strawberry, an internet people-searching site or a sport, it must be as relevant in Alice Springs as it is in the Colombian jungle.

Funnily enough, however, the biggest problem is America – the only country in the world that calls football 'soccer' and insists on playing rounders and netball instead. So, if you have developed, say, a pillow that absorbs dribble, you stand a better chance of selling it to a pygmy with a dinner plate sewn into his bottom lip, than you do to Wilbur and Myrtle from Sacramento.

It's a bit like the 'special relationship' Tony Blair always talked about so much. The Americans can build a nuclear-missile warning station in Britain to protect them, but it makes us the ideal first-strike target. They can extradite people from Britain, but we can't do the same from them. They can get our immediate help in the Gulf, but we had to beg for assistance against the Nazis and the Argies. With America, the world is a one-way street.

We must have their computers, their jeans and their eating habits, yet there are more Made-in-Britain labels on the moons of Jupiter than there are in South Dakota. To the average American, 'abroad' is Canada or Mexico. Any further than that and you need Nasa. Over there, a Brit is simply someone to shoot by mistake. So it's certain that Hank J Dieselburger isn't going to be buying a jar of Bovril any time soon.

Nor will he be watching a British-made car show. *Top Gear* is screened all over the world, from remote Himalayan villages to the bullet-ridden boulevards of Lebanon. It is a genuine, bona fide export success. But in the US it is watched only by half a handful of expats who diligently follow BBC America, and a few torrentists on the interweb.

This is partly because, when it comes to motoring, the English language makes more sense in Albania than it does in Alabama. Almost every word in the Americans' automotive lexicon is different from ours, so when we talk about motorways, pavements, bonnets, boots, roofs, bumper bars, petrol, coupés, saloons, people carriers, cubic centimetres and corners, they have no idea what we're on about.

Our forward commanders can call in a tactical airstrike in southern Afghanistan and their pilots will know precisely what's needed. But review a Fiat Punto 'hatchback' on the 'bypass' and you may as well be speaking in dog. Even their gallons are as odd as their spelling of 'centre'.

Then there's the pronunciation issue. Jagwarr, Teeyoda, Neesarn, Hundy, Mitsuboosi, BM Dubya, V Dubya – it's all completely mangled.

However, while they don't understand our car show, when it comes to the cars themselves, the one-way street works in the opposite direction. Just six months ago, and for the first time ever, foreign car makers sold more vehicles in America than those made by Brad, Todd and Bud.

And what of American cars over here? Well, if we exclude Cheshire from the equation, most people in Europe would rather have syphilis than a Buick. We'll buy their Coca-Cola, their iPods and their Motown sound, but the cars that gave Motown its name? No, thanks. Driving an American car would be like making love to Jade Goody when you had a choice.

It's odd. Why can Bill Gates sell his binary numbers to the world when General Motors can't sell its cars? I wish I had the answer, because then I might understand why I don't want to own the Callaway Corvette I used on a recent trip to Los Angeles.

Callaway is an engineering company that has been tuning and fiddling with Corvettes since the year dot, sometimes without much success. The first example I tried, way back in the sixteenth century, was owned by a murderer and had two turbochargers. This made the engine extremely powerful. So powerful, in fact, that when I tried to set off, it turned the clutch into a thin veneer of powder and shot it like talcum powder into the wind. The murderer was extremely displeased with me . . .

Since then, however, Callaway has continued to beaver away, helped along by the average American's deep-seated belief that all cars can be improved by a man in a shed – understandable when the cars in question were made in Detroit. So, today it makes the Corvettes that race at Le Mans (which they can't say properly either). Furthermore, Callaway has sheds all across America, and even in Germany.

It has become a big business. And I'm delighted to say it has stopped upping the power without uprating any of the other components.

The car I drove, a one-off demonstration vehicle, was garnished with an Eaton supercharger – chromed, of course – that was about the same size as Antigua. It's so big that a special bonnet with a huge hump in the middle has had to be fitted. In the past it would have got the car from 0 to 60mph . . . just once, before the chassis snapped in half and the wheels fell off.

Not any more. The car is fitted with Stoptech racing brakes, Eibach Multi-Pro suspension, wheels made from magnesium and carbon fibre, and other beefed-up components from the tip of its slender nose to the back end of its Plasticine arse (which they also can't say). So it's actually designed to handle the 616bhp produced by that force-fed V8, although the standard car, which is also available as a convertible, has 580bhp.

Yes, 616bhp is a lot. It's the sort of power you get from a Ferrari 599. And yet the car you see in the pictures this morning costs just over $92,500. At today's exchange rate, that's about 35p.

At first, I was too jet-lagged to drive, so I tossed the keys to a colleague who was part gibbering wreck and part Michael Schumacher. We'd kangaroo away from the lights, stall, lurch up to about 400mph and then zigzag through the traffic like Jack Bauer in pursuit of a Russian nuke.

As a result, on our way back from Orange County to Beverly Hills, I snatched the keys . . . and had exactly the same problem. The clutch is like a switch and the gearbox like something that operates a lock on the Manchester Ship Canal. And if, by some miracle, you do get them to work in harmony, you are catapulted into a hypersonic, Hollywood blockbuster world of searing noise, bleeding ears and speeds so fantastic that you mark the instrument panel down as a born-again liar. I absolutely bloody loved it.

Most European and Japanese cars these days hide their thrills behind a curtain of electronic interference and acoustically tuned, synthetic exhaust noises. Driving, say, an M5, is like having sex in a condom. Driving this Corvette is like taking it off.

Oh sure, it has the same problems that beset all Vettes. A dash made from the same cellophane they use to wrap cigarette packets, a sense it's been nailed together by apes, the finesse of a charging rhinoceros and the subtlety of a crashing helicopter. But the Callaway power injection masks all this in the same way that a dollop of hot sauce turns a slice of week-old goat cheek into a taste sensation.

On the El Toro airfield, deserted since it was attacked by aliens in *Independence Day*, it would slide and growl like it was the love child of Red Rum and a wild lion. On the snarled-up 405 on the way back to LA, it made rude gestures to other road users, urging them to take it on, knowing full well that it could beat just about everything up to a Veyron (pronounced 'goddam cheese-eating Kraut junk').

Then, when the traffic got too bad, we cut through downtown LA, where it pulled off the most fabulous trick of them all – absorbing the bumps and potholes that would disgrace even the Zimbabwean highways authority. Simply as a result of this, I have to say it's an even better car than Chevrolet's own hot Corvette, the Z06, which rides the bumps like a skateboard.

Let us look, then, at the Callaway's strengths. It is ridiculously cheap, immensely powerful, much more comfortable than you would expect, beautiful to behold and blessed with handling that belies the fact that it was designed in a country that has no word for 'bend'. It also redefines the whole concept of excitement.

If I lived over there, be in no doubt that I would have one like a shot. It suits the place very well. It is Bruce Willis in a vest. Over here, however, I'd rather go to work in a scuba suit. As a car, it would work fine, apart from the steering wheel being on the wrong side. It would be fun. It would be fast. And, unlike most American cars, it isn't even that big.

As a statement, however, I fear it would sit in the Cotswolds about as comfortably as Sylvester Stallone would belong in an EM Forster novel. It isn't brash – at least not compared with a Lamborghini. But like all American cars, it does feel that way. And a bit stupid, too.

Funny, isn't it. American cars, more than all others, are built to travel and yet that's the one thing they really don't do at all well.

20 April 2008

. . . catch me if you can

Mitsubishi Lancer Evolution X FQ-360 GSR

Having my photograph taken has always been like having extensive root-canal work done on my soul. I hate it with an unbridled passion. A photograph of me serves as a permanent reminder of the simple fact that I am just a stomach and a very large chin with a small piece of wire wool growing out of the top.

Unfortunately, these days everyone has a camera phone, so everyone has become an amateur paparazzo. And that means I have my photograph taken about four hundred million times a day.

I understand why, of course. If you could get a snap of Cliff Richard mowing his lawn, then – ker-ching! – I bet it'd be worth a grand. If you could get a Formula One boss having his hair checked for lice by a girl dressed up as a Belsen inmate, you might even be able to afford a new car.

Of course there are drawbacks. First of all, you have to have the morals of a woodlouse, and second, you might drive your prey to crash into a tunnel. But that doesn't seem to be stopping anyone.

Just recently I was snapped by a member of the public while driving along the M40. He claimed the snap showed I was using my mobile. My phone records prove that I wasn't but, no matter, he sold the picture to the *Mirror*. It ran it on the front page and as a result the young man probably earned enough to buy himself and his girlfriend a slap-up meal at the local Harvester.

On holiday this year someone took a picture of me going snorkelling. And because it showed a chin and a stomach in a face mask the *Mirror* bought this one too, paying the lens-man enough for him to buy himself a jolly nice piña colada.

Now it's open season. Some kid took a picture of me while I was asleep, and when I told him to eff off his dad went immediately, you've guessed it, to the *Mirror*. It's got to the point where my wife never actually bothers to ring and ask where I am. She just looks in the redtops.

I'm thinking of cashing in myself; maybe I'll sell them a picture of me checking my prostate.

It's at its worst, though, when I'm imprisoned by a flash and noticeable car. Recently, I drove my Lamborghini from Guild-ford to Chipping Norton. It's about 90 miles and I had my picture taken 107 times. I counted. This meant I couldn't use the phone or pick my nose or break the speed limit or sing along to the radio or even, on the straight bits, catch forty winks. It was so wearisome that when I got home I sold the car.

And I can assure you that I most definitely will not replace it with a Mitsubishi Lancer Evo X FQ-360. Because, I swear to God, you couldn't get more attention even if you were Jade Goody and you stood on a bridge over the M1 motor-way and had full sex with a cow.

Now if you're looking at the picture above, wondering why such a vulgar little thing could possibly cause anyone to look twice, then you know nothing about cars and, frankly, you'd be better off reading about something else.

If, on the other hand, you do know about cars, then you will also not be very interested to hear what the Evo is like. Because when it comes to four-wheel-drive turbo cars for the PlayStation generation, all eyes are currently on the Nissan GT-R – the most eagerly anticipated new arrival since God stuck a pin in a map and decided on Bethlehem.

The fact is, though, that the Nissan is going to be upwards of £50,000, about 15 grand more than the little Itchypussy. And I'm sorry but I cannot see, with the current laws of physics in place, how it can possibly be that much better.

The previous nine Evos were always exquisite to drive, nicer even than their great rivals from Subaru. But they were also woefully flimsy, stylistically challenged and hard to the point of hopelessness. For one lap of the Nürburgring, you'd use an Evo every time. For the journey home, you'd take the Scooby-Doo.

Now, though, everything has changed. The new Subaru is about as much fun as a church service. And it doesn't look good in photographs because, like me, it doesn't look good at all. I've seen more attractive things in medical books.

The Evo X, on the other hand, looks fab. Peel away the bulges and all that carbon fibre flotsam and jetsam – all of which gives other road users an impression that, for you, driving may be a hobby, like trainspotting – and the basic shape is very good. And then . . . Oh. My. God. There's the way it drives.

I fear I may have to get a bit technical here. When you turned into a corner in an old Evo, initially there'd be a dribble of dreary understeer. In a normal car this is a speed-scrubbing health and safety warning that soon there will be ambulances and fire engines, but in the Mitsubishi it was simply a portal through which you had to pass to get at the car's heart and soul.

The heart and soul in question was its ability to remain composed and absolutely controllable in a lairy, tyre-smoking four-wheel drift. No other car I'd driven was able to do this, even slightly. It was exquisite.

The new car is even better because when you turn into a corner it's the back that steps out of line. This means that even the portal through which you must pass to get at the meat and veg is full of hair-tingling joy.

Of course, there are lots of buttons you can press to make the handling different, but those are for geeks and bores. All I can report is that the basics of this car – the core – are monumentally, toweringly, eye-wateringly brilliant.

Then there's the speed. Yes, a Ferrari 430 is full of brio and passion, but get an Evo X on your tail and I guarantee that, unless it's being driven by a complete spanner, you will not be able to shake it off.

And now comes the really good news. When you have finished at the track, the ride home is not bad either. Certainly, it is way softer than the Evos of old, much more comfortable. Also, the X doesn't require a service every 300 yards. And it's garnished with higher-quality plastics as well. Oh, and I nearly forgot. It has the single best touchscreen central command sat nav system I've found in any car. It'll even give you the average speed, in a graph, of each of your past 20 journeys.

And, of course, it's got four doors, seating for five and a boot which, despite the fitting of a Grateful Dead bass speaker, was still large enough last night to accommodate my daughter's back-to-school requirements.

There are, however, some drawbacks that you might like to consider before signing your name on the dotted line in dribble.

First of all, it has only a five-speed gearbox. This means that on the motorway the all-new super-light 2.0-litre turbo engine becomes awfully drony. It's like listening to Alistair Darling make a speech. And, worse, because there's no cruising gear the fuel consumption is dreadful.

That's bad in any car, but when the tank is only the size of a Zippo, you will struggle to do 200 miles between fill-ups.

Almost certainly, then, you'd be better off with the less powerful but more economical FQ-300. I tried this, too, and missed the savage acceleration. But I liked the twin-clutch six-speed flappy-paddle gearbox, which is not available on the 360. Furthermore, it has the same top speed and it's at least £6,000 cheaper. Of the two, this is the one I'd buy.

Unfortunately, however, I can't. I'd become fed up with the flotilla of camera-toting rats more quickly than I became fed up with the never-ending trips to the pumps.

Happily, my wife has come to the rescue. She's going to buy one and, being an organized soul, will keep it topped up with fuel. This means that when it's dark and all the *Mirror* readers are in the pub fighting, I can take it out for a little drive. It'll serve as a constant reminder of what cars can, and should, be like.

27 April 2008

Look, mums – a 4x4 planet saver

Mitsubishi Outlander 2.2 DI-DC Diamond

All black men are thieves. All Jews would sell their mothers for a pound. All Muslims are suicide bombers and everyone in Ireland is as thick as a slab of cheese. Yes. Right. And everyone with a Chelsea tractor is a stick-thin blonde whose head is so full of useless social engagements that she can't actually be bothered to steer round other cars, street furniture or bus shelters.

It ain't necessarily so. All sorts of people buy 4x4s for all sorts of reasons. And contrary to what the global warmists would have us believe, only some are stick-thin blonde women who won't actually stop until the underside of their car is so jammed up with run-over pedestrians the wheels won't go round any more.

The wave of hatred, then, that engulfs the off-roader is nothing more than ill-informed prejudice. And what makes my blood boil is that things are getting worse.

I do not have much time for people who get dressed up in camouflage clothing and take to the countryside in their Land Rovers to see who can get most covered in mud. This is known as 'green laning' and it's as ridiculous as pushing a kettle over a frozen lake. I wouldn't want to stop them doing it, though, partly because they'd all be at home otherwise, downloading unusual images from the internet, but mostly because it's fairly harmless.

Oh no it isn't, say the ramblists. They argue that green laning is noisy and causes polar bears to drown. One group, the Yorkshire Dales Green Lanes Alliance, says that taking a vehicle for the purposes of fun onto a green lane should be 'an offence'.

Now, even if we ignore the difficulties of policing such a law, or of making a case stick in the courts – 'I wasn't doing it for fun' is hard to disprove – we are left astounded at the narrow-mindedness of these people. Not even the Communists or the Nazis attempted to make 'fun' an offence.

And, unfortunately, it doesn't end here because those of a four-wheel-drive disposition are being targeted, not only in the countryside, but in towns as well, with local councils saying now that anyone who drives a large car on the school run must pay £75 a year for the privilege.

This is insane. Like many parents, my wife and I have a big, seven-seater Volvo, not because we used to lie awake at night dreaming of the day when we could own such a thing, and not because we always wanted, more than anything, a car that sounds like a canal boat. No. We have it because we are part of a school run car sharing scheme.

And the fact is this: by filling our Volvo with six children every morning, we are keeping three other cars off the road. So why should we pay more than someone who takes just two kids to school in a Mini?

In reality, a Mini takes up exactly the same amount of space on the road as a Volvo XC90, so therefore, it should be the Mini driver who's made to pay a premium while those of us with large, high-occupancy vehicles, are allowed to proceed for free.

I mean it. I would far rather own a Cooper S than a Volvo. It is better looking, nicer to drive, cheaper to run and cheaper to buy. But I don't. I sacrifice my love of driving, my love of cars and the contents of my bank account for the public good. I should, therefore, be rewarded with gifts, free passage and some thank-you letters from the world's polar bears.

Yes, I know I'm supposed to make my children go to school on the bus, but I can't – for three reasons. One, they'd get lost. Two, they'd catch a disease. And three, there isn't one.

So, if you are in the same boat as me, and you fancy the idea of a school-run-sharing seven-seater, there are many choices, and almost all of them are terrible in some way. The Audi Q7 is ugly. The Land Rover Discovery weighs more than the moon. The Vauxhall Zafira is a Vauxhall, and the Ford S-Max, while attractive and good to drive, is a mini people carrier . . . and I'm sorry but nothing says you've given up in life quite so spectacularly as a car designed entirely to be practical. It's motoring's equivalent of a tartan zip-up slipper.

Small wonder, then, the XC90 is almost a part of the school uniform these days. It's practical. It's reliable. It has a reputation for safety. With a towbar on the back, it'll pull a horsebox. I even have a friend who has fitted winter tyres and uses it for shooting. But there is one problem. When it first came out, it was good value at less than £30,000. But now the top models are nudging £50,000 or more. And that makes it even more expensive than a packet of pasta.

Which is why my eye was drawn last week to the new Mitsubishi Outlander. Here we have a car that seems to do everything the Volvo does, in a smaller package, for less money. A lot less. The range starts at less than £20,000 and even the most expensive model is only £27,000.

I do not know how such a low price is possible when, so far as I can see, a cut of the profits will be going to every car firm in the world.

The Outlander, amazingly, is based on the same platform as the Mitsubishi Evo X that I reviewed last week. But the car itself was designed in conjunction with Mercedes-Benz when it was in bed with Chrysler, so it shares a great many bits and pieces with the Dodge Nitro, a silly car for silly Americans.

Then there's the French connection. The Outlander, having been designed in America, Japan and Germany, is being built in conjunction with Peugeot and Citroën, who offer their own versions of the same car. And the 2-litre turbo-diesel engine is made by Volkswagen.

No matter: despite the United Nations nature of the background, the end result is quite good.

We'll deal with the drawbacks first, and that means we have to start in the boot, where there is an essay on how the rear seats should be raised and lowered from the floor. I think it's designed to be difficult, because then you'll never actually discover that when the seats are in place there's no rear legroom, at all, and not much boot left either.

It's best, then, on a shared school run, to put the kids you don't like very much back there.

Next is the four-wheel-drive system. Most of the time you're in two-wheel drive and that doesn't really work when the car is fully loaded. Every time you put your foot down, the front end goes light, the driven wheels lose their grip and everything, for a little while, goes all wobbly. Best, I think, to hang the extra fuel consumption and leave it in 4WD all the time.

And that's it. Those are the drawbacks. All two of them. The rest of the car is well made, well equipped, well trimmed and, like the Evo, fitted with Mitsubishi's brilliant sat nav system. I also think it is good-looking and, despite the fact you can only have it with a diesel engine, quite good to drive. It feels much lighter and more responsive than you might imagine.

Of course, it's not as much fun as a Mini, it's not as practical as a Volvo and it won't be as cheap as its sister car from Citroën . . . not if they do their usual trick of offering customers £1m cashback and the chance to sleep with the managing director's wife every other Saturday.

But as an overall package, it's a good way of getting into a car-sharing scheme. Yes, you'll be charged £75 by idiotic, blinkered councils, but look at it this way – you'll save the planet, keep the polar bears alive, cut congestion and, best of all, on the mornings when it's not your turn, have a lie-in.

4 May 2008

Press a button and pray it's the right one

Citroën C5 2.7 HDi V6 Exclusive

My eyes don't work any more. When I dial a number on my mobile, it's only through sheer blind luck that I get through to the right person. And as for texts – forget it. Then there's the bothersome business of going out to eat. Most restaurants provide mood lighting, which is wonderful if you are dining with a moose but not so wonderful if – as is normal – the menu is printed in the sort of typeface that's usually seen on microdots. Mostly, I just point and hope that I've managed to miss the marzipan pie with grated butter beans.

Of course, I should go to the opticians but I'm afraid this isn't possible because, before giving me a pair of spectacles, they will look into my eyes with machinery . . . and here we hit on the problem.

I'm not a squeamish man. I am never unduly troubled by scenes on the news that the BBC's editorial policy unit has deemed worthy of a warning about 'graphic violence and bloodshed'. I can kill a chicken. I could amputate a gangrenous leg. I can even graze the internet and not be constantly fearful that I'm going to be so revolted by something that pops onto the screen that I'll vomit into the keyboard.

But eyes? No. I can't even think about them without going queasy. When my daughter needed an operation to correct a squint, the doctor explained the procedure to me, after which I had to be brought round with smelling salts. I have to fast-forward 'that bit' in *Kill Bill 2*, and I have never once used eyedrops. It would be impossible.

As a result of all this, I buy my reading glasses from the only shops I ever visit, which are in airport departure lounges. This is not easy because the instructions you have to follow before deciding what sort of lens you need are printed in a typeface smaller than most bacteria.

Consequently, I usually end up with a pair of specs that require me to position a book six seats in front of where I'm sitting on the plane. Or so close to my face that it actually squashes my nose.

And here's the really bad bit. The glasses you buy over the counter are a big joke – one that's being played by the Chinese, I expect. They are held together with nuts and bolts so small that when they come undone – and they do, all the time – you need a carbon nanotube to do them up again. And, of course, you don't have a carbon nanotube with you because you're on a plane, and such things – along with shampoo and tennis rackets – aren't allowed on planes. What's more, you don't even have your reading glasses because they're in four pieces on your left knee.

I wouldn't mind, but even if you are not squeamish about eyes, and you make regular trips to the opticians and have a pair of lenses that are perfectly suited to your particular condition, you will look like an ocean-going idiot.

Everyone chooses their specs to make a statement – to make them look interesting or sexy or wise – whereas in fact all spectacles do is tell the world that your body doesn't work properly. Choosing purple frames merely highlights that fact. It's like being diagnosed with erectile dysfunction and then buying trousers that have no fly.

So, maybe the only solution is that we do without glasses and spend the rest of our lives with a headache from the strain, eating marzipan and butter beans. Or that the worlds of industry and catering accept that half of their customers struggle with anything smaller than 72-point bold type, and that they reprint their instructions and menus to suit.

This brings me nicely to the dashboard of the new Citroën C5. My demonstrator had a 7-inch 16:9 television screen with a built-in GSM telephone, a radio, a CD player, iPod connectivity, a 10GB hard drive to store music and GPS navigation with traffic alerts and a bird's-eye-view map.

In addition, there was an electronic parking brake (complete with a system that prevents the car rolling back on hill starts), cruise control and an adjustable speed limiter. And then, in no particular order, I had parking sensors, electrically adjusted seats that vibrate if you stray out of your lane, directional headlamps, switchable suspension, ride-height adjustment, traction control, a dual-zone air-conditioning system, hazard warning lights that come on when you brake hard, an electronic stability program, an electrochrome rear-view mirror, rain-sensing wipers, dark-sensing headlamps, a trip computer, a tyre-pressure monitor . . .

This car made a Mercedes S-class look like the back end of a Cornish cave, and while that's wonderful, unfortunately all of these things have to be operated with buttons that are mostly the size of pinheads because that's the only way they can get them all in. It is therefore impossible to find them and even more impossible to read what any of them do, at least not without reaching for your reading glasses, which is tricky when you're on the move.

Honestly, in a whole week I was unable to activate the sat nav, and any attempt to set the cruise control usually resulted in Ken Bruce being replaced by traction control. To operate the horn you ideally need a head torch and a cocktail stick.

However, I could clearly see that the new C5 was a very handsome car. It sits among other four-door saloons – from BMW, Audi, Ford, Honda, and so on – looking much like Angelina Jolie would while sitting in a Wakefield bus queue.

What's more, we are told it's no longer built by uninterested Algerians in a factory made from straw, and that as a result it is somehow German. Obviously, there's no way of knowing at this stage whether any of this is true, but I doubt that it is. The French have never been able to make a car that lasts, any more than the Germans have been able to make a soufflé.

What is certain is that the C5 is more comfortable than any German rival. My test car had hydropneumatic suspension, which really does isolate you from the pain of a badly made road. It also means it handles like a blancmange, although to get round that problem you can reach for the 'sport' button – which turns on the CD player.

I liked driving this car. I liked looking at it. I liked the sheer surprise of pressing a button and then trying to work out what I'd done. There's one obstacle, however, that I'd have to jump before I signed on the dotted line.

In the past few years, Citroën has struggled to make its products popular in Britain. Or indeed anywhere where people walk on their back legs. So, to get round that, it's indulged in a business strategy that most experts would call 'a bit daft'.

First, it has offered its cars at enticingly low prices and then garnished them with cashbacks, 0 per cent finance and the promise of a Thai massage for everyone buying one before the end of May. I sometimes get the impression there are so many incentives on a Citroën C3, for example, that if you buy one the dealer will give you £40. And some of his daughters.

Of course, this policy doesn't really work for you because if you can buy a Citroën new for minus £40, what's it going to be worth when you want to sell? And obviously, it doesn't work for Citroën either, but that hasn't stopped the company. In about five minutes I found a Citroën dealer willing to offer me a new C5 with well over a thousand quid knocked off its list price.

Of course, there was probably some detailed small print attached to the offer. But, needless to say, I couldn't have read it.

11 May 2008

Face lifted, clanger dropped

Mercedes-Benz SL 63 AMG

Over the past century there has been a handful of cars that stand out as especially innovative, brilliant and important. If they were paintings, they'd be in the Louvre. If they were animals, Texans would have their heads on a wall. These are the Mozart motors. The Mona Lisas.

And sitting comfortably in the mix is the Mercedes 300 SL gull-wing. People in baggy jumpers and worn shoes speak in reverential whispers about how the futuristic engine was canted right over to one side so that the bonnet could be low and sleek. They talk of its light but immensely strong tubular frame and how 29 of the 1,400 made were fabricated entirely in aluminium. And when you get them onto the racing car that spawned the gull-wing, many are so overcome with emotion, they have to go to the lavatory.

This gives me a problem because if I were to draw up a list of the five most important cars ever made, the gull-wing wouldn't be on it. I'm afraid I can't see what the fuss is about. And that, if you're a motoring enthusiast, is a bit like an art collector saying he doesn't see why people get in such a flap about the Sistine Chapel.

To me, the gull-wing is a bit like *Meddle*, the Pink Floyd album that gets enthusiasts of the band all hot under their kaftans. Yeah, yeah, yeah. Very advanced. Blah, blah. Revolutionary. As far as I'm concerned, however, the SL dynasty didn't kick off until the pagoda-roofed model came along in 1963. This was the brand's *Dark Side of the Moon*. If you'll forgive the mangled rock references, this was Genesis.

The 1963 SL did not have a canted-over engine or a fuel-injection system that was forty years ahead of its time. It had no racing brother that scored memorable victories at Le Mans. It was just a very, very pretty car with an engine and some wheels.

It was also, I think I'm right in saying, the first car ever made that looked feminine. It was a miniskirt with windscreen wipers. A man in one of these looked as wrong as a man in a thong. But put a girl behind the wheel and the effect was profound. I once saw Kate Moss drive by in a 280 and I had to pull into a lay-by for a while.

Sadly, after eight years, Mercedes stopped making an SL for girls and aimed its new model at Bobby Ewing.

Bobby liked the new SL very much. He used it to drive around Dallas being unfaithful. But then, one day, another character from the show used an SL to run him down. This made him very angry and he spent the next two years in the shower.

Like the pagoda-roofed version, Bobby's SL was not very sporty. Even the 5-litre V8, which came along in 1980, produced only 237bhp, which meant it had a fairly miserable top speed of 135. It wasn't very pretty either, but despite these drawbacks the SL remained in production for eighteen years. A record for any Mercedes, except the G Wagen.

The car that eventually replaced it in 1989 rather stretched the SL concept. It's supposed to stand for 'Sport Light', and this version was sporty and light in the same way as an East German Olympic shot putter was sporty and light. It weighed about the same as the moon, which meant that if you drove along the Pacific Highway at more than 83mph you could make the tide come in.

This was one of the first cars I road-tested on *Top Gear* and because I was a bit naïve I loved it, especially the adjustable suspension, which was a new idea back then, and the clever electric roof, which was operated by eleven motors. I also liked the hugeness of the thing and the wall of gadgetry. Weirdly, however, despite the buttons and the bulk, the femininity was back, and as a result this model was bought largely by extremely wealthy orange ladies in Cheshire and Harrogate.

It was in 2002, nearly forty years after it had last done a decent SL, that Mercedes got the recipe right again. It built a version for debonair, good-looking, modest and interesting people. And despite this I bought one. Again, it wasn't sporty or light but the SL 55 AMG version I bought did go, and sound, like thunder. I liked it very much, although there were one or two details that I hoped would have been addressed when I drove the facelifted model last week.

First of all, there was the suspension. Most of the time it was fairly soft and comfortable, even when you asked it to be hard and sporty. That was fine. It suited the lazy, cruising nature of the car. But because it was designed by someone with a laptop, rather than someone with a lathe, it couldn't cope when it was presented with a sharp ridge or pothole. The whole car would skip sideways in a move that was not dangerous, but was unsettling and uncomfortable.

Next, there was the woeful choice of colours for both the interior and the exterior. When you are spending £100,000 on a car, the dealer should be able to make the seats from his wife's pubic hair if that's what the customer wants. But no. You get more choice of colour and materials in a Turkish prison.

Then there was the laughable 'linguatronic' system. In theory, you could speak instructions and the car would obey. In practice, it never had a clue what you were on about. So when you asked the sat nav to set a course for home, it would tune the radio to some shouty man on Fox FM. And when you asked it to ring the office, it would call up pretty well everyone but.

Strangely, Mercedes has not changed any of these things on the new SL 63 AMG. It still plays hopscotch on badly made roads. It still isn't available in flame orange or the colour of my wife's eyes. And the linguatronic can still speak only Klingon.

So what has Mercedes done? Well, it's ditched the iron lung of a supercharger and fitted a normally aspirated 6.2-litre V8. This means you get about one more brake horsepower, but before you grow too excited about that I should point out that you get a lot less torque. And it's developed right up the rev range, exactly where you don't want it. The engine produces more carbon dioxide, too.

In addition, it has now fitted a seven-speed automatic gearbox, which is two more cogs than you need. Or want. On the plus side, the gearbox does come with a feature called 'sport+', which drops you down the box when you are approaching a corner. What's more, if you specify the £2,230 driver's package, you get to go on a training course. And Mercedes ups the limited top speed from 155mph to 186mph.

The car I drove was also equipped with an £8,230 performance package, which meant I had larger front brakes, a limited slip differential and a steering wheel that wasn't circular.

If you steer clear of the options list, the new car is broadly similar to the model it replaces, except for one thing. A huge thing. For some reason it's been littered with boy-racer carbon-fibre tinsel and, at the front, given a hare lip. I spent hours examining this design detail, wondering if I was missing something. I wasn't. Mercedes has – and there's no other way of putting this – cocked up.

I'd love to think that this morning the entire team of designers is busy at work in Stuttgart, correcting its mistake. But as we know from the SL's history, the process of evolution is slow. It's therefore likely we are stuck with that gargoyle until 2015. And that is a problem for someone who wants a large, comfortable and fast two-seater convertible.

The Aston Martin DB9 doesn't work as a drop top. It doesn't look or feel right. Its little sister, the Vantage V8, is great but it's far more hardcore than the Merc and that might become wearing. The Bentley Continental is a good alternative, provided you don't mind having eggs thrown at you as you drive around. It is awfully pompous, somehow. And the BMW 6-series. Hmmm. This has exactly the same problem at the back that the Merc has at the front.

I'm therefore forced to conclude that the best of the bunch is the Jaguar XKR. It doesn't have the clout of the Merc. It doesn't have the Airscarf, which wafts warm air onto the back of your neck as you drive along. It doesn't have a lot of the Merc's breathtaking range of toys, in fact. Crucially, though, it doesn't have the Merc's ruined face either.

18 May 2008

So awful even the maker tells you to walk

Kia Sedona 2.9 CRDi TS

It's hard to understand why so many people watch *Top Gear*. Some say it's the cinematography. Some reckon there's a chemistry between the three presenters. Most think it's because there's nothing else on at that time on a Sunday evening.

I think, however, that its main appeal is this: when something goes wrong for one of us, the others don't rush over with furrowed brows, concerned tones and a silver post-car-crash blanket. Instead, we point and laugh. 'Ha ha ha. Look. James's head has exploded.' And that makes a refreshing change in a world full of counsellors and sobbing footballers.

Of course, you might imagine that this is all done for the cameras; and that after they've all been turned off we put our arms round one another and behave like women. 'Fraid not. In fact, when the cameras are turned off, we're even worse.

Just last week, the three of us were waiting for a delayed plane in Belgium. Or it could have been Holland. Or Japan. Whatever, we found a copy of what is basically *Asian Babes* for petrolheads. It's called *Top Marques* and is stuffed full of classified ads for cars you can nearly afford.

Naturally, we decided to see what our own cars are fetching in these times of rising fuel prices and eco-mentalism. This turned out to be a rich comedy gold mine because two-year-old, ultra-low-mileage Porsche 911s, just like Richard Hammond's, are going for 75p.

His little face was destroyed. He sat there working out how many crappy awards ceremonies he'd hosted to buy that car and how it had all been for nothing. He may as well have simply lobbed his money on a bonfire. Christ, it was funny. James May and I laughed that dangerous life-threatening laughter; the sort where your brain starts to run out of oxygen. At one point, I coughed up my own liver.

Eventually, after about two hours, we'd calmed down enough to see how much James's Boxster might fetch. And this, unbelievably, was even funnier. Not because of the drop, which was mighty, but because most of the enormous depreciation was not as a result of market forces or events beyond James's control. No. He'd brought the massive hit on himself by being an idiot.

It hurts, I know, to tick all the options boxes when buying a car. But the simple fact of the matter is this: if you don't, it is going to be worthless when the time comes to sell.

Think about it. A combination of events in the Middle East, sub-prime mortgages in California, Northern Rock and a galactically stupid government has caused all Boxsters to lose half their value in ten minutes. So the only way you can make a car with wind-down windows and unicycle tyres appeal in the pages of *Top Marques* is to sell it for even less than the going rate.

And boy did James scrimp. He didn't even fit satellite navigation and who wants a Porsche with no sat nav? No one. Not unless they deliberately live in a house with an outside bog.

What's more, James – as we know from his hooped jumpers – likes an unusual colour combination, which is why his steel-wheeled, understudy Porsche, with its gramophone and no guidance system, has a brown roof and a brown interior.

There is simply no call for a car like this. It could only be part-exchanged for some used butter. Plainly, James was very hurt by this. He'd worked hard for his car and now it was worthless. If Richard and I were girls, we'd have put our arms around him and hugged some sympathy into his system. Instead, Richard fell off his chair and my kidneys came out of my nose.

There is a serious message hidden in all of this. When buying an expensive new car, accept, like a man, that it will plummet in value in the manner of a fat man plummeting from the top of a tower block. Accept, too, that unless you spec it up with every conceivable extra there will be nothing to cushion the fall. And, most important of all, avoid bonkers colour combinations. You may think that a brown roof makes you look sultry and interesting, but in the long term it will make you look more sort of bankrupt.

Of course, you might think that the best way of avoiding depreciation problems in expensive cars is not to buy one in the first place. Unfortunately, if you go down this route, you may well end up at the wheel of a diesel-powered people carrier like the Kia Sedona. Billed by Kia as a slice of luxury at a down-to-earth price, it comes with seven seats that whiz about in all sorts of interesting ways, rear doors that slide electrically back and forth, an MP3 player, various airbags and braking systems that, they say, 'help you stop'. And you can have the all-singing, all-dancing top model for less than £20,000 if you haggle hard.

This, then, sounds a brilliant substitute for a proper car . . . in the same way that a bunch of flowers from your local petrol station sounds a brilliant substitute for a proper bouquet from a florist – right up to the moment you give them to your wife as an anniversary present. And then, all of a sudden, they are not brilliant at all. They are an affront to everything in life that matters.

And so it goes with the Sedona. Behind the veneer of common sense and good value beats the heart of a wizened chrysanthemum. Its 2.9-litre turbodiesel engine pulls with all the vigour of a primary school tug-of-war team. The suspension is absolutely unable to deal with imperfections in the road surface. It jolts and shudders, and sometimes you get the worrying impression that the body is going to come off. Then your children will be sick.

It gets worse. The Sedona is thirstier than you might imagine, there is wind noise on the motorway, the interior appears to have been made from plastic that Lego rejected and the exterior has the visual appeal of a smashed dog.

I hated this car in the same way that AA Gill would hate microwaved meat. Or Brian Sewell would hate The Crying Boy. I hated it in the same way that I hate own-brand stereo systems. They have all the buttons and they have the low price tags but they have no soul. They were designed simply to milk people who know nothing about the subject. The Sedona is a white good. It is a fridge-freezer with windscreen wipers.

And if you don't believe me, consider this. Kia Motors is heavily involved with getting kids to walk to school. It will provide free high-visibility jackets along with information on how it can be done safely, and how you can get in touch with other parents to form 'walking buses'.

It is actually saying that its Sedona is so terrible that you are better off taking your kids to school on foot. And it's right.

And now I'm going to knock the final nail in the Sedona's coffin. You might imagine that, because it's so cheap to buy, you cannot possibly lose much money. Really? I've just been on the *Auto Trader* website and as far as I can work out, a Sedona sheds half its value in about eighteen months. Not even a wattle-and-daub Boxster can manage that.

Happily, there is a solution to all this. Much to the annoyance of James May and Richard Hammond, it seems there's one car out there that is able to sit in an oxbow lake, away from the turbulence of the mainstream and its vicissitudes – a black Mercedes SLK 55 with red leather seats and all the trimmings. Coincidentally, that's what I have.

1 June 2008

The problem is . . . it's out of this world

Nissan GT-R

Fifteen years ago, I went to Japan, sat in a traffic jam for a fortnight and came home again, a bit worried that this festering, superheated example of unrestrained car ownership would one day spread right round the world, causing everyone to think Ken Livingstone might have had a point.

The traffic did not crawl. It did not move at all. The only way you could garner even half an idea of what it might be like to be stationary for so long is to blow your head off. Tokyo, in 1993, really was twinned with being dead.

So you might imagine that after fifteen years of almost continuous global economic growth, things today would be even worse. That I could go back there now, and find the taxi I used for the airport run all those years ago still at the terminal, queueing to get back on the expressway. That there'd be people in jams all over the city with no idea the twin towers had come down.

But, in fact, Tokyo now flows like the arterial blood in a newborn baby. There are no fatty deposits, no furred-up tributaries, no clots. Recently, at two in the afternoon, I tore up Tokyo's equivalent of London's Marylebone Road at 100mph. And there was not a single car in sight. Not one.

A Communist might argue that this has something to do with Japan's excellent public transport system, which classifies a train as late if it arrives more than fifty-nine seconds behind schedule. But the system was just as good fifteen years ago.

A hippie might suggest that in the nation that gave us John Prescott's Kyoto treaty, the average workaday commuter has hung up his wheels in shame and bought a bicycle instead. 'Fraid not, Mr Hillage. And nor have the city burghers invented a congestion charge that somehow cuts down on congestion, rather than just send a rude and impertinent bill every five minutes.

No. What's happened is very simple. Elsewhere in the world, cars have been getting larger. The current 3-series BMW is 4 inches longer than a 5-series from the late eighties. Today's Polo is bigger than the original Golf. And the twenty-first century's Rolls-Royce Phantom is bigger than an Egyptian's house.

Whereas in Japan, the law says that you must prove you own a parking space before you can buy a car, unless the car is less than 3.4 metres (11 feet 2inches) long and powered by an engine no larger than 660cc. And because almost no one owns a parking space, demand for cars that would fit in a budgie's lunch box has gone berserk. There are currently fifty-eight different models on offer with the bestselling, the Suzuki Wagon R, selling to 250,000 people a year.

Seriously, the cars they sell to us in Britain, which are the size of farms and skyscrapers – you hardly see them at all in Japan. Almost everyone has a car so small, many aren't actually visible to the naked eye.

The result is very simple. A traffic jam made up of normal cars will be twice as long as one made up of these Japanese 'kei' cars. And a kei jam will clear more quickly, because in a car the size of a bacterium you don't have to drive round and round the block looking for somewhere to park. You just pop it in your pocket and the job's a good 'un.

Sadly, there are some drawbacks. First of all, because these cars are so tiny on the outside, they are not what you'd call spacious when you step inside. This isn't so bad in a country where most people are 18 inches tall but if you are, say, Dutch, you will struggle. Certainly, there is no way that two people could sit alongside one another in a Daihatsu Mira if either of them had shoulders.

This brings us on to the next problem. Because the kei car can only be 3.4 metres long, there's no point wasting any of that length with a bonnet. So the microdot engine sort of fits under the dash and you sit right at the very front of the car. This must be strange when you are having a head-on accident because your face could be less than a foot from the face of the chap coming the other way and you still wouldn't have hit one another.

Then there's the styling. Or rather, there isn't. Any attempt to give these cars a tapering roofline or a curved rear end is wasteful of precious capacity, which means all of them look exactly – and I mean exactly – like chest freezers. And because they have such tiny wheels they actually look like chest freezers on casters. And that, in turn, means they look absurd. And no one is going to spend their money on something that makes them look foolish.

To get round this, the car manufacturers try to inject their chest freezers with a bit of funkiness and personality by giving them unusual names. They do this by getting the English dictionary and picking out words with pins.

This means you have the Mitsubishi Mum 500, the Suzuki Alto Afternoon Tea, and from Mazda, the Carol MeLady.

Would you go to work in a chest freezer called the Afternoon Tea? No. Neither would I, which is why, when I went to Japan last month, I got myself a 193mph, 473bhp four-wheel-drive, trixied up, hunkered down, road-burning controlled explosion. I got myself the new Nissan GT-R.

It's funny. In Japan, among the termite hill of kei cars, it felt like I was in a heavy metal blast from the past. It felt like I was blasting through a Girls Aloud gig in a rock dinosaur. But over here, things ought to be very different . . .

The last time Nissan did a GT-R, it was based on the old two-door Skyline saloon. The company couldn't do that this time round because the current Skyline saloon is too ghastly. So instead, a small team, in a hermetically sealed factory, set to work on a ground-up, handmade machine that would take the laws of physics and simply break them in half.

The attention to detail has been extraordinary. For instance, the GT-R's tyres are filled with nitrogen because ordinary air expands and contracts too much. And each gearbox is specifically mated to each handmade engine.

It goes on. Japanese car companies rarely buy equipment from the round eyes. They always feel they can do better themselves. On the GT-R, though, you'll find Brembo brakes. You'll find a chassis that was developed initially by Lotus. You'll find the best that Europe can offer mated to a computer control system that could only be Japanese.

On the road, then, this £53,000 car – with its rear-mounted double-clutch gearbox and its handmade 3.8-litre twin turbo motor and its infinitely variable four-wheel-drive system – is, quite simply, how can I put this . . . very underwhelming. The noise it makes is normal. The ride is normal. The steering is normal. You can adjust all the settings as much as you like but it'll make no difference. It still feels like a big Sunny.

It's not pretty, either. I know every shape and every crease serves an aerodynamic purpose, but it's like free-form poetry. It's like it was conceived by Bartok.

Annoyed that Nissan could have lost the plot so badly, I drove it a bit harder. And then a bit harder still. And still it refused to reveal its hand. It was like driving a car that had fallen asleep. Like there was nothing that I, a mere human being, could do that would cause it to break into a sweat.

There were no clues that I was driving something that could lap the Nürburgring faster than a Koenigsegg or a McLaren Mercedes. That I was in a car that can stop just as fast as a much lighter, ceramic-braked Porsche 911 Turbo.

Even when I found a mountain road and went berserk, the GT-R remained utterly composed, absolutely planted. Occasionally, you'd catch a faint whistle from the turbos or maybe there'd be a little chaffinchy chirrup from the semi-slick tyres. But that was it. There was absolutely no drama at all. No sense that I was in something incredible. And the brakes, even after I'd pummelled them for half a day, were still ice cold and sharp.

This, then, is an extraordinary car, quite unlike anything I've driven before. You might expect it, with all its yaw sensors and its G readout on the dash, to feel like a laptop. Or you might expect, with all that heavy engineering, for it to feel like a road-going racer. But it is neither of these things. It certainly doesn't feel like it could do a 7.29-minute lap of the Ring. Even though I've seen a film of it doing just that.

I dare say that if Michael Schumacher were to find himself in the eye of an Arctic blizzard, escaping from an exploding volcano, he might discover 10 per cent of this car's abilities. But you? Me? Here? Forget it.

Nissan, then, has done something odd. It has built a car for a time and a place and a species that simply don't exist.

8 June 2008

Fair Porsche, my sweet Italian lover

Boxster RS 60 Spyder

If I were to walk round a modern-day motor show featuring all the latest cars with all their clever electronic gizmos, there might be one, or maybe two, that I'd think seriously of buying. While walking round a field in Leicestershire recently, I found about 200 cars that I'd have gladly swapped one of my kidneys for. There were a few I'd have swapped my heart for.

It was the Auto Italia festival, an event at which thousands of car enthusiasts spend the day demonstrating who is best with a vacuum cleaner. They even have a competition to see who has the cleanest car. It is ridiculous.

If you delve behind the preposterously lacquered paint and the Mr Sheened dashboards, however, you are left with acre after acre of machinery that will leave you breathless with desire. I wanted everything.

And I'm not talking here about the fields full of Ferraris. Mostly, they were crummy 348s, which had wooden tyres and suspension made from old pianos. Nor was I overly bothered by the Lambos either. Owning a Countach or a Diablo is just another way of saying that you are deformed.

No. The stuff that blew my trousers off was the humdrum 1970s cars from Fiat, Alfa Romeo and most of all, surprisingly, Lancia.

Let us begin our romp down the autostrada of yesteryear with the Lancia Montecarlo. Early models were plagued with a tendency to lock up their front brakes and so Lancia took the unusual step of removing it from production while the problem was addressed. A year passed and everyone assumed the little sports car had gone for good. But no. Lancia then rereleased it, saying it had cured the issue by removing the servo. In other words, it had simply made the back brakes perform as badly as those at the front. Brilliant.

Provided you never want to stop, you can buy a Montecarlo these days, in good condition, for about £4,000. And for that you get a 2-litre twin-cam mid-engined sports car with, if you want, a folding canvas roof, tweed seats and looks that could melt a girl's face. I decided after about ten minutes that I didn't want one at all. I needed one. It was more pressing than my next breath. I even started offering one owner some money and then, when that didn't work, some quiet threats. 'Look,' I whispered. 'This car will be no good to you if you have lost your legs. And you will, sunshine, if you don't sell it to me . . .'

His dignity was saved because, while threatening to burn his house down, I noticed out of the corner of my eye a selection of Fulvias. By modern standards, the Lancia Fulvia is not much to write home about. It has carthorse suspension at the back, a set-up that's weirdly complicated at the front and a 1.6-litre V4 engine that, in the HF, develops just 115bhp. Fast? Well, yes, but only if you are a visiting Victorian, or you are used to driving a Motability shopping scooter.

However, they are balls-achingly pretty and one of the show cars belonged to an old mate. 'Hello, John,' I said cheerily, but with a hint of Stanislavski menace. 'Would you like to sell me your car or would you like me to stab you in the throat and get the crowd to cheer as you gout arterial blood all over everywhere? Because those are your only choices.'

Happily, from his point of view, I realized that I was actually leaning on the bonnet of a Delta Integrale at the time. And I decided that what I really wanted, more than anything in the world, was this ludicrous, left-hand-drive superstar from the original Sega Rally machine.

Of course, people with blazers will explain that Lancias are old rot-boxes that fell to pieces long before anyone had a chance to drive them to the shops. But having driven across Botswana in a Beta last year, I can assure you this is bunkum.

A classic Lancia will have no more problems than a classic Mercedes. Automotive time is a great leveller. So I'd made my mind up. I was going to buy, having buried the owner in a motorway bridge, a supercharged Lancia Beta HPE. Right up to the moment I spotted a right-hand-drive Fiat 124 Spider.

Or no, hang on a minute. Isn't that a 131 Mirafiori over there – the car that was advertised in a cage, growling? And it's parked next to a 132. My head was starting to swim. And that's when I spotted the Alfa Romeo Montreal.

You may remember, at the beginning of the film *True Lies*, Arnie breaks into an embassy cocktail party at a snowy Austrian schloss. There are lots of cars outside but the only one that's recognizable is a Montreal. And you can forget Morse's Jag or Bond's Aston. That's the best bit of car casting yet. It is the perfect way of saying, without saying anything at all, what sort of people were at the party. People with style.

This 2-litre coupé was first shown at a motor show in Montreal, hence the name, but by the time it reached production it had been given a road-going version of Alfa's quad-cam, fuel-injected V8. Now with 2.6 litres, it developed 200bhp and had a top speed of 137mph. In 1970 that was lots.

Above the racing heart was a body that had been styled by Bertone and garnished with all sorts of beautiful adornments it simply didn't need. Such as six air vents in each rear pillar and grilles over the headlamps that retracted when the lights were switched on. Or, rather, being Italian, didn't retract when the lights were switched on.

Of course, the Montreal was a catastrophic sales failure. Fewer than 4,000 had been made before it was officially discontinued in 1977. But most people believe they stopped making it years before that and had simply spent the time shifting unsold stock.

This is what makes it stand out today. It's what made so many of those cars in that Leicestershire field stand out. They were not made to make their makers money. They were made by enthusiasts because making cars, when you're a car maker, should be fun. They were, in short, Italian.

Did the world need a Fiat X1/9 or an Abarth version of the 500? Cars such as this and the Montreal, the Montecarlo, the Fulvia and countless more besides were, in the 1970s and 1980s, dream cars. And they remain so. I yearn to own them all because they are beautiful and they are interesting and they were designed by people who truly loved cars.

And that, rather late in the day, brings me on to the Porsche Boxster RS 60 Spyder. I have a sneaking suspicion that Porsche is now the only car maker left that's still motivated by the same things that motivated the Italian car companies of yore. There is no Porsche econo-box. The 911 still puts its horsepower at the back. And when the firm did finally follow fashion and build a 4x4, it gave it a sodding great turbo.

Porsches do not sound like other cars. And they do not drive like other cars. They drive . . . how can I put this? Better.

This is not a volte-face. For reasons I don't understand, I still do not want one, but that is not relevant here. If I put on the hat of an impartial reviewer, ignore the badge and concentrate on the RS 60 as a piece of machinery, I'm forced to conclude it's wonderful.

Yes, it looks silly, the driving position is cramped and the interior colour on this limited-edition special is exactly the same colour as a cow's bottom just after it's given birth. I must also say I cannot see how it's worth £5,405 more than a normal S. All you get is bigger wheels, a button to make the exhaust noisier and a dribble of extra power. But those are details. The package is superb. The way it steers, the way it rides, the way it grips. It makes you fizz and shiver in a way other cars do not.

I drove it on the Fosse Way with the roof down the other evening. There was no other traffic. The sun was out. The countryside looked stunning. And then, as 'Nessun Dorma' came on the radio, I started to smile. Because – and this is the highest compliment I can give to any car in these profit-and-loss times – it felt Italian.

15 June 2008

Mr Weedy comes up with the goods

Mercedes-Benz SL 350

It's no good. I can't sit here any more pretending that there's nothing wrong. Because there is. A man came to my house yesterday to fix the computer and he had a worried look on his face. He lives twenty miles away. The fuel tank in his little van was perilously close to empty and he simply didn't have enough money to fill it up again.

In the past I only ever stopped for fuel when the yellow light had been on for a month and the engine was starting to cough. Yesterday, I stopped at a garage simply because its petrol was 4p cheaper than usual. That's a £2.80 difference per tankful. Which works out at £300 a year. That's fifty-five free packets of cigarettes.

Except, of course, these calculations are meaningless because oil, as I write, is $139 a barrel and no one thinks it's going to stop there. Not with Mr Patel on the economic warpath and Johnny Chinaman part-exchanging his rickshaw for a shiny new Toyota. They say it'll be $150 a barrel by the end of summer.

Global warming was never going to get people out of their big cars because we could see it was all a load of left-wing tosh. But when petrol is £3 a litre – and anyone old enough to remember 1973 would not discount that as a possibility – you'd have to be a bit bonkers to drive around like your hair's on fire in a car that does only eight miles to the gallon.

Oh, it's all very well now. You may be a footballer or a Sir Alan. You may see expensive petrol as a jolly good way of getting the poor and the weak off the roads. Soon, though, you will be hit, too.

Think about it. When you have to have a fist fight with an old lady over the last loaf of bread in the shop, and your electricity bill looks as though it's been written in liras, you are going to find yourself in the same boat as my computer man: with a nice car on the drive and no wherewithal to make it go.

Of course, there are lots of things you can do to lessen the impact of spiralling fuel bills – all of which are dreary.

Weight is one issue. If you remove that rolled-up old carpet from your boot, you'll be surprised at the impact it'll have on your bills. You could go further and remove your spare wheel and jack too. Maybe you could even go on that diet you've been promising yourself.

Then there's all the equipment. If you use a lot of electrical stuff while driving, the alternator will need to work harder, which means more fuel. Even Terry Wogan needs a bit of petrol. Your heated rear window needs an alarming amount. And air-conditioning? Turn that off and your fuel consumption will improve by as much as 12 per cent.

Making sure that your tyres are inflated properly will save another 5 per cent, and you know the roof bars? If you can manage without, there's another 3 per cent saving right there. At this rate, you are well on your way to turning your Range Rover Sport Nutter Bastard into something with the thirst of a newborn wren.

By far the biggest savings will come if you change the way you drive, though. Take the Audi A8 diesel as an example. Officially, it will do 30.1mpg. Realistically, it'll be nearer 25. With a bit of care, however, you can do 40. Maybe more.

Audi says that its big V8 oil-burner can go 580 miles between trips to the pumps but I managed to get all the way from London to Edinburgh and then back again on a single tankful. That's a whopping 800 miles. It wasn't much fun, at a fairly constant 56mph, with no radio, no air-con and no sat nav. But the savings were massive.

Things I learnt? On a downhill stretch, ease up on the throttle pedal and work with gravity to build up speed. Similarly, you can ease off the power and use momentum to get you up the next hill. A cruise control system will not do this. It is a sledgehammer when what you need is the scalpel sensitivity of your right foot.

Look far ahead. If you think you will have to slow down, start the process early. If you use the brakes you are simply wasting the fuel you used to reach a speed that was unnecessary.

Already I'm bored with this. The notion that you have to drive at 56mph, with sweaty armpits, stopping every five seconds to check your tyre pressures just to save a pound fills me with horror and dread. It would be like being told to lose weight by your doctor – and sawing your arm off. Effective but annoying. Which is why, when it comes to the price of fuel, I want to have my cake and eat it, too. And then I want second helpings.

This brings me to the Mercedes-Benz SL 350. Ordinarily, I'd dismiss this, the baby of the range, and suggest you bought the mountainous twin-turbo 6-litre V12 version instead. But in these dark and difficult times, I thought I'd give the weedo-matic version a chance.

The fact of the matter is this. Officially, the V12 version will return 18.7mpg, whereas the 350 will do 28.5. That is a colossal difference. And handy too. On my old SL 55, a quarter of a tank would not get me from London to my house in the Cotswolds. A quarter of a tank in the 350 gets me there and back.

But while the fuel savings are obvious, I wanted to know if the price was too high. Would the SL 350's performance be just a bit too wet?

The figures don't look brilliant. The brand new 3.5-litre V6 engine develops 311bhp, which, officially, is 'not enough', and 266lb ft of torque, which is about what you get in a nine-year-old's forearm. Couple that with the SL's thunder-thighed weight and you might imagine you'd be going everywhere at 4mph.

In fact, it will get from 0 to 60 in six seconds or so. That's fast. And the top speed is 155. Exactly the same as it is in the SL 65.

One area in which you might imagine the 350 would be left lacking is when you're on the outside lane of a motorway. You're in a long line of cars doing, say, fifty, but despite this a mouth-breather in a Renault Clio is crawling all over your rear end. Then the road clears . . .

We've all been there. You mash your throttle into the carpet to show that his aggression was pointless. Big-engined SLs are very good at this, humiliating the young and the stupid. And guess what. The 350's not bad either. You don't get the Gatling-gun soundtrack, but the pace is there all right. And this is an engine that likes to spin, too. Up at the top of the rev range, it sings, whereas the bigger V8s and V12s lumber.

Then things get better. Whereas more expensive SLs come with computerized suspension, the 350 has conventional springs and dampers. It is much, much, much, much, much better as a result. It doesn't crash through potholes and the steering is more accurate too. You would never call a sixteen-ton, two-horsepower car 'sporty', but it gets perilously close, this one.

If you are somehow immune to the SL's flashy new Wagtastic nose, you'll find that most of the time the 350 is very nearly as good as the version you were dreaming about. And that some of the time it's quite a bit better.

You can, if you want, order the car with no 350 badge on the back. I recommend, however, you leave it in place. Last year it advertized to the world that you were a bit Gola League. Today, it tells everyone you're actually pretty smart.

22 June 2008

Herr Thruster's gone all limp and lost

BMW M3 convertible

It's my job, each week, to come here and write about flowers, frogs, foxes and fornication and then, towards the end, say a little bit about the car I've been driving. It is not my job to tell the motor manufacturers what to do.

Some of my colleagues in this auto journalism malarkey are an extension of the car industry, shaping its policy and directing future operations. They are clever. They can understand and explain torque. I can't. I'm just a punter, test-driving cars and saying whether I like them or not.

Normally, then, I would say that the satellite navigation system used by BMW is rubbish and move on. But with petrol at £400 a litre, we can't afford to be wasting the stuff by driving to the shops via Dorset every morning. So, today, I shall break with tradition and urge BMW to talk to its sat nav suppliers, with some steely-eyed, Germanic sternness.

The system in the M3 I had last week did not know about the A43. It has no clue that the M25 is connected to central London by the A40. And it had never heard of the Fosse Way, even though it's been around for 2,000 years.

Last Wednesday, I needed to drive from London to Corby, which, in my mind, was just a few miles from the A1. But the madman in the M3's dashboard had never heard of the Great North Road and was adamant I should use the M1. So I did.

Big mistake. Back in 1959, the M1 was a wondrous thing;

a big grey superhighway for people on the move. It had a point. It had a purpose. Back then, the government took our money in taxes and used it to make our lives better with new roads. Now, it uses those roads as a device for making money to fund the government. The M1 has become nothing more than a cash cow.

They say that they are widening the carriageways from London to Watford, and they probably are. But when work moves this slowly, it's hard to be sure that they're telling the truth. What we do know is that by putting cones on the hard shoulder, they can claim that roadworks are happening and this means, of course, they can impose extra-low speed limits to protect the workforce.

How this is possible I don't know, since the workforce is all in Dublin, drinking Guinness. But no matter. To enforce the 50mph limit, they have erected average speed cameras not just over a short stretch but for nearly twenty miles.

And so, onwards you trudge, at caveman speeds, not daring to look up from your speedometer in case you accidentally do 53 for a while. This would then require some mental maths to work out how far you'd have to travel at 47 to bring your average down again. And since we know we can't use a mobile phone while driving because it's a distraction, we can be fairly certain calculators aren't allowed either.

It's absurd. Plainly, the M1 is no longer what the politicians now insist on calling 'fit for purpose'. Endlessly widening it means it's endlessly narrower and even more useless than if they'd left it alone in the first place. They should give up and simply build another six-lane highway that runs parallel.

There is time to think about all this, and exactly where you'd shoot objectors, as you crawl along, in a slow-moving maths exam, with no one looking where they're going, all the way to Watford, where the limit ends and everyone hits the loud pedal. Scientists say it is impossible to go faster than the speed of light. It isn't. Not when you've just spent half an hour doing 50 and you're late. Everyone, even people in Nissan people carriers, bursts out of the cones doing 670,616,629.7 miles per hour. And away from Corby.

Like all sat nav systems, you can choose in a BMW the criteria for your journey. Do you want the fastest route or the shortest? Do you want to avoid motorways or toll roads? All good stuff. But plainly the unit in the M3 was jammed on a setting that took the car past as many forward-facing speed cameras as possible.

So once I'd turned off the M1 in Northampton, which is officially listed in the AA road map as being 'nowhere near Corby', I was faced with mile upon interminable mile of tedium in the face of Big Brother. And the car wasn't much good either.

I like the new M3. As a coupé, it is a surprisingly elegant thing of understated charm. It's fast, too. Really fast. At the Ascari track in southern Spain last year, it was a full five seconds a lap quicker than the ever-so-shouty 6.2-litre Mercedes C-class.

Best of all, though, you no longer have to be a pushy oik to buy one. Today, people with Take That haircuts, Oakley sunglasses and short-sleeved shirts are to be found in fast Audis, leaving BMWs to people who simply want a fast, practical means of getting from A, via Dorset, Aberdeen and the Kamchatka peninsula, to B.

The saloon version is even better. It doesn't have a carbon-fibre roof, which makes no difference at all, but it does have four doors and a bigger boot, which means your children can come too. And it's a little bit cheaper.

The new convertible version, however, has a problem. Taking the roof off, say, a Peugeot doesn't really matter. Who cares if it's all floppy as a result. It was never built to be the ultimate driving machine in the first place.

The problem is that BMW's M cars are built to be the last word in precision, handling, fun, grip and speed. And if you take the roof off, you are sacrificing torsional rigidity, which means you are sacrificing precision, handling, fun, grip and speed. You are therefore removing the whole point of the car. It's much the same story with the Porsche 911.

You can feel the floppiness as you drive along. There's a vibration in the steering wheel and a sense that all is not quite right in the corners. You can feel the weight too. It feels all the time like you're dragging an anchor.

It wouldn't be so bad if BMW had stuck with a canvas roof, but due to perfectly sensible market demand, it's gone instead for the folding metal option. It really doesn't work because apart from the extra metalwork this requires, the styling is hopeless. To get the back window to fold into the boot, it doesn't slope like it should. Instead it rises like a small cliff from the base of the boot. This allows the roof itself to split in two and stack underneath it before folding into the boot. It's all very clever, but you don't half feel like a show-off if you press the button in public. And good though the Germans may be, you just know that, five years from now, it's going to jam.

Other things? Well, although back seats are fitted, God has not yet made a creature that would fit in them, and with the roof stowed, the boot is useful only if you are a naturist.

So, to conclude. The new 4-litre V8: very good. Lovely. Nice noise. Lots of power and bags of torque, whatever that is. The ride: excellent. Here at last is proof – are you listening,

Mercedes? – that a sporty car does not have to shake your eyeballs out of their sockets.

I also like the system that uses energy from the brakes to power the electrical appliances. This means the alternator has less to do and consequently takes less power from the engine. That's good for fuel economy, slightly.

But there's no getting away from the fact that if you want a convertible, you are better off with an Audi RS4 or a Mercedes. And if you want an M3, you are better off with the coupé or saloon.

Just be aware. Until BMW sorts out the stupid sat nav system, you will also have to invest in a portable TomTom. Because if you rely on the idiot in the dash, you're going to spend the rest of your life in Guildford, looking for Edinburgh Castle.

29 June 2008

It takes you to the edge . . . and shoves

Porsche 911 Carrera GT2

Golf is not mysterious. I understand absolutely why someone would play it once . . . and then decide to play it again. It's not because they have a Rupert Bear fixation or because they dislike the company of women or because they secretly want to be a Freemason. No. It's because they think that if they keep playing, they might get a bit better.

Luckily, I was born with a body that renders me quite incapable of doing anything very well. Which means I never suffer from this.

Chess? I'm rubbish. Tennis? I'm so spectacularly bad, I can only just beat Jimmy Carr. DIY? For me this is simply impossible. Even if I attempt something simple, such as hanging a picture, I end up in casualty, the painting ends up ruined and the wall ends up in the garden.

So when I played golf for the first time, I knew there would never be a second. There would be no point. Even if I played every day for 1,000 years, the ball would still never travel more than six inches. And in all probability I'd end up with a severed jugular vein. That's what happened when I tried to help my boy make an Airfix model the other day.

This is a good thing, of course, because it means my life is varied and interesting. I never do the same thing twice, whereas someone who has a hobby does exactly the same thing day after interminable day. James May, for instance, enjoys taking old motorcycle engines to pieces and then putting them back together again, as slowly as possible. Consequently, this is all he does.

Chris Tarrant, meanwhile, likes to spend all his free time standing up to his testicles in dirty water trying to outwit a fish; a creature with less brain capacity than a washing machine.

This brings us on to the Porsche 911, a car aimed at people for whom the drive to work every morning is not a chore or a pleasure. It is a pastime, a hobby. Something that can be improved and finessed with practice. Sometimes, I imagine that 911 people go to work, turn round and then go to work again.

People buy Ferraris and Lamborghinis because cars like this effervesce. They fizz and crackle and they're as much about style and panache as they are about generating G in the bends. A 911, on the other hand, is not about style at all. It's fishing, with a steering wheel.

When you buy a normal car, you choose the model, choose the engine size you'd like and then add as many extras as you think you can afford. Then a few you can't.

It is not so simple with a 911. The range is mind boggling. It starts with the simple Carrera, which has no frills, no spoiler on which the RAF could land a jet, no wide wheel arches, no turbocharging. You get a simple 3.6-litre flat six that drives the rear wheels. This, then, is the starting point. My little pony.

If you go for the 3.8-litre S model, it is the best of the 911s. It offers all of the design's best features with none of the drawbacks, at a reasonable price. But sadly, once you've stuck your toe into the world of the 911, pretty soon you are going to be as hooked as a golfer; believing that if you spend more and more on better equipment, your game will improve.

Pretty soon, then, you're going to be back at the dealership wondering out loud if perhaps you could take the round-about outside TGI Fridays a little bit faster if you had four-wheel drive. (You can't.)

Then you'll start to wonder about the GT3, which is like the simple Carrera S but with scaffolding in the back and a thin back window. Around a track, this is an incredible car. You'll like that. You'll start doing track days. And there you'll be overtaken by people in turbos, so you'll think that maybe you should have one of those. Pretty soon, you'll be sub-scribing to the 911 magazine for enthusiasts. And then all you'll be able to do, day in and day out, is dream of the day when you can have a GT2. The £131,070 GT2 is Everest. It has the engine from the turbo but with more power and only two-wheel drive. It has scaffolding in the back. It is light. It is, to Mr Porsche-Man, what the very best woods are to the world of pro-am golf.

It is also immensely fast. The 530 horsepowers feel as though they're coming from a gigantic muscle rather than an engine. So if ever you feel the need to mash that throttle into the carpet, you'd better be ready . . .

Just yesterday, I pulled out to overtake four cars on a nor-mal A road and by the time the manoeuvre was complete, I was doing 165mph. That is not a boast. That is a fact. And if anyone asks, I shall say I was on the Isle of Man.

I then went to the track, where I discovered that the GT2 can lap more quickly than a Ferrari Scuderia. This is aston-ishing. A Ferrari has no carpets, an electronic differential, sophisticated traction control, adjustable suspension and a flappy paddle box that can shift gears in 60 milliseconds. The Porsche has none of these things. Just its big muscle and a basic six-speed manual. And yet it was faster.

This alone would be enough to get the hobby-boys chortling into their G and Ts. And there's more.

The GT2 handles like an old-school 911. Push it hard into a corner with the traction control turned off and you have yards of nasty understeer which, no matter what you do to correct the problem, results in a violent lurch from the rear: 911 fans love this. They reckon that being able to tame this problem makes them men among men. But for me, as a man who can't do anything properly, it's a bloody nightmare.

The grip from a GT2 is biblical. In a bend, you can feel the G-forces peeling your muscles from their mountings. But when you exceed the limits – and what's the point of a car like this if you don't at least try – you are almost certainly going to spin.

On a road, the problems are even worse – principally it's all far too firm. Anyone who knows where the A40 blends, in a nice right-hander, onto the M40 just outside Oxford, knows about the bump at the apex of the corner. In most cars it's nothing to worry about. In a GT2, however, you take off and don't land till you're in Hillingdon. Good for the fuel consumption, I guess. But bad for your nerves.

It was much the same story last night. There's a crest on a B road near where I live, and in most cars the traction control light flickers as you go over it. The GT2, however, slewed sideways. Suddenly. It was extremely alarming. I may even have wet myself a bit.

And then there's the tyre roar. The GT2 has giant 325/30 rear tyres and, boy, do they make a racket. Even on a smooth modern motorway you cannot hear yourself think.

I hated this car. Yes, the speed is mesmerizing. Epic. But the price is too high. It's too difficult, too much like hard work, and the only rewards if you push it are a series of terrifying and unpredictable lurches.

Think of it as a carbon fibre fishing rod. It will make you look serious and keen among your peers. But one day, you're going to snag it on an overhead power line. And as you lie in hospital afterwards, with no face and melted feet, you're going to wish you'd stuck with a bamboo cane and a piece of string.

6 July 2008

The Devil's done a fruity one

Mercedes SLR McLaren Roadster

Fortunately, my economics teacher at school never really shook himself properly after a trip to the urinals. This meant that instead of listening to his endless droning lectures on Smith and Keynes, I sat there, transfixed by the growing splotch of darkness on the front of his trousers.

This meant I was never tempted to leave school and get a dreary job in a bank. And better still, because I learnt about the importance of taking care while in the lavatory, I have never once been caught by the paparazzi with an embarrassing trouser stain.

What's more, it means that, today, I do not concern myself with Dickensian theories and Victorian idealism when it comes to the question of business. I rely instead on common sense. For instance: if you have a product that people want to buy, you will do well. If it is too expensive, or ugly, then you will not. The end.

I have some sound theories on investment, too. When times are good, put your savings in property, and when times are bad, put them in a high-interest account at the bank.

Unfortunately, in the wake of Northern Rock, entrusting your money to the men in braces is more dangerous than using it to fund coups in Equatorial Guinea. And here's the thing. It is impossible to predict which bank will fold next, which means it's not safe to give your money to any of them. And because the police are too busy filling in health and safety forms to investigate burglaries, it is not safe to put it under the mattress either.

Gold has been the traditional recourse of the terminally scared but that's expensive at the moment. So's art. Someone recently paid £17m for a painting of a fat jobcentre supervisor on a sofa, so we aren't really going to get much more than a Hallmark greetings card with our life savings.

Land's a no-no too. Clever people whose economics teachers did not routinely wet themselves have already noticed that just 8 per cent of the world's landmass is suitable for growing crops, and with the food crisis in full swing, much can be made from this.

So, farm land in Britain has gone from less than £2,000 an acre a couple of years ago to nearly £9,000 an acre today. By the time you have found someone willing to sell, you're going to end up spending all your life savings on an allotment.

I have, therefore, been thinking about what can be done, and I'm delighted to say, the answer is very enjoyable. If we are about to enter a period of great economic turmoil with bankers hurling themselves out of the Empire State Building and stockbrokers selling their children for medical experiments, money will become worthless. So you may as well spend it now on things that will make you happy. A Fairline Targa 52, for instance. Or a villa adjacent to Lake Como. Or a nice car.

This, for once, really does bring me neatly to the semi-gullwing door of the Mercedes SLR McLaren Roadster.

I am more familiar than most with the original coupé version, having driven one nonstop – apart from a health-and-safety-enforced break in Copenhagen (which wasn't as long as the TV pictures suggested) – all the way from London to Oslo. It took twenty-four hours.

Apart from the woeful brakes, I liked it very much. Unlike most hypercars, this one was not built by an enthusiast, in a shed, on an industrial estate, and as a result it never gave even the tiniest hint that it was about to break down or disintegrate or explode.

It was also very, very fast. At one point, in Germany obviously, I hit 200mph. And there was more to come. This was, and remains, the fastest automatic car in the world.

And that brings me on to its strongest suit. Because the engine was at the front, and it had an auto box, and because the dashboard was pretty much the same as it is in all Mercs, you never felt overwhelmed by the simple experience of getting in and doing up the seatbelt. In a Koenigsegg or a Zonda, your heart is thrashing about in your ribcage like a coked-up and cornered dog before you've even started the engine. But because the SLR felt so normal, you were relaxed, which made it easier to exploit the immense power from that 5.5-litre supercharged V8.

Unfortunately, for McLaren anyway, the world's superrich heard what I had to say and promptly bought something else. Maybe because the McLaren race team outfits are so terrible, or perhaps because the SLR didn't capture the heart in the way that a Ferrari can. Who knows. But the SLR was not a sales success and as it failed to achieve its targets we now have the Roadster.

My God, it's got presence. People suggest that if the devil were ever to pay us a visit, he'd have small horns and maybe some numbers in his barnet. But there is some evidence to suggest that he's here now, with an SLR badge and no roof. And terrible, terrible brakes.

Other car makers have got carbon ceramic discs to work properly, but McLaren, which I think was the first to put them on a road car, has not. They operate like a switch, doing nothing at all when you first press the pedal and then smashing your nose into the steering wheel when you press it a bit more.

This is fine in a Formula One car when you never want to slow down 'a bit', but when parking, you do. And in the SLR McLaren, you can't.

In time, you do get used to them, in the same way that you can get used to having no arms. And when you do, the rest of the car is a big slice of bonkers joy.

Some say that you can achieve much the same from a normal Mercedes SL. They say that the standard car comes with a folding metal roof, rather than a strip of canvas, and that it's a third of the price and that it has more toys. But this is like saying, 'Why buy a private jet when for so much less you could have a washing machine?'

The McMerc feels so much more exciting, so much more like a racer, albeit a heavy and enormous one. Lumber is not a word you normally associate with a car like this, but that's what it does. Lumber quickly. A Ferrari feels light and technical. A Koenigsegg feels like it isn't finished. A Zonda feels like you're on acid and you've fallen down some stairs. The SLR feels like Jonah Lomu. And the noise is extraordinary. No car sounds like this. It's a big, dirty, bassy rumble. My daughter said it sounded like a big fart. She's right. A massive, amplified fart from hell.

It is unique. Nothing else combines genuine blitzkrieg power with such everyday normality. Seriously. As you are carried by the Devil's Wind, you have the leather seats, the sat nav and all the usual Mercedes bits and pieces. My only real gripe in this department is the roof, which is only partly electric. 'That's to save weight,' said the man from McLaren. Yeah, right.

I liked this car even more than I liked the coupé; but normally, of course, I would never dream of urging anyone to actually buy one. And not just because of the penny-pinching roof mechanism and the braking system. I wouldn't recommend it because if I had £350,000 sitting about, I'd use it to buy a bond of some sort.

Now, though? Would you rather give your money to a banker so he can go bust with it or would you rather drive through the recession at 200mph in a big black Mercedes SLR McLaren?

13 July 2008

Eat my dust, Little England

Jaguar XKR-S Coupé

It's hard to find a point in history when a man sound in mind and body could have bought a Jaguar. Certainly it wasn't possible in the 1970s, when they were made either badly or not at all by a bunch of Trotskyites who spent most of the working day at the factory gates round a brazier, popping inside occasionally to leave their lunch in an inlet manifold and then going on strike again when a foreman asked them to take it out.

There was even a time when the weak and stupid British Leyland management thought seriously about renaming Jaguar the Large Car Division. Hmm. I can see that someone might buy a piece of farm equipment from the People's Tractor Factory, but that's mostly because they'd starve or be shot if they bought something else. I cannot see, however, why anyone would want to drive round in a Large Car Division XJ12 when they could have a, er, Bavarian Motor Works 735i instead.

Eventually, though, Jaguar's management was sent off to live on plastic inconti-armchairs on the south coast, the workforce was given a clip round the ear by Mrs T and the company was rescued by Ford.

And then, briefly, there was a time – it was 3.15pm on October 12 – when a sensible chap might have thought, 'No. I won't buy a Mercedes or a BMW or an Audi or a wheelbarrow. I'm going to get one of those supercharged Jaguar XJRs.'

Right up until tea time the next day, Jaguar even managed to do well in the JD Power customer satisfaction surveys. Although this result, you have to suspect, was born of amazement rather than solid build quality. 'Jesus. I've bought a Jag and it's got all the way home without exploding or turning inside out. And there isn't a single sandwich in the inlet manifold.' It's for much the same reason that, at the same time, Skoda was doing well too.

Sadly, the honeymoon didn't last. Jaguar launched the S-type, which was about as relevant as Terry and June. And then the X-type, which was very nice. As well it should have been because it was a Ford Mondeo with a fancy radiator grille and a bigger price.

To make matters worse, Jaguar had decided to shake off its wood'n'leather image by going into Formula One. Brilliant, except its cars, which were also Fords behind the green paint, either came last or crashed into one another. Then Ford ran out of money.

The result is that, apart from at 3.15pm on October 12, the only people who have bought a Jaguar since about 1970 did so because they were buying something British. That's not a good enough reason. That would be like someone from Ankara buying a car 'because it's Turkish'.

Given the choice of two similar products, I'll always buy the one with a Union Jack on the label. But who says, 'No. I will not buy a Riva Aquarama speedboat. I shall buy this lump of dog dirt instead. Because it was made in Pontefract'?

Of course, we know exactly who says that sort of thing. Golfers. The ruddy-faced little Englanders who refer to everyone by their initials and become aroused whenever anyone mentions Enoch Powell.

Now, though, since Jaguar was offloaded to the Indians, it

is very obvious that the little Englanders have had enough. They could just about stomach Jag being American-owned. But with Mr Patel in the hot seat? 'Better have another G and T, Maurice. I think I'm going to have a coronary.'

You must have noticed the result. In the past few months the whiff of the nineteenth hole has been lifted from the Jag range. No longer do you open the door to be knocked sense-less by a nauseating cloud of Eau de Belfry.

The smell of Nick Faldo's trousers has now settled on the Lexus range, and Jags, for the first time since the E-type was given a V12, are being bought by people you'd have round for dinner. And so, with a spring in our step and hope in our hearts, we arrive at the door of the Jaguar XKR.

When it was launched, our heads told us that it was a very fine car. Faster, more practical and cheaper than the Aston Martin V8 Vantage. And not exactly a minger, either. Of course, the power of the badge is strong in us all, so while our heads said Jag our hearts said Aston and off we all tod-dled to buy the Vantage.

Why not? Astons were all glamour and James Bond, and Jaguars were full of Jim Davidson.

That, though, has now changed. Astons are bought largely by people who can't even park properly, and the XKR is an extremely good way of saying, 'I know I'm not James Bond. I'm not having a midlife crisis. I just wanted a good-looking two-seater and I bought this one because it's the best.'

It is. I recently said that 15 per cent of me wants an XKR convertible, but as each day goes by, that climbs. It's up to 36 per cent now and that's the point when you go on the web-site to see what colours are available. Green, I'm thinking. With a fawn hood.

The only problem is the engine. When it was designed in

1435, 400bhp was lots. But since then the Germans have been engaged in a power war and now we have the Audi RS6 wading into the fray with 572bhp. That makes the Jag's 416bhp look weedy and vegetarian.

I know that, as we speak, a 500bhp 5-litre Jag V8 is being tested, but it won't be here for a year. So you either have to buy a Merc or a BMW. Or you have to think, 'Actually, with fuel costing more than lobster, maybe 416bhp isn't so bad . . .'

It certainly isn't so bad in the limited-edition XKRS I drove last week. At no point did I put my foot down and think, 'Mmmm. Has it broken down?' The only thing I did think was, 'Mmmm. I wish it made a bit more noise.' I know that, from the outside, the exhausts crackle and rumble, but from behind the wheel, all you can hear is the whine of the supercharger. It's a bit like being in Nigel Mansell's nose.

I also wished the sat nav was a bit more funky. Doubtless, an all-new command-and-control centre is on the drawing board and that's probably a year away as well. Memo to Jag, then. Ring Mr Patel. Ask for more rupees.

It's important because, God, this is a lovely car. I parked it next to my wife's Aston Vantage and there's no doubt in my mind: it's better looking. It's likely to be more reliable too, as well as still being cheaper, faster and fitted with two (albeit useless) seats in the back. And nicer to drive.

The S model's engine has been tweaked so the top speed is up to 174mph. And, underneath, you get revised springs, dampers and antiroll bars. It's stiffer than the normal car but you're hard pressed to tell. It still rides the bumps beautifully – better than any other car in the class, by miles – and it still handles with a smile-on-your face simplicity.

Sadly, only fifty of these cars have been made for the UK. All are hard tops. All come in black and all have been sold.

But it's really not the end of the world, because it felt very similar to the standard car, which costs £9,000 less, comes in any colour you like and is available as a convertible, too.

You've probably never thought about buying a Jaguar before. Trust me, though. You should now.

20 July 2008

Calm yourselves, campers

Ford Kuga 2.0 TDCi Titanium

Interesting news from the quagmire. Sales of tents and camping equipment are up by 40 per cent as the credit crunch bites and families appear to ditch their annual pilgrimage to the Mediterranean.

According to tenting enthusiasts, a fortnight in Mallorca costs a family of four about £3,000, whereas they can spend two weeks under canvas in Devon for as little as £500.

I don't doubt this is true. But I'm not sure the comparison is relevant, because they aren't really comparing like with like. Arguing that a holiday in Mallorca is more expensive than a holiday in a field full of cow dung is the same as arguing that a Rolls-Royce Phantom is more expensive than hitchhiking.

Tenting works well when you are in Afghanistan, fighting the Taliban, but I find it extraordinary that a family should say, 'Well. Things are tight. So let's spend our holiday this year soggy and quarrelling in a room none of us can stand up in properly.'

If you are that hard up, and you are so desperate for a change, then why not simply stay at home and cut your legs off?

It's claimed by medical experts that we cannot remember pain, but that isn't true, because forty years ago my parents took me on a tenting holiday on the west coast of France, and I remember every little detail of it – so much detail that sometimes it makes me cry.

I remember the rain, and the way it cascaded down into the hollow where our tent was built. I remember the wind that knocked it down. I remember the Germans laughing at us. I remember the hateful food – mustard-encrusted salmonella entombed in the pungent aroma of Calor gas.

I remember the soggy sleeping bags, the sloping floor, the stones that dug into my back, the lack of sleep, the arguments, the discomfort, the pain, the misery, the mosquitoes, the desperation, the homesickness and my poor little sister's confused face asking, 'Why have our parents done this to us?'

At home we had headroom and walls. We had space. And when we wanted to go to the lavatory, we didn't have to tiptoe through the ooze to a filthy shower block full of yet more Germans with faulty bomb-aiming equipment. I can see them now if I close my eyes. All those massive Germanic turds; some not even close to the centre of the 101 bogs they had in France in those days.

I don't doubt for a moment that it hadn't cost very much money, but even today I cannot work out why it cost anything at all. Nor can I work out why a fortnight's holiday under canvas today could possibly cost £500. Killing yourself would be so much cheaper and more pleasant.

In every single walk of life technology has made things easier since the 1960s. We have dishwashers, computers and oven cleaners that wipe away grime in a flash. So you might imagine tenting had come on in leaps and bounds as well.

It hasn't. As I discovered on my trip to the North Pole, it's still an impenetrable maze of zippers, flaps, straps, exploding cookers and tent pegs that have the structural rigidity of overboiled pasta. Oh, and the skin of the modern tent is still exactly one inch smaller than the frame over which it must be stretched. This means that when you finally get it up you will have no fingernails, no wife, no children, no voice and not a shred of dignity either.

And where will you be? In a wood? Then you won't sleep because every noise at night, among the trees, is Freddy Krueger. In a field? Nope. You will wake up dead with a cow on your head. On a campsite? Ha. Well, then, you've really had it because women, and I have no clue why, think tenting is erotic. Which means you're going to have to spend the night listening to a hundred wizened ramblers bouncing around on the only pole in all of tenting that's still upright.

Naturally, this brings me to the Ford Cortina. This, too. came from a time when Mallorca was an impossible dream. When film makers could be guaranteed a box office smash if they could only persuade Barbara Windsor's bra to ping off. With hilarious consequences. We know it now as the Swinging Sixties, but unless you were on Carnaby Street, with a Moke, and you were intimately friendly with Twiggy, they weren't swinging at all. They were crap.

No, really. I bet it was a hoot in northern California in the summer of '68. But I wasn't on the corner of Haight and Ashbury. I was picking my way through a puddle of German urine on a campsite in the rain. If you were going to San Francisco, you would have been wise to wear some flowers in your hair. If you were on your way to a camping holiday in the family Cortina, you'd have been better off with some wellies.

The Cortina was Britain's most popular car back then because there was no choice. You couldn't buy an Austin because it wouldn't work, and Japan hadn't been invented. It was *Carry On Camping* with windscreen wipers. Four seats and a boot. British Rail tea.

Today, however, there is simply no need to buy a modern-day Cortina, because Terry's dead, June's in *Ab Fab*, Mallorca's only two hours away and British Rail, or whatever it's called these days, can rustle up a skinny latte instead. That's why you've got an MX-5. Or a RAV4. Or a Prius.

The thing is, though, that somewhere deep down inside us is a fear that all this choice is frightfully un-British. That we're not really cut out for being tall poppies. That we should be washing our clothes in a mangle. That's why tenting's made a comeback. And it's why we all still have a secret soft spot for the family Ford. You might imagine that if you traced the Cortina's bloodline, you'd end up with the Mondeo, but that's not so. Today, the modern family likes a high driving position and four-wheel drive, which means that actually today's 1.6 Deluxe is the Ford Kuga.

Ooh, it's a good-looking thing: nicely proportioned with just the right amount of styling trinketry. It's good underneath, too, with independent rear suspension like you get on a Focus.

However, it has none of the things you might normally associate with a four-wheel-drive vehicle. There is no hill descent control, no low-range gearbox, no little button to lock the centre differential. It's almost as though Ford is embarrassed that it has four-wheel drive at all. Perhaps, in these mad eco times, that's sensible.

Instead, Ford makes a great deal of noise about what a small amount of carbon dioxide the Kuga produces. I guess that's more important these days than an ability to climb every mountain and ford every stream.

It's well thought out in other ways, too. There are two boot doors, easy-to-fold back seats, a good, solid feel to the interior and an impressive ride. Unlike most high-riding cars, this one neither rolls nor bounces. If you have a Subaru Forester or a Honda CR-V, you'd be amazed at how much better the Kuga feels.

Except for one thing. Ford has a habit of fitting its cars with ridiculously hard seats and in the Kuga it's gone mad. I've sat on comfier kitchen chairs. Actually I've sat on comfier spikes.

When it comes to beds, I appreciate that some people like the firmer feel, but in a car, no one does. Unless, of course, they are used to camping, in which case anything with a roof and a heater and chairs – no matter how back-breakingly solid they may be – is going to feel fine.

More than fine, because the model I tested had a neither-here-nor-there diesel engine. And it was as brown as an alderman's sideboard. In this set-up the Kuga is perfect for the modern age. It's oxtail soup in a Tetrapak carton.

27 July 2008

Très bien – a plumber in a tux

Citroën Berlingo Multispace

Sarah Brown, the wife of our prime minister, is a complete mystery. For all I know, she collects fish, is qualified to fly fighter jets, has two left feet and sounds exactly like that woman with the broom in the Tom and Jerry cartoons. You even have to say 'Sarah Brown, the wife of the prime minister'. Which was unnecessary with Cherie Blair or Denis Thatcher.

All I do know is that she looked at the country's twenty-eight million men and thought, 'No. They are all horrid except for Gordon.' Which must mean she's a bit odd. And let's be honest here, shall we; like all women in and around British politics (with the notable exception of Samantha Cameron), she's not exactly a purring sex kitten.

Things are very different in Italy where Silvio Berlusconi has filled his entire cabinet with ex-glamour models. And, naturally, this brings me on to France's President Nicolas Sarkozy.

Unlike anyone in British politics, he attained high office and responded immediately by replacing his wife with the almost impossibly gorgeous Carla Bruni. Her mother is a concert pianist, her sister an actress and film director, and she's an heiress to an Italian tyre fortune. We're talking good genes here. And you can see them all in those cheekbones. I'm very much in love with Carla.

More than that, I'm very much in love with the French

for taking her into their hearts. That'd never happen here. Imagine, if you will, Gordon Brown winning an election (hard, I know) and then ditching Sarah for Abi Titmuss. He wouldn't last a week.

Weirdly, however, while the French like a good-looking woman in the Elysée Palace, they plainly have trouble with aesthetics in other departments. Take the oyster as an example. I have no idea who first cracked one open, peered at the snot inside and thought, 'Mmm. I'm going to put that in my mouth.' But I bet he was French.

Of course, Paris is a fine and handsome city, but the man who dreamt up those twelve wide boulevards radiating from the Arc de Triomphe was called Haussmann. And while he was born in France, his parents were from the disputed province of Alsace. Which technically makes their son an Alsatian. Which means he was a dog.

It's also true, of course, that Parisian women are very elegant, but I always think they were put on earth to make Italian clothes look good. And have you ever been in a Frenchman's house? Holy cow. It's an orgy or horror: antimacassars, Dralon, floral wallpaper, Formica and chintz. The minimalist Danish look completely passed them all by, leaving them all stuck in Huddersfield, in 1952.

France itself is a beautiful part of the world and the French language is spoken honey – unless it's being used in a pop song, obviously; in which case it's as attractive as an inside-out horse.

But just about everything the French make or do is lumpen, ugly or odd. This is especially true of their cars.

If you asked anyone to name the ten best-looking cars ever made, not a single person with functioning retinas would put a French car on their list. Renault occasionally does something appealing like the Avantime, but mostly it believes we'll buy its cars specifically because they've got big arses. Peugeot can do a good-looking car but only when it pays Pininfarina to design it. Left to its own devices, it mostly does bland, with occasional gusts of awfulness like the 309. That really was a mobile wart.

That leaves Citroën and, of course, what it has done mostly over the years is best described as, er . . . brave. It's hard, really, when it presents a new car, to find the right word. It's best to imagine Heston Blumenthal has just asked you, eagerly, to try his new dog-turd-flavoured ice cream. You can't be honest and say, 'That was terrible.' So you go for 'brave' or 'very striking'.

Today, though, Citroën is starting to buck the trend. The C5 is exceptionally good-looking. The C6 has great presence, and if you drive through town in a C4, no one is going to point and laugh. But then, just when you think Citroën has got the idea, out pops the new Berlingo.

The old one was just a van with windows and it struck a chord. Oh sure, it looked like a frog that had sat on a spike, but there was something rather appealing about the no-nonsenseness of a box with seats. Especially as it retailed for about 60p.

Sadly, with the new version, they've tried to disguise the window cleaner origins with chrome this and flared that. What they've ended up with is a plumber in a tux. It looks and feels completely wrong. Almost certainly, then, you will see it and immediately decide to buy something else. This would be a very big mistake.

I'll start with the problems. Um . . . Well, the tailgate is so huge that when you push the button it will rise up, and unless you're standing well back – which you won't be because you've just pushed the button – it will smash into the underside of your chin and remove your whole head. This would become wearisome. But aside from this upside-down guillotine feature, and the British female politician looks, the rest of the car is an object lesson in common sense.

Prices start at less than £11,000, which is very low for something with this amount of interior space. It rides more smoothly than a Jaguar XJ8 – they should have called it the Aeroglisseur – and it is the first car ever to come with a loft. I mean it. There is an internal roofbox into which, I'm fairly certain, you could fit a pair of modern-day skis. And that's just the start. There are so many cubbyholes and oddment stowage boxes that you could hide a priest in there and never find him again.

The car I tested had a ninety horsepower diesel, which meant I couldn't go very fast. But on the long straight between Shipston on Stour and Chipping Norton, I did get past a tractor in just eighteen minutes. So it's not the end of the world. And better still, it should do 40mpg easily.

It's a good car, the Berlingo. And in these difficult times, it makes even more sense than usual.

3 August 2008

This is an epic car. Every single atom of every single component is designed only to make your life as quiet and as comfortable as possible. Dreaming of a . . .

Rolls-Royce Phantom Coupé

Recently, I wrote in another part of the paper about the difficulties of trying to work while staying for the summer at your bolthole in the country. There are too many distractions, the view is too consuming, the children too needy and the constant longing for a beer too overwhelming.

Well, soon all the problems will be erased because a government think tank has looked carefully at the question of second homes and has announced that the rich bastards who have them should be forced to rent them out to underachieving, fat people.

Hmmm. I wonder. Did it deliver its findings to Gordon Brown at Number Ten, or to his second home in Buckinghamshire? And how does it think such a scheme could possibly work?

Many people, for instance, claim they live in Monaco for tax reasons. Whereas, in fact, all they do is buy a small flat and employ an estate agent to pop in every morning to make a few phone calls. The bills are then used as proof that they were there.

Second-home owners would adopt similar tactics here. Or they'd say their country cottage is their primary residence and that their apartment in London is a pied-à-terre. Then, the local council would have to prove otherwise by going through everyone's knicker drawer and employing men with binoculars and coffee breath to follow us about.

I fear the government think tank hasn't considered any of this because it was so consumed with bitterness, hatred and envy for people with money. It is not alone.

Just the other day, I read a report that said musicals in London's West End are bucking the trend with higher-than-ever audiences. This, you might think if you were a normal, well-balanced soul, is a good thing. But, sadly, the red top reporter was not. He was just bothered that bigger audiences meant Andrew Lloyd Webber would have even more money. And that made him incandescent with fury.

Why? It's not like Andrew Lloyd Webber spends his evenings being carried around council estates in Slough in a sedan chair, waving his jewels out of the window. He just gets on with his life in a way that has no effect whatsoever on the way you live yours or I live mine.

It's like being kept awake at night with a burning sense of envy about Cliff Richard's youthful good looks. What should we do? Take a Black & Decker sander to his cheekbones? Why? Because disfiguring Cliff's face won't make any difference to your own.

I don't yearn for many aspects of the American way but they do seem to have this dreadful bitterness under control. When they see a man pass by in a limousine, they say, 'One day, I'll have one of those.' When we see a man pass by in a limo, we say, 'One day, I'll have him out of that.'

All this past week, I've been driving around in a Rolls-Royce Coupé and it's been a genuinely alarming insight into the bitterness of Britain's obese and stupid underclass. Because when you drive this enormous monster past a bus queue, you realize that hate is not an emotion. It's something you can touch, and see and smell.

Just yesterday, a man in a beaten-up van deliberately straddled two lanes to make sure I could not get past. It would have made no difference at all to his life if I'd done so, but there was no way in hell he was going to let a Roller by. I find that shoulder-saggingly depressing.

I also find it wearisome that I must now go on to say what the car is like. Because I know this article will appear on the website, where readers will be invited to have their say. And some will wonder why, once again, I'm reviewing a car that so few people can afford.

Well, yes, I could tell you all about Hyundai's new supermini, which, let's say, 5 per cent of the country could buy. But what's the point because the other 95 per cent aren't interested.

Perhaps 0.01 per cent can afford a Rolls but a huge number of those that can't are still interested in knowing what it's like. Because contrary to the teachings of Britain's think tanks, there's no harm in dreaming . . .

The Rolls-Royce Phantom has been a success story. More than a thousand have been sold already and, much to the surprise of everyone, a great many are actually driven by their owners. The Maybach is for chauffeurs. It feels all wrong in the front. But when you're in the back of a Rolls, you spend most of your time dreaming up reasons for firing the man in the peaked cap and taking the wheel yourself.

It is an epic car, quite unlike anything else in the world. Because every single atom of every single component is designed only to make your life as quiet and as comfortable as possible. There is no sportiness in the mix whatsoever.

I imagined that the coupé would continue to amble down

the same road. But no. BMW, which owns Rolls, says it's aimed more at 'the driver'. And because of this, it is the first Rolls-Royce ever to be fitted with a sport button. That's like putting Prince Philip in training shoes. Pointless. Just leave it alone. I did.

There are some other issues as well. You cannot see much out of the tiny rear window, the backward-opening suicide doors are a nuisance in tight spaces, and the interior is polished so vigorously that everything reflects everything else. You spend half your time being startled by shadows. And when the sun is low in the sky it bounces off the dash in a glare so vivid it can detach your retinas.

Then there's the sat nav, which comes from BMW. It's hard to fathom, is devoid of any useful information and powered by a program that's part fiction, part comedy. Oh, and when you want to tighten the scale when approaching a complicated junction, the whole screen goes blank until you're on the other side, going the wrong way.

Worst of all, though, are the seats. They are too hard, there is no side support at all and after one four-hour drive, I had backache. 'Good,' you might be thinking, if you are in a government think tank. 'That means the rich bastard won't mind when we force him to rent his stupid car to a fat woman in the north.'

Ah, but you see, in a Rolls all of these faults are lost in a sea of unparalleled joy.

Providing you leave that sport button alone, it will sashay down a motorway in such a way that there's no need to worry about whether it is better to arrive or to travel hopefully. It doesn't feel like you're doing either. It's like you're in a big kapok ball.

Mind you, it is still pretty fast. Its performance figures are nearly as good as those of a Maserati GT. And it would be faster still if the slushmatic box didn't take a full second to make sure each gear change is as smooth as possible.

It's equally relaxing in town. While everyone else frets, the only thing you need worry about in the Rolls is keeping your eyes open. Speed bumps? Bah. Take them as fast as you like.

It must have half killed BMW to make a car this way because it, like every other manufacturer in the world, always puts a bit of hardness into its products. This means they are compromised everywhere just so they can take Stowe Corner at Silverstone without falling over.

Because the Rolls cannot take Stowe Corner very well, it is sublime in the real world. The big 6.75-litre V12 blows up its fuel in such a way you don't know it's happening. It's like being moved around by a muscle. The suspension feels like six miles of silk and everything you touch inside the car feels like it was made over a period of several years by a man from the nineteenth century in a brown store coat. Let me put it this way. The trim alone weighs more than an entire Triumph Herald.

Complaining, then, about poor rear visibility is like Arthur Negus complaining that one of the doors on a Georgian tallboy is a bit sticky. It's part of the price you pay for something that feels, looks and is genuinely beautiful.

So there we are. If you are the sort of chap who likes to drive his own Rolls, there's no point dragging around the six acres of empty shag-piled splendour you get in a Phantom saloon. Yes, the coupé is £27,000 more expensive but it is easier to park. And it does come with a Range Rover-style drop-down boot lid you can sit on when having a picnic.

The only proper drawback is the loathing from other road

users. But you know what. That's their problem, because style and comfort are not deadly sins. Envy, on the other hand . . .

10 August 2008

Oh, tell me it's not too late

Aston Martin Vantage

Over the years, we've been told by solemn-faced experts that life as we know it is about to end. Strange to report, then, that we've managed to survive Communism, particle accelerators, fascism, asteroids, Cuba, bird flu, global warming, terrorism, nuclear war, various tsunamis and Aids, and now we are going to be finished off by Fannie Mae.

I don't even know what Fannie Mae is. Apparently, it's not a bank and it's not a building society, but it seems to have been buying mortgages and debts from various institutions. And then, one day, it appears to have woken up and thought, 'Oops.' Quite how it was allowed to get in this mess, I'm not sure. Did nobody think it odd that a mysterious organization was stomping around the world buying debt? Did nobody stop for a moment and wonder if, perhaps, Fannie Mae was a home for mentals? I mean, we're talking here about an operation named after the human bottom. How did it sign its deals? With crayons?

Seriously, if I set up a business called Arse and went around buying outstanding loans on the nation's never-never-land three-piece suites, I wouldn't get very far before someone with a soothing voice and a corduroy jacket put me in a padded room for the rest of time.

Whatever. We have now arrived at a point where the world is going bankrupt. Politicians keep explaining that Britain is well placed to face the future, but we're not. Not when the food in our fridge is worth more than the contents of our jewellery box and we're scared witless that Bradford & Bingley is about to go belly up with all our life savings.

The net result is that half the country can't afford to buy anything and the other half daren't. This means companies can't sell anything, which means they can't employ anyone, which means everyone will fail to pay their mortgages, which will increase the likelihood of Bradford & Bingley going bust, which will accelerate the downward spiral to such an extent that it will be spinning faster than the atom-basher in Geneva. In short, we are all on the *Titanic*. It is holed. It is a mathematical certainty that it will sink. And all Gordon Brown can do is offer the ship's most elderly passengers a few extra winter logs as they drown in a sea of disease, debt and destitution.

Needless to say, cars are an early casualty of the meltdown. Having seen orders plummet by 44 per cent in July, Aston Martin sold just nineteen cars in the whole of August, according to the Society of Motor Manufacturers and Traders, down from fifty-eight in the same period last year. Porsche sales, meanwhile, were down by 58 per cent, Land Rover also by 58 per cent and Jaguar by 41 per cent. Potential customers, then, are split into two groups: those who can buy but won't, and those who want to buy but can't. Because no loans are available.

It's all such a shame. Not just for the 800,000 people who earn their living from cars in this country, but because for 200,000 years, human beings – with the notable exception of eco-activists who want to go backwards – have strived to improve the quality of their lives: to travel more quickly, to enjoy better health, to live longer and to be more comfortable.

The labour-saving, fast-acting television remote control is a classic case in point. It is just so human: no dolphin would even begin to see the point.

And it's the same story with cars. Just last night I left the *Top Gear* test track in the new Aston Martin Vantage, and, using just a couple of cubic feet of petrol, it brought me right to my door, ninety miles away, in just ninety-five minutes. That, in itself, is an achievement that any migrating wildebeest would kill for. And yet this snarling, sculptured machine is so much more than an auxiliary transport module. It's also a feast for your eyes, an electrode for your heart and a song for your soul. And now, thanks to Fannie Mae, we may be about to kiss it goodbye. Pity, because for the first time since it came out three years ago, the Vantage can be classed as a genuine player, and not just a pretty-boy 911-substitute for cocks with a James Bond fantasy.

Oh, some of the old niggles remain. The dash, for instance, looks lovely, but like so many things that look lovely – loon pants, for example – it doesn't work very well. Because there's no central command unit, such as you find in a BMW or a Mercedes-Benz these days, the buttons are all over the place, and because there are thousands of them, they have to be small. Hitting the right one while on the move is like trying to stab mercury with a cocktail stick while standing on a power plate.

Then there are the seats, which are far too hard, and the manual gearbox, which is fine . . . except that to engage second and fourth you need to dislocate your elbow. And the iPod connection, which has never heard of an iPod. And the Volvo sat nav system, which, no matter what you tell it, simply picks a destination you've been to recently and sends you there instead. The other day I tried to go to a *Top Gear* shoot and ended up at my mother's house, having phoned someone I hate on the way.

It sounds like I am not enamoured of Aston's Vantage, but the simple fact of the matter is this. All of these problems existed in the old car, and that was hugely popular before Fannie Mae did a Bear Stearns and Northern Rocked its Freddie Mac.

Truth be told, I don't really care about little faults like this. What I did care about on the old car was that its mouth kept writing cheques its engine couldn't cash. You put your foot down and there was a huge bellow, but not much extra speed.

The problem was that Aston Martin and Jaguar were both playing for the blue oval. And politics meant the Aston couldn't be as fast as Jaguar's XKR. Now, though, Jaguar belongs to Mr Patel, and Aston is in the hands of some Kuwaitis, so the politics have gone. In their place stands a 4.7-litre version of Jag's V8. The result is 420bhp instead of 380, and some proper get-up-and-go. Accelerate hard and the driver of a Porsche 911 Carrera S – it was R Hammond last night – is not going to see where you went. And not only because he can't see over the steering wheel.

The amount of carbon dioxide produced by the new engine is less than before. Not that it'll make any difference to your tax bill. Or the weather. More importantly, the suspension has been tweaked such that it's still firm on a motorway but much softer at low speed. And while the body remains the same, the wheels are wider, so the car looks even better.

But the best thing about this car is that because it's so brilliant at some things and so awkward at others, it has a human quality. Some cars you can like. Some you can use. And some you can respect. This one, though, you can love. I do. And that's why I'd be so sad if Aston were to wither and die in the current economic climate.

However, while I am pessimistic, I suppose we should look more carefully at the perils we've faced these past fifty years. War. Asteroids. Jonathon Porritt. Russia. The IRA. And so on.

They've come. They've frightened us. And then, contrary to the teachings of the scaremongers, they've all just sort of fizzled out and gone away.

14 September 2008

An old flame returns to relight my fire

Volkswagen Scirocco

In its latest glossy press information pack, Volkswagen says the original Scirocco Storm was sold with a 1.8-litre engine. This is a mistake. It is referring to the 1781cc unit that was, in fact, not introduced until October 1982, by which time it was making the Mk 2 Scirocco. The Storm, like all fuel-injected Mk 1s, was sold with a 1588cc engine. I'm surprised the people at VW didn't know this.

I, on the other hand, know everything about those early cars. I even know what sort of fuel injection system they used and how big the tyres were. Bosch K-Jetronic and 175/70/13s, in case you're interested. Furthermore, I know the leather-lined Storm was available in only noisette brown or silver green.

The Scirocco, for me, is very important. I was interested in cars long before VW thought about making a coupé version of the Golf. But it was the result of its efforts that caused me to want to write about them.

Here's why. Back in 1980, I lived up north, in the flatlands around Doncaster, and most of my friends were in the Young Farmers, which was not so much a club as a way of wife. You had dirty fingernails, stout shoes, a dislike of the south in general and London in particular, and either a Ford Escort RS2000 or a Dolly Sprint. One chap had a TR7 and we all thought he might be a mental.

I didn't really fit either, because while they all understood the art of ploughing and drilling, I thought fields were something for crashing into. And I wanted a Golf GTI. 'It's what they're all driving in London these days,' I said one night in the Carpenter's Arms. This was a mistake. A deathly hush fell over the bar. Heads turned. A dart slammed into a wall. Admitting that I might in some way be interested in the buying habits of people in Fulham was the same as admitting that I was interested in the sexual orientation of Larry Grayson.

The silence was broken after several agonizing moments by one chap who was wearing especially stout shoes. 'Are you a poof?' he said menacingly. Which is the catch-all northern prelude to someone having their head kicked off.

The lure of the GTI, however, was strong. So I agonized over what colour I'd like and precisely what sort of modifications I could afford if I took it to the GTI tuning centre at Silverstone. And then my eye was caught by the Scirocco. Underneath, it was the same as the Golf, but it had just the most agonizingly pretty body. So should I have this instead?

Unable to talk to anyone about this, in case they thought I was a southerner, I turned to the various motoring magazines, all of which were completely useless. They told me how big the boot was and the benefits of fuel injection and the precise dimensions of the rear seat, but I didn't care about any of this. All I wanted to know is whether, if I bought a Scirocco, it'd cause me to have more sex than if I bought a Golf.

I decided pretty much there and then that, one day, I'd write about cars in a whole new way . . . but in the meantime I moved to London and bought the Scirocco – a GLI with a tan interior – and in a year I clocked up 54,000 miles in that car. I loved it. I can even remember the numberplate – PUA 516W – and I can definitely remember how heavy the steering became when I fitted 205/60 tyres.

Eventually, I replaced my beloved Mk 1 with a Mk 2. This was a terrible car, partly because I fitted a white steering wheel to match the white paintwork, and partly because the damn thing was a fully paid-up member of Exit. Over a period of six painstaking months, it used its own clutch cable to saw itself very nearly in half.

However, in the same way that we cannot remember rainy days from our childhood, or pain meted out by dentists, I tend to forget the dismal Mk 2 when I think of the Scirocco and remember with a dreamy fondness all the good times I had with (and in) that wonderful Mk 1.

And that's why, as much as anyone else alive, I was so pleased to hear that VW was going to revive the name and bring the old girl back.

To drive, the new model feels pretty close to the Golf GTI, on which it's based. Which means it feels pretty close to perfect. The only weirdness is that it takes 7.2 seconds to get from 0 to 60, which is just half a second less than my old Mk 1 took twenty-eight years ago.

More important than the speed, though, is the way it looks, and I'm not sure. The original Scirocco was designed by Giugiaro, who is a modern-day Leonardo da Vinci. This new one was done in-house, and from some angles it's what Michael Winner would call historic. But from others it's a bit wet. And you should definitely be aware that in white it looks like a Stormtrooper's helmet.

In the past, this would have been a big problem because the only reason for buying a Scirocco, rather than a much cheaper Golf, was the extra style. Now, though, things are a bit different because, incredibly, the coupé is only £90 more than the hatch.

And you'll soon offset that because even though the two cars have a 2-litre direct-injection turbocharged engine, the Scirocco produces less carbon dioxide than the Golf. And is therefore in a lower tax band.

For even bigger savings, you could wait until VW introduces new versions of the car. One will have a 1.4-litre unit, which comes with a supercharger and a turbo, and the other – God help us – will be a diesel. Frankly, though, these cheapo models will be a bit like the fake Prada handbag my daughter bought on a recent day trip to Thailand. It looks like the real thing, but because it isn't, it's actually a bit crap.

Eventually, I am sure, there'll be a 3.2-litre, four-wheel-drive version – they could call it the Storm – but for now, the TSI is the model to go for, and you should spend an extra £1,300 on the DSG system. It's the only flappy-paddle gearbox that actually works in the real world.

Frankly, there aren't that many other boxes to tick. You get, as standard, multi-adjustable suspension that allows you to make the ride uncomfortable, you get climate control, you get a million bouncy castles that boing out of the dash if you hit a tree and you get a brilliant central command system that can be hooked up to your iPod. The only option I'd bother with is the smoker package. It's only £15, and choosing it would irritate the sanctimonious bastard who decided not to fit ashtrays as standard. If they offered a chlamydia pack, they couldn't sound more holier-than-thou.

Drawbacks? Well, the Scirocco is 97mm lower than the Golf, a point that becomes blindingly obvious every time you try to get inside. You really do have to pull your head into your ribcage if you don't want to bang it on the roof. To get in the back, it's best to cut yourself in half.

And that's it, really. I suppose I could mention the boot sill, which is a bit high, but then I'd sound like those old motoring hacks who drove me into this business all those years ago.

To make me sound nothing like those guys: the new car is like an old girlfriend you meet after hooking up on Friends Reunited. To everyone else she's just an ordinary middle-aged woman, but to you she's a bit more than that . . .

That's the new Scirocco. To most people it's just another car. But for those of us who had the old one, it arrives on the scene, after a fifteen-year period of nothing but grey skics and drizzle, like the warm, fast wind from which it takes its name.

21 September 2008

A one-armed man with a twitch can go fast in a Gallardo

Lamborghini Gallardo LP560-4

In the current economic conditions, the number of people who might want to buy the car you see photographed this morning – a new, even more powerful Lamborghini Gallardo – is about six. In fact, I don't know why I'm bothering to fill the rest of the page. It'd be easier and cheaper to send them a letter.

Then we could ignore the snarling, fuel-sucking, speed-busting supercar and look instead at how the streets of Britain might be when everything has gone bust, no one has a job and the government has decided to build a huge dam in the Cheddar Gorge just to keep everyone busy.

I do not believe there will be significantly more buses. The fact is that once you have been exposed to the freedom of personal transportation, it is impossible to retreat to the misery of veal-style collectivism. Buses are a safety net, a device civilization uses to move around the poor and the weak. Nothing more.

Nor do I believe there will be that many electric cars. They enjoyed their rise in popularity when times were good and we could all afford to have guilt about ecoism. But when you are forced to eat your dog to stay alive, it is very difficult to spare a thought for the polar bears and the cedar trees of Lebanon. And anyway, they don't work.

For guidance on the future, it's tempting to look at France.

Many years ago, when my head was full of hair and sixth-form politics, I argued that, in Paris, a car is not used to show off the wealth of its driver, only his level of interest in all things motoring. It is quite normal, I said, for a rich man who has no interest in cars to drive a beaten-up Clio, while his secretary, who loves to drive fast, has a big BMW.

It was a lovely theory, but it was wrong. Because, if we exclude the Côte d'Azur, which is now Moscow-on-Sea, we find that in fact no one in France has a nice car, no matter how interested they may be in motoring. This is because France is essentially Communist and anyone who displays outward signs of wealth is fearful that soon a mob will come and his head will be in a basket.

Here, there has never been a successful revolution. Oh, we've cut a king's bonce off but it only lasted a couple of days before the Paddy Basher was gone and Mr King's offspring was sitting in the hot seat. Today, the country is full of people who dislike the rich but they stick to vandalizing Range Rovers rather than beheading the Queen. And anyway, it's equally full of Essex and Cheshire; places where people will sleep on bare floorboards before they stop driving into town in the Bentley.

Britain is fundamentally middle-class. There are no walnut-faced sons of the soil with hate in their hearts. Basically, we all want a plasma television. We're all show-offs. We strive to be tall poppies. And, as a result of this, the car, whatever form it may take in the future, will always be mired here in mammonish k rather than cornering g.

So, in order to decide what sort of car Britain will be using in the near future, we must examine exactly what we require it to do. It must be considerably cheaper and less expensive to run than the cars we have now. Power will not matter due to the government's latest moronic wheeze to put average-speed cameras on all motorways. It must be available in a range of versions so that Chelmsford can continue to demonstrate its superiority over Wakefield. And with half of Africa and eastern Europe living here, it needs to be small to deal with the congestion.

Japan is already there. Yes, there are big Lexuses and yakuza Mercs prowling the streets, but most people drive what they call kei cars: extremely small, extremely light, extremely fuel-efficient personal modules. Some have Rolls-Royce radiator grilles. Some have ladders on the roof. Anyone who sets up a business importing these cars to Britain right now will do very well. Frankly, I'm amazed Honda, Toyota and Subaru haven't cottoned on already.

Perhaps they know what I know: that actually Japan is ahead of us but still some way behind Vietnam, where everyone has a small motor-bike. They are used as family saloons, lorries, pose-mobiles and taxis. And the system works, even when it rains, which it does, hard, and often for nine months of the year. I really can see a day when London looks much the same as Hanoi does today.

Funny, isn't it? Vietnam never quite caught up to the West but now it's accidentally overtaken us. Even as we speak, I have a small Vespa in my garage. Soon, I may be forced to go out there and see how the damn things works.

In the meantime, let's get back to the Lamborghini Gallardo that may be bought by only half a dozen people in the next century. Look at it this way: very few people will ever take a holiday on the international space station. But that wouldn't stop me reading about what it's like up there . . .

There's a very good reason why the baby Lambo is always seen as a poor relation to Ferrari's F430. It's because the

Ferrari is a better car. Drive them back-to-back around a racetrack and the difference is immediately obvious. The red car feels tight, sharp, pointy and modern. The orange car with the lime-green seats, feels, in comparison, like a canal boat. It rolls more in the corners, pitches more under braking, is less immediate in the way it accelerates and less responsive through the steering.

However, here's why I love the Lambo. To get the best out of a 430, you need to have testes like globes. Whereas a one-armed man with a twitch can go just as fast in a Gallardo while eating a sandwich and having a spasm attack.

And now he can go faster still because Lamborghini has upped the size of the V10 from 5 to 5.2 litres. That means you now get 552bhp, and that, coupled with a weight saving of 44lb, means you arrive everywhere in a cacophony of barking, wailing exhaust noises slightly before you set off. It is ridiculously quick. Mad quick. Eyes-on-stalks bonkers. Way, way faster than a standard Ferrari 430, massively louder, too, and because of the squidge-matic suspension and four-wheel-drive system, just as easy to drive as its predecessor.

Some have said in the past that the Gallardo's sister car, the cheaper Audi R8, was very similar. Not any more it isn't. It is David Miliband in the face of Russian aggression.

There's more. The Gallardo has always been a lovely-looking car, much more striking and desirable than the Ferrari. And the new model, with its new Reventón-style nose, is even better. The fact is that curves on a car never look as good as straight lines. The old Ford Scorpio proved that and the sharp, super-creased Lambo hammers the point home. We see the same thing with women. A fat girl's curvy round face does not have the same appeal as the straight lines found on Keira Knightley or Kristin Scott Thomas.

Pointlessly, I shall now run you through the costs. They are very high. But at least the fuel consumption has been improved by 18 per cent. Oh, and don't bother with the manual version. If you want a Gallardo, get the one with the flappy paddles.

If, then, you like to dream as you commute to the dole office on your Yamaha FS1E, dream about the Lambo. Lamborghinis have always been the heart and soul of the supercar scene and this is the most Lamborghinish model that has ever been made.

28 September 2008

Oh no, this is the world's worst car

Chrysler Sebring Cabriolet 2.7 V6

Many people imagine when they rent a convertible in America that they'll be thumping down Highway 1 under a blazing sky in a throbbing Corvette or an evocative Mustang. Yum yum, they think. Freedom. Sunshine. A V8 bass line. Engineer boots, leather jackets and tight blue jeans. The American dream.

Sadly, however, most tourists end up with a Chrysler Sebring convertible, which is almost certainly the worst car in the entire world.

My journey in this automotive horror story began in Wendover. Famous for being a base used by the *Enola Gay* back in 1945, it lies on the border between Utah and Nevada. So, half the town is full of man mountains emptying what's left of their savings into MGM's shiny and very noisy slots. And the other half is full of Donny Osmond. As you can imagine, I was in a hurry to leave and so I piled, along with my *Top Gear* colleagues, into the rented Sebring and set off for Denver.

Immediately, I was annoyed by a non-stop whining sound from the back. This turned out to be Richard Hammond, who, despite being 8 inches tall, claimed that he had never been so uncomfortable in his life, apart from when he was being born. 'Only that,' he said, 'was more spacious.'

After several hours of continuous moaning, he changed his tack. I'd selected a 'classic vinyl' station on the car's satellite radio and this did not meet with his approval. As a fan of Westlife and Girls Aloud, he didn't see why James May and I were air-drumming our way across the salt flats to a non-stop selection of brilliance from Supertramp, Yes and the Allman Brothers. Eventually, 'Hocus Pocus' by Focus drove him into such a frenzy of whingeing, we could take no more and drowned him out by turning up Steve Miller to the max.

I can only presume that when Steve went from Phoenix, Arizona, all the way to Tacoma, he was not at the wheel of a Sebring, or the song would have been rather different. 'I went from Phoenix, Arizona, to the other side of the city and then I went home again.'

Certainly, we only got as far as Salt Lake City in our rented car before we ditched it and resorted to the services offered by Delta. It had been 120 miles of abject misery, and not only because of the unswervingly pissed-off Richard Hammond.

Let us look, first of all, at the car's only good point. The boot is bigger than the hangar deck of a Nimitz-class aircraft carrier. However, the drawback of driving a car with an aircraft carrier on the back is that it doesn't look very good. No. That doesn't cover it. It looks terrible. Hysterically awful. Anyone thinking of drawing up a list of the ugliest cars ever made will be forced to put this one at the top. I have seen more attractive boils.

And disappointingly, if you push the button that lowers the roof – and then push it again because it isn't working properly – you will find that a) all of the carrying capacity is lost, and that b) with no roof in place, everyone can see you at the wheel. This is very bad. Some, for sure, give you pitying looks. Mostly, though, they point and laugh.

So how much do you have to pay for the privilege of being

a laughing stock? Well, in the US, it's around $29,000 (£16,400). You could buy a clown suit for less and achieve much the same effect. Here, however, a 2.7-litre drop-top Sebring is £25,100 and at that price, I simply don't know how the salesman keeps a straight face.

Power? There isn't any. Spec sheets show that in Britain, a 2.7-litre V6 will do 121mph and 0 to 62mph in 10.8.

But 10.8 what? Years? Let me put it this way. It develops 185bhp, which is pretty much what Volvo can get these days from a 2.4-litre diesel.

I'm afraid I have no idea which engine was fitted to my rental but I can tell you that all it did was convert fuel into noise. Put your foot down hard and after a while of nothing happening, the gearbox would lurch down a cog and the volume would increase. That was it.

Sadly, there's more bad news. Turning petrol into motion, as we know, is an expensive business, but turning it into sound is even worse. We managed just 18mpg. Quite why anyone would buy this rather than, say, a Volkswagen Eos, I simply do not know. You'd have to be so window-lickingly insane that you'd be banned from handling anything other than crayons.

A Sebring can do nothing well. It was hopeless in crosswinds and the only option you need on a twisty road is sick bags. Interestingly, however, while the ride is very soft, the suspension still manages to crash about like a drawer full of cutlery when it is asked to deal with a small pothole.

And of course, being an American rental car, it came with a warped disc brake and steering that was so out of whack it kept making a beeline for Wyoming. But the worst thing was the overwhelming sense from everything you touched that it had been built by someone who was being deliberately stupid or who was four years old. Life inside that bag of crap plastic gave me some idea of what it might be like to be a boiled sweet.

We see this with so many American cars. Dynamically, some of them are pretty good these days. One or two are even a match for what the Chinese are doing. And by and large they are still extremely cheap. But there's a very good reason for this. They are simply not built to last.

I spent most of my time in America this time in a new Corvette ZR1. It is a fabulous car. Mesmerizingly fast, good looking and amazing value. But after three days the damn thing was beginning to disintegrate. It made me growl with annoyance and despair.

But I think I know the problem. Because America is a new country, the people who live there have no sense of history. And if you have no concept of 'the past', it is extremely difficult to grapple with the idea of 'the future'.

If you think a bar established in 1956 is 'old' then you will not understand the idea of next week. So why bother building for it?

We see this short-termism in everything from the average American house, which falls over whenever the wind gets up, to the way chief executives are treated. In Japan, you are given twenty-five years before you are judged on whether you've turned the company around. In America, bosses are given two months. And if there's been no financial about-turn, they are fired.

AIG and Lehman Brothers got caught out because they were being run by people who live only in the here and now. They couldn't see that it would all come crashing down in the future because there's no such thing.

I suppose eco-mentalists would use this argument as a

stick to beat the pickup-driving masses. But how can Hank and Billy-Bob think about the world ending in a thousand years when everything they know, everything they are, began a week ago last Tuesday?

And this brings me on to the war in Iraq. They went in there, knowing that pretty quickly they could depose Saddam Hussein. But nobody in power stopped for a moment to think about what might happen next. And there you have it. The insurgency problem in Baghdad and the wonky gear-lever on the Chrysler Sebring. They are both caused by exactly the same thing.

And the only cure, frankly, is time. Give them 2,000 years and they might just start to understand what I'm on about. Until then, do not buy a Sebring. Do not rent one either. Close your eyes, hum and, hopefully, we can make it go away.

5 October 2008

A Wilmslow pimp with class

Cadillac CTS-V

The Stig's car has blown up. It's not surprising, really, given the way he drives, but whatever, he now needs a new one. His requirements are very simple: it must have a 'loose back end', several hundred horsepower, almost no suspension, extraordinary acceleration, a vivid top speed and a traction control system that can be turned off, completely and for ever.

Lewis Hamilton's tail-happy McLaren would be ideal except for one minor, but important, detail.

The Stig also insists that his new car must be capable of at least thirty-five miles to the gallon.

Yes, even *Top Gear*'s peculiar racing driver, a man who eats raw mince and fills his spare time by chasing sheep, has noticed that the economy has gone wrong and that he must have an everyday car that is economical.

You may think he has a point. Buying fuel is surely the most painful experience known to man, partly because petrol pumps deliver it so unbearably slowly, and garages are such unpleasant places, with their horrible pies and silly country and western CDs on special offer, and partly because the cost is just so enormous.

It costs nearly £100 to fill my car, and 210 miles later I have to spend another £100 to fill it up again. And for why? It's not like spending £100 on a delicious supper, which would be memorable and pleasant. We only use fuel to get us to work, which is boring, or to the shops at weekends, which is hateful.

Fuel is like washing-up liquid: something you must have in your daily life but that is extremely boring. And that's why all of us want to go as far as possible between fill-ups. And that's why most people think it makes sense to make fuel economy a central pillar of their new-car-buying decision.

Don't be so sure. The figures put out by governments and car manufacturers are theoretical, which is a Greek way of saying 'wrong'.

You are therefore basing your buying decision on nothing but hot air and probabilities. And this can lead to much disappointment.

Making the situation worse are the bores you bump into occasionally at the local Harvester. They always tell you that they manage to get 80mpg from their old Vectra. This is not true. They are making it up in a desperate bid to appear clever – which they aren't, or they wouldn't have a Vectra.

Whenever someone, and they always have a branded bomber jacket, says they achieve more than 70mpg from a family saloon, stick your fingers in your ears and hum. Because all they are doing is trying to make themselves feel better about the awful hand God has dealt them.

Sadly, however, people believe preposterous mpg figures like this are possible. And that the official government figures are accurate too. Only the other day, I received a letter from a Mr Disgruntled of Kent, who had bought a Mercedes Smart car, expecting to drive for several years between trips to the pumps. And then found to his horror that it was doing only twenty-something miles to the gallon.

He has taken his car back to the garage, which says there

is nothing wrong with it. But the garage is wrong, too. There is, I'm afraid. It's called 'the person behind the wheel'.

Unlike Bomber Jacket Man's Vectra, a Smart car is capable of 70mpg but only if you drive it with extreme care. And plainly, Mr Disgruntled, you are not doing this.

It's not easy, and it's not pleasant, indulging in what the Americans call 'hypermiling', but the effect on your wallet can be profound. If, for instance, you have a BMW 5-series and you get twenty-five to the gallon, I reckon you could pretty much double that. Without your journeys becoming appreciably longer.

It's all to do with how you brake and how you accelerate. It's about finesse, reading the road ahead, anticipating, treating the pedals and the steering wheel as though they are made from stained glass. It's about the shoes you wear, and turning the air-conditioning off.

Maybe it would be a good idea to make all this a part of the driving test. At present you are told how to stop and how to reverse round a corner, but at no point will an instructor tell you to accelerate briskly, and to build up speed when going down a hill so you can ease off the throttle when going up the next one.

You may be tempted by all of this, but I'll warn you. It is extremely boring and unbelievably tiring. Popping into town for a pint of milk can become more exhausting than trying to hop there on one leg. And for what? So that you achieve 50mpg, which is still twenty less than Bomber Jacket Man claims to get from his old Vectra without really trying.

It's probably better, then, if you want to save money – and we do – to choose a car, and then see if another manufacturer can sell you something similar for much less.

And that brings me, briefly, to the BMW M5. It's a little

bit complicated, perhaps, with all its various settings, but provided you have the time to set it up properly, it goes, stops and steers with a panache and a zest that are extremely rare among four-door saloons. Lovely, except it costs £65,890, and these days you could buy an island for less.

So now we arrive at the Cadillac CTS-V, which you can buy, in the UK, for about £47,000. That's a saving of roughly £19,000. And that equates to approximately 3,800 gallons of fuel. You could drive an M5 as though it were made from bits of your children from now to the end of time and you'd never make up the difference.

So what, then, are the drawbacks to the Cadillac? Well, first of all, it's a Cadillac, so everyone will think you are a Wilmslow pimp. And second, this hot version will be available with only left-hand drive.

Depreciation? Yes, a Cadillac will plummet as though it's being fuelled by melted-down Bradford & Bingley executives. But the M5 is not exactly a ten-year government bond, is it?

So make no mistake: financially, the Cadillac smashes the M5, completely and utterly. And here's the next part. Round the Nürburgring, it smashes it again. With an ordinary part-time racing driver at the wheel, an automatic version of the hottest ever Caddy went round in seven minutes fifty-nine seconds – a record for any four-door saloon.

Part of the reason is its 6.2-litre supercharged V8, which develops a dizzying 556bhp. That's forty-nine more than you get from an M5. The Cadillac is mind-bogglingly fast. The manual version I drove will hit 191mph. And it accelerates with a verve that truly leaves you breathless. It also makes an utterly irresistible growl. Like an AMG Mercedes but more refined. More muted.

And now you are expecting the 'but'. But there isn't one. Maybe the steering is a bit too light, but other than this it handles beautifully when you have the Ferrari-style magnetic dampers in 'sport', and rides soothingly when you switch the knob to 'comfort'. This is unusual for an American car, which usually can do neither thing properly.

Even more surprising is the interior. Trimmed by the people who do the Bugatti Veyron, it is – and you won't believe this – a nice place to be. The seats are by Recaro, the leather is hand-stitched and the graphics don't appear to have come from Amstrad circa 1984. You would swear you were sitting in something European.

Of course, you'd expect the illusion to be gone when you look at the exterior. It isn't. There are no badges written in the typeface used on northern wedding invitations. There's no onyx. Maybe the chicken-wire radiator grille is a bit sudden, but then again, have you seen the front of a Bentley recently? No. I'm sorry but it's a good-looking car, this.

As you may have gathered, then, I like it. I believe that ultimately an M5 would be more satisfying, a touch more crisp. But if you had an M5 you'd have to drive it carefully, to save fuel. With the Cadillac, you can blast through the recession at 191mph, knowing you made the savings when you bought it.

12 October 2008

Misery, thy name is Vespa

Vespa GTV Navy 125

Recently, various newspapers ran a photograph of me on a small motorcycle. They all pointed out that I hate motorbikes and that by riding one I had exposed myself as a hypocrite who should commit suicide immediately.

Hmmm. Had I been photographed riding the local post-mistress, then, yes, I'd have been shamed into making some kind of apology. But it was a motorcycle. And I don't think it even remotely peculiar that a motoring journalist should ride such a thing. Not when there is a problem with the economy and many people are wondering if they should make a switch from four wheels to two.

Unfortunately, you cannot make this switch on a whim, because this is Britain and there are rules. Which means that before climbing on board you must go to a car park, put on a high-visibility jacket and spend the morning driving round some cones while a man called Dave – all motorcycle instructors are called Dave – explains which lever does what.

Afterwards, you will be taken on the road, where you will drive about for several hours in a state of abject fear and misery, and then you will go home and vow never to get on a motorcycle ever again.

This is called compulsory basic training and it allows you to ride any bike up to 125cc. If you want to ride something bigger, you must take a proper test. But, of course, being human, you will not want a bigger bike, because then you will be killed immediately while wearing clothing from the Ann Summers 'Dungeon' range.

Right, first things first. The motorbike is not like a car. It will not stand up when left to its own devices. So, when you are not riding it, it must be leant against a wall or a fence. I'm told some bikes come with footstools which can be lowered to keep them upright. But then you have to lift the bike onto this footstool, and that's like trying to lift up an American.

Next: the controls. Unlike with a car, there seems to be no standardization in the world of motorcycling. Some have gear levers on the steering wheel. Some have them on the floor, which means you have to shift with your feet – how stupid is that? – and some are automatic.

Then we get to the brakes. Because bikes are designed by bikers – and bikers, as we all know, are extremely dim – they haven't worked out how the front and back brake can be applied at the same time. So, to stop the front wheel, you pull a lever on the steering wheel, and to stop the one at the back, you press on a lever with one of your feet.

A word of warning, though. If you use only the front brake, you will fly over the steering wheel and be killed. If you try to use the back one, you will use the wrong foot and change into third gear instead of stopping. So you'll hit the obstacle you were trying to avoid, and you'll be killed.

Then there is the steering. The steering wheel comes in the shape of what can only be described as handlebars, but if you turn them – even slightly – while riding along, you will fall off and be killed. What you have to do is lean into the corner, fix your gaze on the course you wish to follow, and then you will fall off and be killed.

As far as the minor controls are concerned, well . . . you

get a horn and lights and indicators, all of which are operated by various switches and buttons on the steering wheel,
but if you look down to see which one does what, a truck
will hit you and you will be killed. Oh, and for some extraordinary reason, the indicators do not self-cancel, which means
you will drive with one of them on permanently, which will
lead following traffic to think you are turning right. It will
then undertake just as you turn left, and you will be killed.

What I'm trying to say here is that, yes, bikes and cars are
both forms of transport, but they have nothing in common.
Imagining that you can ride a bike because you can drive a car
is like imagining you can swallow-dive off a 90-foot cliff
because you can play table tennis.

However, many people are making the switch because
they imagine that having a small motorcycle will be cheap. It
isn't. Sure, the 125cc Vespa I tried can be bought for £3,499,
but then you will need a helmet (£300), a jacket (£500), some
Freddie Mercury trousers (£100), shoes (£130), a pair of
Kevlar gloves (£90), a coffin (£1,000), a headstone (£750), a
cremation (£380) and flowers in the church (£200).

In other words, your small 125cc motorcycle, which has
no boot, no electric windows, no stereo and no bloody heater
even, will end up costing more than a Volkswagen Golf. That
said, a bike is much cheaper to run than a car. In fact, it takes
only half a litre of fuel to get from your house to the scene
of your first fatal accident. Which means that the lifetime cost
of running your new bike is just 50p.

So, once you have decided that you would like a bike, the
next problem is choosing which one. And the simple answer
is that, whatever you select, you will be a laughing stock.
Motorbiking has always been a hobby rather than an alternative to proper transport, and as with all hobbies, the people

who partake are extremely knowledgeable. It often amazes me that in their short lives bikers manage to learn as much about biking as people who angle, or those who watch trains pull into railway stations.

Whatever. Because they are so knowledgeable, they will know precisely why the bike you select is rubbish and why theirs is superb. Mostly, this has something to do with 'getting your knee down', which is a practice undertaken by bikers moments before the crash that ends their life.

You, of course, being normal, will not be interested in getting your knee down; only in getting to work and most of the way home again before you die. That's why I chose to test the Vespa, which is much loathed by trainspotting bikers because they say it is a scooter. This is racism. Picking on a machine because it has no crossbar is like picking on a person because he has slitty eyes or brown skin. Frankly, I liked the idea of a bike that has no crossbar, because you can simply walk up to the seat and sit down. Useful if you are Scottish and go about your daily business in a skirt.

I also liked the idea of a Vespa because most bikes are Japanese. This means they are extremely reliable so you cannot avoid a fatal crash by simply breaking down. This is entirely possible on a Vespa because it is made in Italy.

Mind you, there are some drawbacks you might like to consider. The Vespa is not driven by a chain. Instead, the engine is mounted to the side of the rear wheel for reasons that are lost in the mists of time and unimportant anyway. However, it means the bike is wider and fitted with bodywork like a car, to shroud the moving hot bits. That makes it extremely heavy. Trying to pick it up after you've fallen off it is impossible.

What's more, because the heavy engine is on the right, the

bike likes turning right much more than it likes turning left. This means that in all left-handed bends, you will be killed.

Unless you've been blown off by the sheer speed of the thing. At one point I hit 40mph and it was as though my chest was being battered by a freezing-cold hurricane. It was all I could do to keep a grip on the steering wheel with my frostbitten fingers.

I therefore hated my experience of motorcycling and would not recommend it to anyone.

19 October 2008

A trolley's the better bet

Renault Twingo Renaultsport 133

Not that long ago, so many people had Ford Sierras that they formed an army large enough to shape the outcome of general elections. And now? They're gone. All of them. You're more likely to see a Model T.

It is the same with all cars. They come. They provide a frisson of excitement for the new owner, they get sold to a minicab driver and when they are so full of hen-night sick that their wheels stop going round properly, they are dismantled and turned into toasters.

The speed at which this process happens is astonishing. In fact, I've just worked out that it takes longer to design and engineer a new car than it does for that car to go from being someone's pride and joy to being the handle on a Morphy Richards kettle.

Just last week I sold my Volvo XC90 because it was getting a bit tired. There was a sense that soon it would start to cost money and that we'd be better off handing that problem onto a minicab driver and getting a shiny new one instead. It was sad to see the old girl go, but hey, within a couple of years, I'll be drinking some fizzy pop from its rear wing and keeping my vegetables crisp and fresh in what used to be its bonnet.

I think, however, that soon this is going to have to stop. In the good times, it's all very well replacing your car because it's got a bit of asthma, but when a burly man from Northern Rock is outside with a removals lorry and an eviction notice, people are going to keep their cars for years after the 'best before' date has expired.

The question is: how long can you reasonably keep a car before it oxidizes, explodes, disintegrates or kills you and everyone within a thirty-mile radius? And the answer is: pretty much for ever.

When the trade embargo slammed shut on Cuba in 1962, it became impossible to get spare parts. So, if the windscreen wiper motor packed up on your Buick, you couldn't go to a dealer and get a new one. Nor could you replace the car. You had to fix it as best you could.

They even worked out that when brake fluid became manky and useless, it could be replaced with a concoction made from shampoo, sugar and alcohol. And to invigorate a dead battery, they simply shinned up a telegraph pole and attached it to the overhead power lines. Only some people were killed doing this.

I saw similar feats in Vietnam back in the early 1990s. One chap had cleverly replaced the suspension on his ancient Chevrolet with scaffolding poles. It wasn't a desperately elegant, or comfortable, solution but it did mean he had a car. Which, as we discovered last week, is infinitely better than the alternative. A stupid motorcycle.

Poverty is the mother of ingenuity . . . unless you were born like me with fists of ham, fingers of butter and a complete inability to fathom how anything that is broken can be repaired. If I'd been living in Cuba in 1962 and my washing machine had broken down, I'd still be wearing the same underpants today.

And if the suspension had collapsed on my 1971 Chevrolet,

I would have sat down at the side of the road and wept solidly until communism went away. So I fear the hard times that lie ahead because when my new Volvo starts to make a knocking noise I will have absolutely no clue what is causing it and no chance of making it go away.

The underside of a car to me is a strange and frightening place full of limitless possibilities for ending up with a dire need for a blood transfusion. None of the bolts can be worked loose and even if you do have the muscles of Samson, there is still an overwhelming fear that what you are about to undo will cause the entire car to collapse in such a way that no man will ever be able to put it back together again.

Once I did take the engine in my old Ford Cortina to pieces in a bold but ultimately unrewarding attempt to see how it worked. And I was never able to enjoy the car again because I knew that I'd rebuilt its beating heart and that there had been one important-looking nut and bolt left over when I'd finished.

I dare say many of you are in the same boat. Which means that you will not be able to mend your car in the hard times. So you will have to replace it. And because money is tight, and you've already eaten all the family pets, your new car is going to have to be much smaller and much more economical than anything you've driven since you were a student.

There are many small cars from which you could choose, but most have got 'cheapskate' written all over them. No. You'll be wanting something with a bit of style, a bit of pizzazz. And that will lead you inexorably to the door of the Fiat 500 Abarth, a turbocharged shoe of a thing that looks good, goes extremely quickly and has just as many seats as a Range Rover Vogue.

In many ways, it reminds me of the original Golf GTI. A

car you would buy even if you could afford a Maserati Quattroporte. It really is extremely appealing with just the right
blend of cuddly cutesiness and naked growling aggression.
A sabre-toothed labradoodle, if you will.

It is excellent. But before you sign on the dotted line, I
thought it might be a good idea to check out the Fiat's only real
competitor: Renault's equally tiny Twingo Renaultsport 133.

At first glance, it looks like a normal run-of-the-mill
micro-hatchback. The sort of thing your geography teacher
might drive. That's bad. But look again. Note the big wheels,
the wider track, the get-out-my-way frontal styling: hints that
if it were to get into a fight with Alien and Predator it might
just emerge victorious. And you can buy it with the cross of
St George painted on the wings, which is eye-catching, if not
very French.

Under the bonnet, there's a 1.6-litre engine that delivers
133bhp to the sole of your right foot. That sounds rather
mouth-watering in a car that weighs about the same as a Lotus
Elise. And it is. It'll do 0 to 60mph in 8.5 seconds and hit
125mph, and that's lovely. But the Fiat is considerably faster,
and more economical, and it produces less carbon dioxide,
which the government thinks is relevant in some way to the
amount of tax you pay.

That said, with the Fiat expected to cost £13,500 when it
goes on sale, the Renault is cheaper to buy. In theory. The list
price is £11,550 but if you want any luxuries at all – and you
will if you are downsizing from a Range Rover – you'd better
break out the Treasury bonds because just about everything
is an optional extra. You even have to pay extra if you want
it to drive well.

The standard car comes with a relatively soft chassis,
which is fine if you want a shopping trolley. But if that's

what you want, why bother with the Twingosport? Why not just go down to Asda one night with some bolt-cutters?

To make the car really fly, you need the £650 Cup chassis, which is lower and firmer. With this, the little Renault is tremendous. Better, in fact, than the Fiat. But the price you pay, apart from the £650, is a ride that would drive you absolutely mad.

It's hard, then, to recommend the Renault. It's got clever rear seats that move about and the dashboard is deliciously mad. But then the Fiat is a joyous place to sit as well. And you can buy it with an SS pack that takes it up to 160bhp.

It's a bit of a one-horse race, if I'm honest. The Renault might be in tune with the times. But the Fiat sings the same song more loudly and better. And, of course, being Italian it'll have become a household appliance by the time the economy is back to normal. So you can get back to your Range Rover.

26 October 2008

Don't go breaking my bones, baby

Alfa Romeo Brera S 3.2 JTS V6

Obviously, you can't buy a Toyota Prius. Quite apart from the acid rain caused by mining the nickel for its battery, and the fact it uses an enormous amount of fuel to cover incredibly short distances, it looks absolutely stupid.

And, interestingly, it looks absolutely stupid on purpose. You see, car makers have got it into their heads that cars that run on holistic, fair-trade technology should not look like normal cars. We saw this first of all with the silly Honda Insight and we see it now with the Prius.

There is, of course, a very good reason for this. It's because the people who are interested in bear-friendly motoring tend to look like you and I. There is no way of knowing as we walk past them in the street that they have bought a wood-burning stove that runs on melted-down bankers and limbs hacked from McDonald's executives.

However, if they have a weird-looking Prius, they stand out. So we can tell they care about the world. It is part of their uniform, worn in much the same way that murderers always have face hair of some sort. So that other murderers can nod, knowingly, when they pass in a crowd.

We see this in all walks of life. Enthusiastic homosexuals, for instance, favour the white vest. People who holiday in Cornwall sport Boden swimming trunks. Golfers enjoy dressing as Rupert Bear. And green people have their odd-looking cars.

The funny thing is that by demanding they stand out, they will actually hurt the world. This is because normal people like you and me don't particularly want to drive about in something that appears to have been designed by the Northampton branch of the Society for the Mad. So we buy a normal car instead.

Take the G-Wiz as another example. I am sure there are lots of people who'd love a silent urban runabout that's easy to park and uses no fuel. Who wouldn't? But you'd have to have the sartorial ambitions of an American tourist to sit in a Wiz and think, 'Yes! I look good.' Because you don't. You look ridiculous.

The fact is that you would not wilfully buy a horrible garden ornament for your front lawn. You would not deliberately select an ugly sofa, and it is the act of a madman, or more usually a nervous wife, to look at all the available au pairs from Finland and think, 'Hmmm. I'll take the moose.' Looks, in everything, are key.

Take my wife's Aston Martin Vantage. This is an extraordinarily beautiful car but, that said, when viewed head-on it appears to have no wheels and as a result it looks a little bit awkward. Therefore, and this I know makes me sound slightly strange, I ensure it's always parked at an angle in the yard so that whenever I see it from a window it pleases me.

Other really good-looking cars on the market today are the Lamborghini Gallardo, which is one of the best-looking cars ever made in fact, the Jaguar XKR convertible – especially in dark grey – the Alfa Romeo 8C, the Citroën C5 estate, the Lexus IS 200, the drophead Chevrolet Corvette C6, the Dodge Challenger and the Maserati Quattroporte.

I've half a mind to include the Volkswagen Scirocco in this list but two things stop me. First, there is rather too much strangeness about its proportions, and second, I have got it into my head that it will be bought exclusively by people who like wife-swapping. I'm not sure why. Maybe it's because it will appeal to those who live in executive housing estates, and in my mind everyone who lives in such places spends all of their time sleeping with their next-door neighbour.

Whatever, before you all reach for the Basildon Bond to say 'it's all right for some' and you don't have a millionty pounds to spend on a set of wheels, I should point out that cars do not have to be expensive to be handsome. The Smart is a fine example. So is the Mini, if you avoid the terrible Clubman. And both these will be much kinder to the environment, and your wallet, than a stupid Prius.

And, finally, we arrive at the subject of this morning's missive from the hills – the Alfa Romeo Brera.

Oooh, it's a looker. Yes, it sits in Alfa's history like a goat would sit in a tank of tropical fish, but while it may not have many traditional Alfa details, there's no getting away from the fact that it's the sort of car that makes you have to bite the back of your hand to stop you crying out.

Unfortunately, there has always been one rather enormous problem with the Brera. How can I put this? It isn't very fast. In fact, it is very slow. Slower than a dog with no legs. You don't need a stopwatch to measure its 0 to 60mph time, or even a calendar. You need a geologist. Someone who thinks the speed of Everest's drift westwards is impressive.

This car, then, is the perfect candidate for a spot of tweaking'n'tuning. And that's exactly what's happened with the limited edition Brera S.

Alfa Romeo took the basic car to Prodrive, the company

behind just about all the world's race and rally programmes since Harold got an arrow in his eye, and said, 'Can you make this thing go as well as it looks?' And what Prodrive did was ignore the engine and set to work on the suspension. Quite why, I have no idea. It's a bit like going to the doctor with a stye in your eye and having your left leg put in plaster.

Describing the end result is difficult, partly because I'm friendly with the chap who runs Prodrive. And partly because our children are friendly too. I'll try to be tactful, then. It's awful.

A normal Brera may not be fast but the ride comfort is lovely. Sitting on tall tyres, it absorbs bumps and potholes with an elegance to match the style. Prodrive, however, ditched the tall tyres, increased the spring rates by 50 per cent, lowered the ride height and ended up with something it says is perfectly tuned for British roads.

What British roads is it talking about? The British roads I know are bumpy, and in the Brera S you feel every single ripple. The ride is not just bad. It is intolerable. And when you couple this to shockingly lumpy seats, you will get out after even the shortest journey in great pain. I certainly did.

The idea, I suppose, was to make the Brera handle more aggressively. And it does. But even here there are problems. The steering is now so direct, you can get yourself into a bit of a muddle when driving quickly, and I'm afraid that despite the best efforts of Prodrive, the chassis it had to work with is a bit of a bender. You can still feel the flex. Not that you worry about it unduly because your back is hurting so much.

And you can't get the journey over quickly because the engine is unchanged. Yes, 100kg has been shaved from the overall weight but the 3.2-litre version still takes seven seconds to get from 0 to 62mph. The 2.2-litre version? God knows. No one would have the patience to find out.

The only nice thing I can find to say about the whole job is that I liked the red stitching on the dashboard.

This car, then, is a bit like having a very beautiful but bonkers girlfriend. You'll know exactly why you got involved, but equally you'll know that the relationship can never last.

2 November 2008

Well, I did ask for a growlier exhaust

Racing Green Jaguar XKR 475

I don't like speed cameras very much so you'd probably expect me to laud the decision taken by Swindon council to remove them from the town's streets. Hmmm. The council says that it currently spends £320,000 a year on cameras and that this money could be better spent on other road safety schemes.

What, exactly? Because in the extraordinary world of government finance £320,000 may be enough, just, to buy a hammer, but it certainly isn't enough to pay for the safety courses people must attend before they're allowed to use one.

One of those solar-powered 'Slow down' signs is £10,000, and by law, in case there hasn't been enough global warming and the eco-sign stops working, there has to be another, conventional sign right next to it, saying exactly the same thing. So quite how many lives Swindon council hopes to save with £320,000 I really don't know.

Don't get me wrong. I don't agree with the communists who say speed cameras have the life-saving properties of penicillin, but who knows what the truth is? I always drive quite slowly through the village of Woodstock because there are two cameras. If they weren't there, would I do 180 and hit a bus queue? Or would I do 180 and not hit a bus queue? Nobody knows.

Except of course for the communists. They take the accident figures every year and claim every single tiny drop is entirely down to speed cameras. They say that were it not for this brilliant enforcement measure, everyone in the land would now be a drooling vegetable or dead.

Really? The fact is that since cameras were introduced, the number of deaths has remained pretty much constant at about 3,000 a year. However, it's also a fact that the number of serious injuries has been steadily falling. 'You see,' say the communists squeakily. 'If everyone is made to drive at the same speed, irrespective of wealth or power, the number of people losing arms and spleens is slashed.'

Unfortunately, they are talking rubbish. The problem is the term 'serious injury'. According to the government, this means fractures, concussion, internal injuries, crushing, severe cuts, lacerations or shock. Technically, then, a broken finger is a serious injury, and some policemen might well record it on their forms that way. Others might not. And there is some evidence that officers are being 'encouraged' to downgrade their assessments near speed camera sites. So it looks as though the so-called safety measures are working.

And no one ever says, 'Hang on a minute. Can't some of the improvements be down to the way cars are designed these days?'

The only accurate way of assessing how we are doing as a nation of drivers is to look at the number of people being killed, because that isn't open to interpretation by a traffic officer. Someone is either dead or they are not. The figures cannot be manipulated. Not even the government can hide a dead body in the bushes for long. Someone's going to find it.

So if we concentrate on deaths, the whole picture becomes extraordinarily blurred. I mean, you'd expect, now that cars have airbags, and bluff fronts to make them almost comfortable when they run you down, that the number of deaths on the road would be falling dramatically. But it isn't. It's constant.

It's not as though the airbags and the antisubmarine seats have been offset because we are driving faster. Department for Transport figures show that in 1997 70 per cent of cars regularly exceeded the 30mph limit. In 2007 it was less than half. Average speeds are coming down, too, by nearly 1 per cent between 2005 and 2007. In the rush hours the average speed in many built-up areas is less than 15mph.

So we're going slowly. Cars are safer. There are speed cameras on every street corner. Pavements are fenced off from the roads. There are more underpasses and foot bridges. Motorways are safer. Road surfaces are more grippy. Tyres are better. Antilock brakes have been introduced. And none of this is making the slightest bit of difference to the number of people being killed.

Why? Well, I racked my brains. Smoked a pack of cigarettes. Walked round the garden twice. And still I could not come up with a plausible explanation. But then along came the Green Party, which seems to have hit on an interesting theory.

It may be woolly on the issue of climate change – it keeps claiming the world is warming up when every single figure shows it's actually cooling down – but on road safety the Green Party seems to be bang on the money. It says casualty figures aren't dropping because the roads are full of gormless morons.

Of course, the Greens don't put it quite like this. Instead, they say that the number of pedestrians being killed on the roads in the least deprived areas (where intelligent people live) is three times smaller than the number in areas of greatest deprivation (where thick people live).

Naturally, they think the problem can be solved with a nationwide 20mph speed limit, but this seems to punish the bright unfairly. I mean, why should a solicitor have to drive his Audi A6 through Godalming at twenty simply because a fat, one-eyed oaf in Pontefract can't get to work in the morning without hitting a hundred prams? Much better, surely, to base the speed we're allowed to drive on our IQ. This way, Stephen Fry would be allowed to travel at 160 while Kerry Katona would be limited to 2mph. I thank the Green Party for its research on this matter and hope the solution I've come up with is implemented as soon as humanly possible. Because we've tried everything else and nothing has worked.

And that in no way brings me on to the car you see pictured this morning. It is a supercharged Jaguar XKR convertible that has been fettled by a company called Racing Green.

The whole thing stems from a review I wrote some months back suggesting that the standard XKR needed a growlier exhaust and a bit more bile in its sac. Well, the Racing Green version has water methanol injection, which costs £905 and means that water and alcohol are added to the fuel and air going into the cylinders. Water keeps the temperature down. Methanol increases the octane rating of the fuel. Yum, yum.

In addition, my test car had lowered suspension, which costs £830, enormous 20 inch wheels (£3,830), a new exhaust system (£1,735) and revised engine mapping (£3,175). Some of these things work quite well. Some don't. The exhaust is tremendous under load but at a cruise it can be a bit irritating because it never stops making the sort of low-frequency drone that can kill dogs. And the massive wheels serve mainly to make the standard brakes look like milk-bottle tops. And you like a purveyor of cocaine.

That said, I did enjoy the extra power. It's nice to know the car is going more quickly because it's drinking and driving. And the lowered suspension doesn't seem to have spoilt the ride at all. It hasn't improved the handling noticeably either, but there's no doubt a lower car looks better than one that's on stilts.

Unfortunately, the effect of this is somewhat overshadowed by a horrible Arden body kit. Adding this kit, which costs £10,850, is a bit like nailing a plank of wood to Keira Knightley's face. They couldn't have done a worse job if they'd fitted the car with a selection of garden gnomes.

Happily, all the modifications are options, so you can pick and choose which ones you want. And, better still, Racing Green will make the alterations to a used XKR, which can be part-exchanged these days for a tin of boiled sweets and a handful of loose change. In short, then, you can have a car like this, without the body kit, for £55,000. That's pretty good.

If you had the body kit, it would be around £65,000, but because you would have demonstrated a serious lack of intelligence, I'm afraid, under the new Jeremy Clarkson/Green Party rules, you'd be limited by law to a top speed of 7mph.

9 November 2008

Just take your big antlers and rut off

Audi RS6 Avant

Sometimes, I think life would be a lot less complicated if we were deer. Because then, all we'd need do to establish ourselves, as the superior being in a group, is to stand tall and wave our antlers around.

Unfortunately, men cannot do this, partly because we don't have horns and partly because the human equivalent is the penis. And if you start waving that around over a game of darts in the pub, no good will come of it.

All men will claim they don't jostle for the high ground in a group of other men, but this is nonsense. We all do. Some by using wit, some with the enormity of their wad and some by demonstrating their cleverness. And then you have those who think it's all down to the size of the engine in their car.

I met one such chap last week. To begin with, I thought he was genuinely interested in my new car, but it quickly became obvious that he saw it as a threat to his dominant position in the assembled herd. 'How many horsepower does it produce?' he asked, sweatily. I genuinely didn't know. When you're 6 feet 5 inches, you tend not to worry about that sort of thing.

But he wasn't 6 feet 5 inches so off he scuttled, only to return the next day with information from the Mercedes website, backed, he said, by a call to the local Mercedes dealership. 'Your car,' he told me loudly, so everyone could hear, 'develops 507 horsepower. Whereas my AMG E-class' – there was a pause – 'trumps that with 518.' The unspoken ending was clear. He was eleven better than me.

I'd like to say at this point that I'd met a weirdo, a desperately sad and lonely man, the sort of chap who buys an enormous underwater laptop despite the inconvenience, simply so he can appear to have the biggest penis in the airport departure lounge. But I fear he may not be alone. I fear there are many others just like him all over the world.

Because, why else have the world's car makers spent the past fifteen years churning out cars that develop more and more horsepower? Someone must be buying all these M5s and AMG Mercs. Even though the power their engines make is only any good when worn on the head like an antler.

I mean it. In a Bugatti Veyron, a car built to smash records and boggle minds, lots of horsepower and torque are absolutely necessary. And it's much the same story with a Ferrari and a Lamborghini too. These are speed machines.

But in a saloon car that is limited to 155mph, the only reason why you might be interested in the power output is because you are penistically challenged.

Most mainstream cars with big engines are limited to 155mph because if they went faster than that, they would need brakes like the rings of Saturn, and so many cooling ducts they'd look like the Pompidou Centre. And this would make them preposterously expensive to make. And, therefore, even more preposterously expensive to buy.

So why buy a car with seven million horsepower when only 200 of those horsepowers are actually needed to get it to the electronically governed top speed? It makes no sense . . . unless you are a small man, with no antlers and a tiny willy. Then it makes all the sense in the world, because now you can go down to the Harvester, and quantify your life.

'I am 518, which means I am eleven better than him and a whopping seven better than him. But I'm not at the top of the tree because he, that man over there who runs the Rotary Club and has an orange wife, he is six better than me. Drat.'

You think I'm being silly. Well, consider this. Why have sales of the supercharged Jaguar XJ languished so badly for such a long time? Because if you buy one, you are 107 worse than someone with a BMW M5. That's like turning up at the urinals with an acorn and finding the man next to you is winching out a fireman's hose.

Worse, you are a massive and humiliating 172 worse than someone with the subject of this morning's missive, the £77,730 Audi RS6 Avant.

It's easy to see what caused this car. Audi looked at the heavyweight horsepower fight between BMW and Mercedes and thought, 'We can stop this once and for all because we aren't going to pussyfoot around with the odd extra pony or foal here. We're going for a whole flock of rampaging mustangs.' The result is an ordinary five-door estate car that produces 572bhp. That's 122 more than Jackie Stewart had at his disposal when he won the Formula One world championship in 1973.

The effect is profound. While this car may be no faster, ultimately, than a hot Golf, it accelerates from 120mph like most cars accelerate from rest. There's a momentary pause as the gearbox does something electronic and then you are pinned to your seat as though you've fallen into a wormhole. This sort of power, I have to admit, is intoxicating.

And the Audi is similarly impressive around a racetrack. There's none of the boisterous bellowing enthusiasm you get from an AMG Mercedes as it slithers about in a cloud of its own tyre smoke. And it doesn't feel as technical or as precise as a BMW M5 either. But ooh, it's clever.

You turn into a corner, at speed, and lift off the power, imagining that you'll be rewarded with the usual Pillsbury Dough trough of traditional Audi understeer. But, no. The back slides round until you apply a dab of throttle and feel the four-wheel-drive system gathering up the mess you've made.

To make a car as big and as heavy as this – it weighs more than two tonnes – fast is not hard. To make it handle so incredibly well on a track is nothing short of astonishing.

Unfortunately, I suspect that very few people who buy this car will ever actually take it round a track. Or feel that Herculean shove in the ribcage by getting up to 120 on the motorway and burying the throttle in the carpet. Which is a pity because at all other times, and in all other circumstances, the RS6 is fairly terrible.

Now I should say from the outset that the wheels on my test car were not balanced properly and reviewing a car with a permanent judder is like asking someone to review a play while being tickled. But I pressed on through the vibrations, and these are my findings.

First, we must talk about the ride. Set the suspension in 'comfort' and it's just about acceptable. But do not, under any circumstances, go for the 'sport' setting because then you will be bounced around so much you will not be able to grab hold of the button to put it back again. The man who thought this option to be a good idea should really leave his body to medical science because, plainly, his skeleton is made from steel.

Then there's the seat. And God Almighty, this is worse. Every time you go round a corner, the side support digs with increasing ferocity into your kidneys until you are weeping with pain. The only place where this sort of seat might work is on the I50 in America. Here, in Curly-Wurly Britain, it's a nightmare.

Not that you want to go round corners all that much because the steering system is so bad. At parking speeds, it is super-light but as you get to a trot it suddenly becomes extremely heavy. This always comes as an unpleasant surprise, and if you are not holding onto the wheel firmly, it'll slip through your fingers and you will bump into the car you were trying to avoid.

Things don't get much better when you're out of town and just trying to get home. You can sense all that power under the bonnet. You can't use it, of course, but you can feel it as a weight, something you are having to manhandle. It's wearing. It's annoying. And it exists only because men don't have antlers.

16 November 2008

Look, a cow running in the Grand National

Infiniti FX50S

I once drove an oil tanker. She was called the Jahre Viking and at 1,504 feet was not only the longest ship in the world but also the biggest man-made movable object. She was so vast, in fact, and drew so much water, that she was unable to get through either the Panama or the Suez canal. Even the English Channel was too shallow.

To drive, she was not sprightly. To pull up and stop in Texas, for instance, the captain had to start braking off the coast of Namibia. At one point, I grabbed the throttle and slammed it forward, but there was absolutely no difference in the pace of our lonesome plod round the Cape of Good Hope. In fact, it took a full half an hour for the speed to creep up from 12.4 knots to 12.5.

Certainly, the Somali pirates could catch this enormous ship, but making it stop? That would be rather more difficult.

In many ways, then, driving the Jahre Viking is a bit like driving the car industry.

In all other walks of life, disaster can be averted at the last minute. 'I smell gas, so I won't light this cigarette.' 'That Taliban insurgent is shooting at me so I shall shoot back.' 'This girl has obviously been torturing her baby so I'll put it in care.' And so on.

However, when you are running a car company, you are not afforded this luxury. 'Oh, God. A recession has arrived so I must immediately stop making large off-roaders and make an urban runabout instead.' This is not something the managing director of Land Rover can do.

The Queen didn't see the financial crisis coming. The government didn't see the financial crisis coming. The banks didn't see the financial crisis coming – and they caused it. So what possible chance was there for a Rotarian in Birmingham? And what can he do now it's arrived? He's in the driver's seat of the Jahre Viking, he's doing 12.5 knots, a cliff has appeared off the bow and there is absolutely nothing he can do to prevent a massive crash.

It takes, if you rush, a minimum of four years to design a new car, to build the tools and the robots on the production line and to make sure the seats don't squeak if the finished product is driven over rough roads in Arizona or on a frozen lake in northern Norway. It is simply not possible to do all this in a moment. When you run a car firm, you have to anticipate a gas leak in your kitchen before the house has even been built.

Look at Jaguar, a company that has spent the past thirty years jumping over thin air and crashing through the fences. It started work in the Loadsamoney Eighties on a hypercar called the XJ220, which went on sale in 1992, just as the world went into reverse. So then it began work on a small car called the X-type, which came out when everyone was eating cash just to get rid of it. And now it is working on a new 5-litre V8, which will emerge into the marketplace in the middle of next year, when most forecasters are saying the unemployment figures will have enveloped everyone up to and including the Archbishop of Canterbury.

Yes, Jaguar could down tools and start on a 1.1-litre ecodiesel. But that wouldn't be ready until 2012, when who knows

what state the economy might be in. Certainly not a businessman from Stourbridge.

It's a complete nightmare and I was, therefore, not surprised
to see a bunch of car bosses descend on Downing Street the
other day with their caps in their hands.

The bankers have been bailed out. It seems likely the car
industry in America will be bailed out. So surely the British
government, represented in this instance by Lord Mantelpiece, would be sure to listen, especially as the car industry
here still employs 780,000.

I bet it didn't, though. Because while an old-fashioned
socialist would have put the needs of the workers before the
composition of the gas in the upper atmosphere, we are currently being ruled by a bunch of new-age Communists, who
almost certainly sat there saying, 'Yes, I'm sure it's all very
sad, the destruction of the motor industry, but we've prom-
ised the electorate a cut of 80 per cent in carbon emissions
so your death is probably for the best.'

It makes my hair itch with rage. Because how can a Rotarian from the Midlands possibly develop an all-new means of
propulsion to stave off a disaster that most right-thinking
people accept isn't happening while the products he is making now pile up unsold on every disused airfield in the land?
It's like being asked to give someone a new hairstyle while
you are drowning.

And now, as a result, Britain's car industry will soon join
the mines and the steelworks in the chapter headed 'Something We Used to Do Before It Was Ruined by Communists'.

Still, there's always an upside. Other countries have decided
the needs of the many are more important than how much
carbon dioxide there is in the air and as a result their car indus-
tries will expand to fill the gap left by ours. In fact, it's already

happening, because soon something called Infiniti is coming to a dealership near you. Possibly one that used to sell Range Rovers.

When Toyota decided to start making upmarket cars twenty years ago, it realized, rather brilliantly, that the Toyota badge wouldn't cut much mustard and came up with the Lexus brand instead. Well, you may not realize that Nissan did exactly the same thing for the American market, creating the Infiniti.

There was, however, one big difference between the two philosophies. Toyota decided that a Lexus should be built to a standard unparalleled in the world and that the cars should drive and feel better than any Mercedes. Nissan, on the other hand, just wrote Infiniti on the back of a Datsun. In crayon. Hoping the Americans would be fooled. Which they were.

Since then, though, Infiniti has apparently been catching up and it now says it is ready to come to the cradle of motoring. Europe.

There will be a selection of models on offer but I began by testing the car that'll get here first. It's called the FX50S and it's a big five-seater, seven-speed, five-litre V8, all-wheel-drive monster. I use that word advisedly. The front, dominated by a radiator full of massive spiky teeth, really does look as if it should be in a cave. It looks like Jabba the Hutt. And from there on, things get worse.

I don't deny that it's quite fast. But it's only quite fast . . . for an enormous off-roader. Which is the same as being quite well behaved . . . for a psychopath. In the big scheme of things, it is not fast at all.

Oh, they've tried to give it a sporty feel. The chassis is lifted from a Nissan 350Z and the suspension is electronic and adjustable, but it doesn't work. Any more than it would work if you entered the Grand National on a cow. And by trying to make it handle, which it doesn't, they've ruined the ride. It is deeply uncomfortable in sport mode and nasty in the standard setting.

Worse, still, is the fact that while this car might work off road – though with those massive sport tyres, I doubt it – you'd never think of going there because all the mud might mess up your shiny paint.

Then there's the interior, which is sort of all right. I even quite liked the clock. But it's no more accommodating than a Ford Focus, the boot is tiny and the front seat is not the sort of place you enjoy sitting especially. Unless it's raining.

What this car did, most of all, was remind me just how fabulous the Range Rover is. That's a car that is sporty, comfortable and handsome, whether you're on the road, off the road or just sitting in the thing, waiting for your children to finish their music lesson.

I don't doubt the Have Your Say bit that's put at the end of this on the internet will be full of Americans saying they've got an FX50 and it's great. But it isn't.

The only thing that would possibly convince me to buy one is if Land Rover went out of business. And with Captain Mantelpiece in the hot seat, we have to accept that this is a possibility. Worrying, isn't it?

23 November 2008

Watch out, this nipper's tooled up

Ford Fiesta Titanium 1.6

The anti-car lobby can never win its argument until it begins to understand that here in the West the car is not a tool. It is not a white good. It is not an alternative to the bus or the train. We do not buy cars like we buy dishwashers and toasters. It's not a decision made on cost or practicality and it certainly has nothing to do with the environment. Otherwise, everyone would have a Hyundai Accent with a three-cylinder diesel engine. Or a bus pass.

The reason we don't is that cars, here, are status symbols, they are penis substitutes, they are cherished members of the family, they are heart-starters, they are art, they are sex, they are glamorous, they are cool, they are something you probably don't need. But, my God, you want one so badly that it hurts. Giving up your car is like giving up an emotion. It's like giving up love, or happiness. And that's why people will sell their children before they'll sell their wheels.

However, in what we must now call the developing world, it doesn't work like that. Cars are not substitutes for empty underpants. They are not glamorous. They are white, made in Korea and really nothing more than vinyl oxen with wheels. Offer anyone in India a transport solution that's cheaper and more convenient and they'll bite your hand off. All the way up to your shoulder.

Working out why this is so does not take much time. It's

because here the car was exciting from the get-go. It was about motor racing and Donald Campbell. It was about glamour and sophistication. Every time you stepped into your Austin Seven you were only a tuned carburettor away from hurtling through Casino Square in Monte Carlo. We've always felt – and still do – that the car is a little bit decadent, a little bit Princess Grace. That every single one of them has the soul of Wolfgang von Trips in its carpets.

This is why, for us, looks are important and speed is more important still. A car stands or falls on the time it takes to get from rest to 60mph. Boys are born in Britain knowing instinctively that a car that does this in four seconds is cool and that one that does it in eighteen is rubbish.

Whereas, in places with earthquakes and mud and flies, zero to 60 is irrelevant. And good looks mean that some of the interior space must have been compromised. A Hyundai van with twelve seats and a diesel engine. That's what gets them going in Nigeria.

This is because cars did not drip down into the African psyche from Princess Grace and von Trips. They came in sideways, as nothing more than tools to prop up the economy. That's why no one in Vietnam wants a Lamborghini. It doesn't have enough seats. It uses too much petrol. The import taxes are too high. The roads are too rough.

I watched this in action on my recent trips over there. In the course of several weeks, I was driven around by a selection of young men who, had they been from Bolton, would have treated their government-owned vans as though they were touring-car racers. This didn't happen, though.

There was one chap – we'll call him Charlie – who was in charge of a Toyota minivan, which is a Saigon supercar, but not once, ever, did he exceed 1500rpm. He would begin in second and switch immediately to fourth, where we would remain, come what may. He even parked in fourth, which meant the engine was turning over at about one rev per hour. For me the pain was excruciating. I would sit gripping my thighs, grinding my teeth, biting my tongue to stop myself turning to him and saying, 'First. For God's sake, man. First.'

On the open road, we plodded along at twenty, each piston moving up and down as though propelled by continental drift, and the whole cabin shaking itself to death. To begin with I asked politely for him to speed up. But after a day I was on my knees in the footwell, begging.

He looked at me as though I might be mad. Why speed up? That would place undue strain on the engine, chew expensive fuel and simply mean he'd get to wherever he was going more quickly. And since he was being paid whether he was there or on the way, he obviously couldn't see the point of hurrying. Certainly, he couldn't see that taking his stupid van to the red line and hanging its tail out in the bends might actually be fun. Spending money on speed is simply not a fun pastime when you earn only £500 a year.

Charlie, then, would certainly not understand the new Ford Fiesta. 'Why does the roof taper like that?' he would ask. 'Surely this makes the boot smaller than it need be.'

This is true. The boot on the new Fiesta could be bigger, but then the outside wouldn't look so good, and that's what got under my skin so much. Being a western boy with a disposable income and a love of fine watches, I was bowled over by the styling of this little car. For that reason alone I'd buy one. And that's just the start.

For a period, beginning with the booted Escort in about 1992, Ford completely lost the plot. Its cars were ugly, unforgivably from a company that had given us lookers such as the

RS 2000, the Mk 3 Escort, the Mk 1 Cortina and even the Zodiac. But worse, they were terrible to drive. It was almost as though the boys from the blue oval had given up.

Then along came a man called Richard Parry-Jones. He is Welsh. But he was in charge of how the original Ford Focus should drive, and it was he who insisted it was given expensive independent rear suspension. The result was amazing. Focuses were just . . . better.

Then, shortly afterwards, they employed someone who isn't Welsh to work on the way Fords look. We saw the fruits of their Biro with the current Mondeo, which is let down only by its familiarity. And we have seen it again with the Fiesta.

I say again. It is a cracker. And, like the original Focus, it is a cracker to drive as well. Demonstrably better than anything else for the same sort of money.

Part of that is down to a fine chassis but some of it is also down to the engine. I tried a 1.6, which has twin independent cam shaft timing. The result is a smoothness you simply don't expect in a car of this type, and 118bhp. That's eight more than you got from the original Golf GTI.

Of course, other engines are available, one of which produces such a small amount of carbon dioxide, it'll kill every plant in your garden. But you won't pay any road tax. I should also say the range begins at just £8,700, although the model you get for this has the luxuries of a cave.

My car, on the other hand, had air-conditioning, cruise control, iPod connectivity, leather seats, blue teeth, parking assistance, a heated front windscreen, a trip computer, traction control and privacy glass. In short, everything you would find on a mid-range Mercedes. And yet it cost only £14,970. It's mind-blowing value.

It's a mind-blowing car. Yes, you can get a roomier Far

East box for less, and you would do just that if you lived in a house made from bamboo. But you don't. And because none of your children has ever been eaten by a crocodile, believe me, this is one of those cars that tick and tickle every one of your western boxes.

It's sensible. It's well priced. It's much more comfortable and quiet than you have any right to hope for in this part of the marketplace, and because it's made by Germans, it's well bolted together too. But most important of all, it's so much more than a tool. So much more than a white good. It's fun. And as a result, I shall do an unusual thing and award it five stars.

30 November 2008

An adequate way to drive to hell

Vauxhall Insignia 2.8 V6 4x4 Elite Nav

I was in Dublin last weekend, and had a very real sense I'd
been invited to the last days of the Roman Empire. As far as
I could work out, everyone had a Rolls-Royce Phantom and
a coat made from something that's now extinct. And then
there were the women. Wow. Not that long ago every girl on
the Emerald Isle had a face the colour of straw and orange
hair. Now it's the other way around.

Everyone appeared to be drunk on naked hedonism. I've
never seen so much jus being drizzled onto so many improb-
able things, none of which was potted herring. It was like
Barcelona but with beer. And as I careered from bar to bar
all I could think was, 'Jesus. Can't they see what's coming?'

Ireland is tiny. Its population is smaller than New Zealand's, so how could the Irish ever have generated the cash
for so many trips to the hairdressers, so many lobsters and so
many Rollers? And how, now, as they become the first country in Europe to go officially into recession, can they not see
the financial meteorite coming? Why are they not all at home,
singing mournful songs?

It's the same story on this side of the Irish Sea, of course.
We're all still plunging hither and thither, guzzling wine and
wondering what preposterously expensive electronic toys
the children will want to smash on Christmas morning this
year. We can't see the meteorite coming either.

I think mainly this is because the government is not telling us the truth. It's painting Gordon Brown as a global economic messiah and fiddling about with VAT, pretending that the coming recession will be bad. But that it can deal with it.

I don't think it can. I have spoken to a couple of pretty senior bankers in the past couple of weeks and their story is rather different. They don't refer to the looming problems as being like 1992 or even 1929. They talk about a total financial meltdown. They talk about the End of Days.

Already we are seeing household names disappearing from the high street and with them will go the suppliers whose names have only ever been visible behind the grime on motorway vans. The job losses will mount. And mount. And mount. And as they climb, the bad debt will put even more pressure on the banks until every single one of them stutters and fails.

The European banks took one hell of a battering when things went wrong in America. Imagine, then, how life will be when the crisis arrives on this side of the Atlantic. Small wonder one City figure of my acquaintance ordered three safes for his London house just last week.

Of course, you may imagine the government will simply step in and nationalize everything, but to do that, it will have to borrow. And when every government is doing the same thing, there simply won't be enough cash in the global pot. You can forget Iceland. From what I gather, Spain has had it. Along with Italy, Ireland and, very possibly, the UK.

It is impossible for someone who scored a U in his economics A-level to grapple with the consequences of all this but I'm told that in simple terms money will cease to function as a meaningful commodity. The binary dots and dashes that fuel the entire system will flicker and die. And without money there will be no business. No means of selling goods.

No means of transporting them. No means of making them in the first place even. That's why another friend of mine has recently sold his London house and bought somewhere in the country . . . with a kitchen garden.

These, as I see them, are the facts. Planet Earth thought it had £10. But it turns out we had only £2. Which means everyone must lose 80 per cent of their wealth. And that's going to be a problem if you were living on the breadline beforehand.

Eventually, of course, the system will reboot itself, but for a while there will be absolute chaos: riots, lynchings, starvation. It'll be a world without power or fuel, and with no fuel there's no way the modern agricultural system can be maintained. Which means there will be no food either. You might like to stop and think about that for a while.

I have, and as a result I can see the day when I will have to shoot some of my neighbours – maybe even David Cameron – as we fight for the last bar of Fry's Turkish Delight in the smoking ruin that was Chipping Norton's post office.

I believe the government knows this is a distinct possibility and that it might happen next year, and there is absolutely nothing it can do to stop Cameron getting both barrels from my Beretta. But instead of telling us straight, it calls the crisis the 'credit crunch' to make it sound like a breakfast cereal and asks Alistair Darling to smile and big up Gordon when he's being interviewed.

I can't say I blame it, really. If an enormous meteorite was heading our way and the authorities knew it couldn't be stopped or diverted, why bother telling anyone? Best to let us soldier on in the dark until it all goes dark for real.

On a more cheery note, Vauxhall has stopped making the Vectra, that dreary, designed-in-a-coffee-break Eurobox that no one wanted. In its place stands the new Insignia, which has been voted European Car of the Year for 2009.

This award is made by motoring journalists across Europe, and, with the best will in the world, the Swedes do not want the same thing from a car as the Greeks. That's why they almost always get it wrong. Past winners have been the Talbot Horizon and the Renault 9.

They've got the Insignia even more wrong than usual because the absolutely last thing anyone wants right now, and I'm including in the list consumption, a severed artery and a massive shark bite, is a four-door saloon car with a bargain-basement badge.

Oh, it's not a bad car. It's extremely good-looking, it appears to be very well made, it is spacious and the prices are reasonable. But set against that are seats that are far too hard, the visibility – you can't see the corners of the car from the driver's chair – and the solid, inescapable fact that the Ford Mondeo is a more joyful thing to drive.

In the past, none of this would have mattered. Fleet managers would have bought 100 of whichever was the cheapest, and Jenkins from Pots, Pans and Pyrex would have had no say in the matter. Those days, however, are gone. The travelling salesman is now an internet address, and the mini MPV has bopped the traditional saloon on the head. I cannot think of the question in today's climate to which the answer is 'A Vauxhall Insignia'. And I'm surprised my colleagues on the car of the year jury didn't notice this as well.

Then I keep remembering the Renault 9 and I'm not surprised at all.

I feel, I really do, for the bosses at GM who've laboured so hard to make this car. It's way better than the Vectra. It looks as though they were bothered. But asking their dealerships to sell such a thing in today's world is a bit like asking men in the First-World-War trenches to charge the enemy's machine-gun nests with spears.

Right now, there are two paths you can go down. You can either adopt the Irish attitude to the impending catastrophe and party like it's 1999. In which case, you are better off ignoring the Vauxhall and buying a 24-foot Donzi speedboat instead.

Or you can actually start to make some sensible preparations for the complete breakdown in society. In which case you don't want a Vauxhall either. Better to spend the money on a pair of shotguns and an allotment.

7 December 2008

Safety first, then rough and tumble

Volvo XC60 T6 SE Lux

In the past, cars were extremely safe, provided you didn't crash into anything. Sadly, however, my father used to crash into absolutely everything, which meant he'd go to work of a morning and come home in a plaster cast. Over the years he had so many bones removed that he actually became a human blancmange and we all accepted this as normal.

For millions of years, the top speed a human could achieve was 40mph and even then only if he had a very good horse. And then, all of a sudden, we found ourselves travelling at sixty. And we all decided the advantages of this – you could go to see your mother-in-law but you didn't have to stay the night – far outweighed the consequences of hitting something while travelling at a mile a minute.

The idea that a car could be safe was laughable. Of course it wasn't safe. It was useful and glamorous and many other things besides, but we were none of us in any doubt: if you were to crash it into a tree, or a bush, or even a bag of fish and chips, your head would come off.

What's more, your right kneecap would be slammed into the ignition key, which would smash it, the engine would be dislodged from its mountings and come careering into the passenger compartment, severing your stomach, the wooden steering column would splinter and send shards of timber into your spleen and the fire crews would be unable to cut your screaming, dislocated body from the wreckage because the car would be so badly mangled. And probably on fire as well.

Then along came Volvo with a simple message. You could have a crash in one of its cars and chances are you'd be all right. My dad was amazed by this and immediately bought an enormous 265, which was fitted with a bumper like the bottom lip of Forrest Gump's mate Bubba.

He loved that car because it meant he could crash into houses, brewery wagons, lamp posts, dogs and anything else that took his fancy, safe in the knowledge that the only bone left in his body – the small one in his right ear – would emerge from the accident undamaged.

Volvo was the first to fit three-point seatbelts, head restraints, childproof locks, seatbelt reminder buzzers, daytime-running lights and anti-submarining seats. Volvo also employed a team of researchers to visit the site of every car accident within a hundred miles of the factory so it could collate information on what had hurt the occupants and what might be done to stop it happening again.

For many years, the Swedes had this corner of the market all to themselves. If you wanted a 'reliable' car you bought a Volkswagen. If you wanted a 'good-quality' car, you bought a Mercedes. If you wanted a 'sporty' car, you bought a BMW. And if you wanted a 'safe' car you bought a Volvo.

But then, every other car maker cottoned on to the idea of safety, so that now even a small Renault has a five-star rating from the Euro NCAP safety testing people. And as a result, to stay ahead of the game, Volvo is now using electronics. And that's why the windscreen on the new XC60 looks like the guidance system on a Hellfire missile.

In other cars, electronics are used to provide better sound

quality, more accurate satellite navigation systems and chilled glove boxes. On the XC60 the computers are used to ensure you cannot crash.

The system is called City Safety, it's fitted as standard to all XC60s and it works like this. A radar 'sees' the road ahead and if it senses that you are about to have a rear-end shunt it will apply the brakes for you.

Of course, I had to try this out and that means I must apologize profusely to the driver of the BMW 3-series whose car I thwacked while he was waiting at a roundabout on the Oxford ring road.

I don't know what went wrong. But plainly, you really should read the handbook before saying to your friends in the car, 'Watch this. I'm not going to brake but we won't hit the car in front.' Because, as I proved, you will.

I know the system is supposed to work only in city traffic at speeds less than 20mph, but so far as I can tell, it doesn't seem to work at all. Mind you, I am a man who claims everything I ever buy doesn't work. The Association of British Insurers thinks differently, as it is apparently considering a 25 per cent discount because the system is so effective.

And City Safety is just the start. The XC60 I drove also had lights in the door mirrors that flash orange when another car is in your blind spot, as well as a system that alerts a driver if they stray out of their lane on a motorway.

Citroën, which pioneered this idea, warns the driver by vibrating the seats, but Volvo has obviously realized that women may deliberately drive on the hard shoulder to create this effect, and alerts you with an irritating bong. As a result, I drove with it turned off.

It sounds as though I have a downer on the systems in this car, and to an extent that's true. I understand mechanical safety, crumple zones, energy-absorbing beams and laminated windscreens. But I don't trust electronics. Think how many times your laptop crashes and you'll understand what I mean.

That said, Volvo must be congratulated for continuing to advance the cause of safety and it must be congratulated, too, for the XC60 as a whole because this is the first soft-roader I've driven that doesn't feel like one.

Now, if you don't like five-seat soft-roaders – and I don't either – then you may think that what Volvo has actually done is solve a problem that needn't have existed in the first place. I mean, why do you need a tall four-wheel-drive car just for doing the school run? It's madness. But at least with the XC60 the ride is car-like, the handling is car-like and if you go for the T6 petrol version the performance is car-like as well. Of course, you could simply buy a car . . .

If, however, you really do want a tall four-wheel-driver, then this is better than the Nissan X-Trail and better even than the Ford Kuga. The interior is Bang & Olufsen cool, the knobs can be operated while you are wearing gloves and everything is intuitive, except of course for the Volvo sat nav system, which only ever takes you to somewhere you went three years ago.

The best thing about this car is how it makes you feel. And how it makes you feel is middle class. Really middle class. Stepping inside this car is like stepping into Johnny Boden's boxer shorts while cheering on your daughter at a gymkhana. This is a car for extremely pretty women, who will use it in the morning for going to the gym, in the evening for doing the school run and in the afternoon for having an affair. I can hear them now. 'Would you like to come for a ride in my Vulva?'

That's probably what the anti-crash system is for. So that

Arabella doesn't have to explain to her husband why the nose on her car is all smashed in and what on earth she was doing on the wrong side of town with her tennis coach at three in the afternoon.

On that basis, not only is this car jolly good, but it might save a few marriages as well.

14 December 2008

Fritz forgot the little things

BMW 330d M Sport

You know the score. Your computer wakes up one morning and thinks it's a cauliflower so you spend two hours on the phone to a man in Mumbai who has a set list of possible remedies, none of which makes the slightest bit of difference. You beg and beg for a technician to come round but the internet provider doesn't have any technicians; only a room full of parrot men in India, who think a wireless connection can be fixed by endlessly typing numbers into a laptop, even though the reason your 'black box' isn't working is because it's in the dog.

That night, the fury in your heart is so vibrant that it has become an all-consuming entity. A big jaggedy spike in your head. Sleep is impossible.

All you can think about is what you would do to the boss of the internet service provider were you to encounter him in the street one day. Last night, in my mind, I spent two hours poking him in the chest, asking how in the name of all that's holy he ever thought a broken box in Notting Hill could possibly be fixed by an uninterested parrot man in India. And then I think I might have set him alight and thrown him on the fire I started by burning the boss who thought flimsy ring pulls on tins of soup are a good idea.

Of course, we have this rage and frustration in so many other areas of our everyday lives as well. Bought a new toothbrush recently? Tried to get it out of the packaging? I have and there is nothing I would like more than for the chief executive of Mouths R Us to come round to my house and show me how it is possible without cutting all his fingers off.

Likewise, I should very much enjoy for George Clooney to drop by one day and explain why each spoonful of the Nespresso coffee he advertises so suavely needs to be wrapped in an individual container. I am no environmentalist, but he is, and I would love to hear his views on why such an enormous amount of packaging is a good idea when a patio heater is not.

Then, you have those extremely expensive corkscrews that you buy at Christmas time because it's 5.25pm and the shops are about to shut and you haven't got anything for your dad. The managing director of the company must know that after three days the action will become so stiff your wrist will snap before the Rioja gives up its cork. He must. But he does nothing about it. So I'd like to see him on fire as well.

I want to see all of them on fire until they learn to say to their design and development teams, 'No. This is not right. You are all blithering idiots, so go away and do it again.'

And hello, banks. Why do you not fit your hole-in-the-wall cash machines with red flashing lights so that we discover they are out of service when we drive by? Not after we have gone to the trouble of parking our cars half a mile away.

Then we get to the airport, where I have another question. Why subject someone to a humiliating strip search when they are a blue-eyed nine-year-old girl, or Paul McCartney. It's a waste of time for you and a waste of time for everyone in the queue that results. If you know someone to be Paul McCartney, then you know he is an elderly singer and not a crazed suicide bomber. So he can be waved through immediately, leaving you time to concentrate on the sweating Afghan with wires poking out of his backpack.

Governments, of course, are fantastically uninterested in the people they are supposed to serve. Which is why you have Gordon Brown committing us all to a target of cutting CO_2 emissions by 80 per cent, which will cost about 2 per cent of the nation's GDP. And not work. While at the same time deciding that the navy's new aircraft carriers will be powered by carbon-rich diesel, and not nuclear reactors, to save £3.50.

I don't mind mistakes; the chap who accidentally forgets to close the doors on the ferry, for instance. These are errors. These are evidence of human fallibility. What I cannot abide is the wilful lack of interest in customers that ruins everything we buy and everything we do these days.

Except smoking. Over the years, I have worked my way through perhaps a million cigarettes and not one of them has ever come out of the packet shaped like a penis, or covered in mud. Not one has ever refused to light, or exploded while I am driving along. You sometimes get a beetle in your chocolate bar or an earwig in your curry. But cigarettes? Every single one is just as you would expect. A perfectly tailored nicotine delivery service.

It would, of course, be unreasonable to expect such consistency from cars. They are made up of 15,000 parts and some of them are made by people who are French. So, naturally, there will be mistakes from time to time.

But these days, for the most part, cars are staggeringly reliable. Tyres are able to run over broken bottles without detonating. Onboard computers get shaken, boiled and rattled around and still continue to function. Honda, for example, has made fifteen million VTEC units over the years and has never had a single warranty claim on any of them. That's a Marlboro-like consistency.

But despite the car makers' ability to build products to a fantastically high standard, I'm always amazed by some of the design faults that make it through the testing and development phase. The seatbelts in my Mercedes, for instance, are almost impossible to fasten. Did the boss not notice this, in which case he is an idiot? Or did he think, like an internet service provider, that not quite good enough will do?

Even if we take the Range Rover V8 diesel, which can do more things to a higher standard than just about any other car on the road, we find a wiper system that collects dirt from the car in front and smears it all over the windscreen so you can't see where you're going.

And now we arrive at the BMW 330d. In many ways, this is a perfect car. Anonymously styled for maximum anti-cock inoffensiveness, it's the right size and it's fitted with a diesel engine of unparalleled smoothness. You can find more power elsewhere, and more economy. But for a combination, with almost none of the tingling you normally get from a coal burner, this big six is the tip of the arrowhead.

And now that our friends with the Oakley sunglasses and the big Breitlings are all in Audis, BMWs are generally driven by enthusiastic drivers who like the balance of a rear-wheel-drive set-up, and the steering feel; people who understand that the stopping distance at 80mph is not 4 inches and drop back from your rear end accordingly.

The best bit of the 330d, though, is not the engine or the way it drives; it's the suspension, which manages to be firm and comfortable at the same time. No other car maker can do this.

And yet, here in this wonderful package we find a sat nav screen made up of blues and greys. It's all very tasteful but you can't read it. Ever. And then there's the headlamp dip switch, which works like the lever in a railway signal box.

But worst of all is the torque. Put your foot down to pull smartly out of a side turning and all you get is an ear-splitting screech as the tyres leave big black lines down the road. On gravel, you just dig a big hole, no matter how delicate you are with the throttle, and go nowhere.

It's the little things, then, that spoil the BMW. It's the little things that spoil everything. Like my iPhone, which was brilliant except that it didn't work in the rain. Or the Sony Ericsson I replaced it with, which doesn't work at all. Nothing does really. It's annoying.

21 December 2008

Out of nowhere, my car of the year

Chevrolet Corvette ZR1

It's been a quiet year for the world's motor industry. There have been no wrecks, nobody drowning; in fact, nothing to laugh at at all. But, hidden in the sea of normality and business as usual, were a couple of gems.

We start with the BMW X6, which must receive my inaugural What Were They Thinking Of award. Have you seen one? No, and I doubt you ever will because in a world that's plagued with recession and run by people who believe the world's polar bears are up at the North Pole sipping pina coladas and slapping on the factor five, it is surely the most inappropriate piece of corporate thinking since Sir Clive Sinclair said, 'Yes. The electric slipper. That's what people want . . .'

However, I cannot say the BMW X6 is the worst car of the year, partly because I have not yet driven it and partly because it cannot possibly be worse than the Chrysler Sebring Convertible. Unless it smells of slurry and the radio is jammed on Rap FM.

The Sebring is an extraordinary car. Ugly to behold and hateful to drive, it is not cheap, elegant, comfortable, practical, prestigious, clever, economical, luxurious, well designed, well thought out or, if the rental car I drove in America this year is anything to go by, especially well made either. Perhaps this is why the boss of Chrysler chose to go to Washington in his private jet. He knew that if he used a Sebring, it would break down on the way. Or worse, it would get there and he'd be a laughing stock among his business-mates from Ford and General Motors.

Strangely, however, the Chrysler is not the worst car I drove all year. That accolade rests with the diesel-powered Kia Sedona people carrier.

With the Sebring, you get the impression that the designers and engineers couldn't be bothered to make a good car. With the Sedona you are left with the distinct impression they simply didn't know how.

I cannot conceive of how empty, pointless and lacking in ambition or style your life must be for the Sedona to be a solution. It is like alcohol-free beer, a pointless car-free facsimile of the real thing and, as a result, it can have no place in the life of a sentient being.

The biggest disappointment of the year is a closely fought contest between any number of cars, but the winner is Audi's RS6. It promises much and on a racetrack it delivers a great deal. But to buy a five-seat estate car simply because it's so fluent through Becketts is like going out to buy a pet goldfish and coming home with a horse 'because it's so good over the Chair'.

The drawbacks you will encounter in real life are too endless. The uncomfortable seating, the weird steering and a very real sense that in a car like this, 572bhp is a lot more than you will ever need. It's said you can't be too beautiful or too rich but you can have too much power. Because one minute you'll be overtaking a lorry and the next you'll go mad and want to invade Poland.

Other disappointments are mostly centred on cars which aren't really as good as others that do broadly the same thing. The Ford Kuga, for instance, is not as good as the Volvo

XC60 and the Renault Twingo Renaultsport is not as good as a Fiat 500 Abarth. And then there's the Vauxhall Insignia, which is massively better than the Vectra it replaces. But not quite as good as the Ford Mondeo. And who says, 'Right. What I want to buy is the second-best four-door saloon with no badge prestige'? Actually, come to think of it; who wants to buy the best?

My main gripe of the year, though, rests with seat designers who have got it into their heads that we only like leather – there's really nothing wrong with pleblon, especially on a day that's hot or cold, and doubly especially if there are any corners between your house and your place of work.

Worse, though, they seem to think that what we really want are seats in our cars that are less comfortable than those in our kitchens. I know that cod liver oil is good for you. I also know you will go to heaven if you only eat weeds and you spend your evenings embroidering kneelers for the local church. But we are not all vegi-vicars. That is why we don't wear hair shirts and it's why we want the seats in our cars to have a bit of give. Are you listening, Vauxhall? Are you listening, Ford? Go and find yourself an old Renault Fuego Turbo. Check out the bean bags it came with and you'll know what I'm on about.

And now we shall move on to the good stuff from the past twelve months. On television, recently, I said the best car from the year was the Caterham R500, but it's important to remember that the criterion we were looking for was very specific. The winner had to do more than you could reasonably expect for the money.

The Nissan GT-R was a contender because it costs almost half as much as a Porsche 911 Turbo and yet around the Nürburgring – and such things do matter with cars like this – it is faster. Then you have the VW Scirocco, which costs, as near as makes no difference, the same as the Golf GTI on which it is based. And yet it's so much more desirable. But the winner had to be the little Caterham, which is faster round the *Top Gear* track than the Bugatti Veyron ... even though it costs about thirty times less.

However, if you broaden the search engine and look simply for the best car of the year, the Caterham isn't in with a shout because it's ugly and geeky and I wouldn't have one even if the option was the loss of my right testicle.

Best car, then? Hmmm. You cannot discount the Rolls-Royce Phantom drophead, because it is exquisite in almost every way. Nor can we ignore the Fiat 500 Abarth, because it's just so bouncy and wonderful and so full of enthusiasm. I don't think it would be possible to be in a bad mood while driving this car. And soon there will be a 200bhp version with a spoiler the size of Middlesex on the roof. That'll make the Mini Cooper look like a brogue.

However, the car I've selected wins because it's just such a surprise.

Over the years there have been a great many Corvettes, and none of them, if we're honest, have been any good. Oh, there have been some fast ones and some with great charisma. Mostly, they have been pretty as well. But to drive? No. They were the automotive equivalent of Big Macs. Cheap, plastic and at the right time, and in the right place, sort of just what you want. But like I said. Just no.

And then out of nowhere came the ZR1, which has a supercharged V8 that manages to be both docile and extraordinarily savage, all at the same time. I've been trying to think of a dog that pulls off a similar trick, but there isn't one. And anyway, this car is not a dog.

Oh, it's not built very well. After just three days in my care, the boot lock disintegrated and the keyless go system refused to acknowledge the keys were in the car, but I didn't mind because there is simply no other car that looks this good, goes this fast – in a straight line and around corners – and that most of the time bumbles about like a forgetful uncle. And when you throw in the price tag of just £106,690 – lots for a Corvette but modest next to a similarly powerful Ferrari – the case for the defence can sit down and put up its feet, knowing that the prosecutor simply has nowhere to go.

It is an epic car and I'm only sad that unless the healthcare and pensions company that makes it can be turned around, it will be the last of the breed.

Indeed, I worry that the next twelve months will bring us many wrecks, many drownings and absolutely nothing to laugh at at all. I shall therefore stop short of wishing you a prosperous new year. Instead, I shall hope that in our new-found poverty, we can still all be happy.

28 December 2008

What bright spark thought of this?

Tesla Roadster

Mostly, the world's car makers realize that I'm a harmless piece
of navel fluff whose opinions make absolutely no difference to
their hopes and dreams. But occasionally, threatening noises
are made if they think I've been unfair.

Once, many years ago, Renault in France told the people
who run its operation in Britain to pull all its advertising
from the BBC. 'Zis will show zem,' said a red-in-the-face
Jean-Claude, unaware presumably that the BBC carried no
advertising.

And then there was Toyota, which, after I compared its
1990s Corolla, unfavourably, with a fridge-freezer, refused to
lend me any more demonstrators until I accepted it was, in
fact, the best car in the world and as important as the second
coming.

Vauxhall was similarly argumentative about its then new
Vectra, and SSangYong in effect banned me from driving its
cars in the first place. When I asked its PR man if I could
borrow a Rexton recently, he said, 'No. We have other pri-
orities.'

If he'd been on fire at the time he took the call, I could
understand this. Because, yes, finding a pool into which he
could jump to put himself out would be a higher priority
than talking to me. But other than this, I cannot think what
might be a higher priority for a car-company PR man than

fixing up a date when a motoring journalist could try out a new product.

Oh, and I can never forget a letter sent by the public relations man at BMW to the *Sunday Times* saying that my dislike of BMWs had nothing to do with their drivers' pushy attitude, their silly sunglasses, their awful short-sleeved shirts, their hair gel, their orange wives, their awful houses, their fondness for golf and their membership of the Freemasons, and everything to do with the fact I had a garage full of free Jaguars.

Mostly, though, all is calm. I don't talk to the car makers. They don't talk to me. I simply borrow their cars. I write about them. They go back whence they came and, whether I've been kind, indifferent or wrong, the world continues to turn.

All of which brings me on to the curious case of the battery-powered Tesla sports car that I reviewed recently on *Top Gear*. Things didn't go well. The company claimed it could run, even if driven briskly, for 200 miles, but after just a morning the battery power was down to 20 per cent and we realized that it would not have enough juice for all the shots we needed.

Happily, the company had brought a second car along, so we switched to that. But after a while its motor began to overheat. And so, even though the first was not fully charged, we unplugged it – only to find that its brakes weren't working properly. So then we had no cars.

Inevitably, the film we had shot was a bit of a mess. There was a handful of shots of a silver car. Some of a grey car. And only half the usual gaggle of nonsense from me shouting 'Power' and making silly metaphors. And to make matters worse, we had the BBC's new compliance directive hanging over us like an enormous suffocating blanket. We had to be sure that what we said and what we showed was more than right, more than fair and more than accurate.

Phone calls were made. Editorial policy wallahs were consulted. Experts were called in. No 'i' was left undotted. No 't' was left uncrossed. No stone remained unturned in our quest for truth and decency.

Tesla could not complain about what was shown because it was there. And here's the strange thing. It didn't. But someone did. Loudly and to every newspaper in the world. The *Daily Telegraph* said we'd been caught up in a new fakery row. The *Guardian* accused us of being 'underhanded'. The *New York Times* wondered if we'd been 'misleading'. The *Daily Mail* said I could give you breast cancer.

This was weird. Tesla, when contacted by reporters, gave its account of what happened and it was exactly the same as ours. It explained that the brakes had stopped working because of a blown fuse and didn't question at all our claim that the car would have run out of electricity after fifty-five miles.

So who was driving this onslaught? Nobody in the big wide world ever minds when I say a BMW 1-series is crap or that a Kia Rio is the worst piece of machinery since the landmine. And yet everyone went mad when I said the Tesla, the red-blooded sports car and great white hope for the world's green movement, 'absolutely does not work'.

I fear that what we are seeing here is much the same thing professors see when they claim there is no such thing as manmade global warming. Immediately, they are drowned out by an unseen mob, and then their funding dries up. It's actually quite frightening.

The problem is, though, that really and honestly, the US-made Tesla works only at dinner parties. Tell someone you have one and in minutes you will be having sex. But as a device for moving you and your things around, it is about as much use as a bag of muddy spinach.

Yes, it is extremely fast. It's all out of ideas at 125mph, but the speed it gets there is quite literally electrifying. For instance, 0 to 60 takes 3.9 seconds. This is because a characteristic of the electric motor, apart from the fact it's the size of a grape-fruit and has only one moving part, is massive torque.

And quietness. At speed, there's a deal of tyre roar and plenty of wind noise from the ill-fitting soft top, but at a town-centre crawl it's silent. Eerily so. Especially as you are behind a rev counter showing numbers that have no right to be there – 15,000, for example.

Through the corners things are less rosy. To minimize roll-ing resistance and therefore increase range, the wheels have no toe-in or camber. This affects the handling. So, too, does the sheer weight of the 6,831 laptop batteries, all of which have to be constantly cooled.

But slightly wonky handling is nothing compared with this car's big problems. First of all, it costs £90,000. This means it is three times more than the Lotus Elise, on which it is loosely based, and 90,000 times more than it is actually worth.

Yes, that cost will come down when the Hollywood elite have all bought one and the factory can get into its stride. But paying £90,000 for such a thing now indicates that you believe in goblins and fairy stories about the end of the world.

Of course, it will not be expensive to run. Filling a normal Elise with petrol costs £40. Filling a Tesla with cheap-rate electricity costs just £3.50. And that's enough to take you – let's be fair – somewhere between 55 and 200 miles, depending on how you drive.

But if it's running costs you are worried about, consider this. The £60,000 or so you save by buying an Elise would buy 15,000 gallons of fuel. Enough to take you round the world twenty times.

And there's more. Filling an Elise takes two minutes. Filling a Tesla from a normal 13-amp plug takes about sixteen hours. Fit a beefier three-phase supply to your house and you could complete the process in four (Tesla now says three and a half). But do not, whatever you do, imagine that you could charge your car from a domestic wind turbine. That would take about twenty-five days.

You see what I mean. Even if we ignore the argument that the so-called green power that propels this car comes from a dirty great power station, and that it is therefore not as green as you might hope, we are left with the simple fact that it takes a long time to charge it up and the charge doesn't take you very far. We must also remember that both the cars I tried went wrong.

In the fullness of time, I have no doubt that the Tesla can be honed and chiselled and developed to a point where the problems are gone. But time is one thing a car such as this does not have.

Because while Tesla fiddles about with batteries, Honda and Ford are surging onwards with hydrogen cars, which don't need charging, can be fuelled normally and are completely green. The biggest problem, then, with the Tesla is not that it doesn't work. It's that even if it did, it would be driving down the wrong road.

11 January 2009

This is by far the best of all the school-run-mobiles. There really is room for seven people, fourteen legs and two dogs in the boot as well

Volvo XC90 D5 SE R-Design

As I'm sure you've heard, the green-eyed madmen of Richmond upon Thames in London have elected a bunch of über-loonies to run the borough's services and now, predictably, everything is falling apart.

Instead of organizing war memorials and better rubbish collection, the super-loons have announced that if you fail to send the council an e-mail before you go shopping, they will assume your car produces a great deal of carbon dioxide and, as a result, will charge you 40p an hour more for parking than someone who has sent an e-mail.

Quite what difference 40p will make to someone who has a £30,000 car, I have absolutely no idea. It will really hurt only the poor. But this is the way with the world's mega-loons. They leap from bandwagon to bandwagon, simply not understanding that bandwagons are transient because they're silly and the tune they're playing always goes out of fashion.

Of course, I quite agree that something must be done to unclog the nation's town centres. And I'm not certain the banks have got the right idea either. By running out of money they are now ensuring that every restaurant, pub, building society, estate agent and shop is closing, so that soon there will be no reason for popping into the local conurbation.

This will definitely ease congestion but the side effects are even more profound than the ideas being implemented in Richmond by the giga-loons.

Happily, however, I have been giving the matter some serious thought and I have devised a plan of my own that might just work.

As we know, Monte Carlo is a fairly horrible place full of prostitutes, wedding cake architecture and greasy little men who've learnt their English from baddies in James Bond films and who meet in bars at night to sell one another machine guns. It rains more than you might think, too.

And yet it is perceived to be a glamorous place simply because of the cars that prowl round Casino Square. Big is good. Low is better still. Red is best. And, plainly, if Simon Cowell lived here, they'd put him on income support.

The cars are what makes Monaco look so good and it's the same story in Tokyo. Mostly, this is an all-grey fifty-mile Lego set with concrete telegraph poles and a wiring system that seems to have resulted from a massive primary school game of cat's cradle.

But, once again, we find ourselves amused and impressed, partly because you are encouraged to smoke indoors but mostly because of all the funny little Postman Pat cars that hop about the place, with their cheeky smiles and their lilac paint jobs.

And then there are the taxis with their antimacassars and their electric-opening rear doors. We know, as soon as we climb into such a thing at the airport and are overtaken by a Mazda Bongo in teenage lip-gloss pink, that we have arrived in a funky go-ahead place and that we shall be happy there.

Exactly the opposite applies in San Francisco. Make no mistake, this is my second favourite city in America – after

Detroit – with its hills and its sharp, clear afternoon skies. I adore the hills and the patisseries, but the whole place is let down by the cars. Because the people who live there like to sit around pretending to be French, they all drive crappy Hondas.

You may imagine as you cross California Street that you will be mown down by Steve McQueen in a Mustang or Nicolas Cage in a faux Ferrari 355, but it's more likely you will be killed by some bespectacled librarian in a VW Beetle who's not looking where he's going because he's too busy trying to be Jean-Paul Sartre.

And that brings me, naturally, on to Huddersfield. Without a doubt, this is one of Britain's most impressive towns. The square in the centre stands as four-square testimony to the fact that money does not necessarily equal a here-today, gone-tomorrow excursion into the shag-pile world of bad taste.

It's gorgeous, especially because your eye is drawn down each of the streets that lead off it to those dark satanic hills that lie beyond.

But you're not looking, because all the streets are lined with such a terrible collection of rubbish. It's hard to under-stand why. The council would insist you got planning permission before painting the roof of your house beige, and yet it does nothing to prevent people from buying a Nissan Bluebird and leaving it on the drive, or in the road, where it can be seen by passers-by.

So how's this for an idea? Each council should allow free parking for people who have a nice car, while those with unpleasant eyesores such as the Bluebird should be made to pay around £1m a minute.

It is much simpler to implement than the gas-based system being used by Richmond because just one person is needed to decide what's okay and what's not. You don't need a computer and an army of traffic wardens with degrees in upper-atmosphere dynamics.

Don't, for a minute, imagine that I'm looking for Ferraris here. Far from it. Anyone who has a Mondial, for example, or a 308 GTB, would be made to pay a great deal because these are terrible cars and nobody wants to see one on their street.

There would be similar penalties for people in disgusting Hummers but anyone with an interesting older car, such as a Rover 90 or a Hillman Hunter GT, would be allowed to park wherever they pleased.

Not only would the system improve the look of a town centre but it would ease congestion, too, because people with Kias and Hyundais would simply be priced out of the market. And here's the brilliant bit. They won't mind.

Because anyone with a Kia is plainly not interested in cars it's no hardship being made to go shopping on the bus. That's the fatal flaw with the system in Richmond. It penalizes cars with big engines, which tend to be driven by enthusiastic drivers who would mind very much being made to go on public transport.

It also penalizes people who drive large school-run 4x4s and that really is idiotic. I've just bought my third Volvo XC90 in a row and the simple fact is this: it takes six children to school in the morning.

If I were forced to swap it for something smaller, we would need to do the run in two cars. And I'm sorry but two Minis produce 256 grams of CO_2 per kilometre. A single Volvo diesel produces just 219. This means the XC90 is actually good for the environment and we should all have one immediately.

Just don't do what I've just done and buy the 'sport' version. Because fitting an XC90 with hard suspension and chunky alloy wheels may make it look good but it will ruin the ride. I've been in more comfortable jet fighters.

I don't know what I was thinking of, really, because I know the Volvo is not sporty in any way. The diesel engine, though better than it was in the early days, is still desperately agricultural. The handling is straight from the playpen and the speed is woeful. Sticking four exhausts on a car like this is a bit like sticking four exhausts on Eamonn Holmes and attempting to sell the end result as a sport model.

Other versions, though, are just epic. People think this car has become such a common sight on the road because it is part of the private school uniform. That may be so. But there's another, bigger reason. It is by far the best of all the school-run-mobiles because there really is room for seven people, fourteen legs and two dogs in the boot as well. No other car maker – and this is strange – has managed to pull off a similar trick without ending up with a bus.

And if it's a bus you're after . . . well, why not get out of my way and use one from the council.

18 January 2009

I'm scared of the dark in this doom buggy

Ford Ka Zetec 1.2

Unlike most motoring journalists, I do not attend ritzy, cham-pagne-drenched, Michelin-starred, club-class car launches at exotic hotels in sun-kissed, faraway places. I'm not being holier than thou here. I'd love to eat a swan at Mazda's expense and spend my life licking the goose fat from the hand that feeds me, but I simply don't have the time.

This means I never get the chance to meet the people who design the cars I drive or the people who are charged with selling them. In one important way, this is a good thing. When I review a car, I am unable to visualize the man who sweated into the night to make it possible. So I can be as rude as I like, because I don't have to worry about upsetting him.

However, there is a downside. Because I don't meet the engineers or sit through the two-hour-long technical press conferences, I am less well informed than my colleagues. And less well fed, for that matter.

And so, because I approached the new Ford Ka in a state of blissful ignorance, I was expecting a very great deal. I assumed it would be a funky, small and cheap alternative to the new Ford Fiesta, a car that does everything very well whether you're on the road, at the shopping centre or taking part in a beach assault with the Royal Marines.

Almost immediately, however, I began to dislike the Ka

very much. First of all, the styling's not quite right. The door – and I apologize to the faceless man who made it – doesn't seem to sit very happily with the lines of the profile. And the wheel arches look as though they were going to be flared but someone dropped the original clay model from a fork-lift truck and they got squashed.

Inside, there are problems, too, including ridiculously hard seats that someone – whom I've never met – at Ford thinks are a good idea. Worst of all, though, is the driving position. The steering wheel, which adjusts for height but not reach, is too far away and, even on its highest setting, too low down.

And the clutch pedal is far too close to the centre console. A small foot rest has been provided inside the aforementioned console but the only way you can actually get your foot in there properly is if you saw it off.

Then I began the test drive and things got worse. Because the old Ka looked like a teapot, you didn't expect it to be very fast. And it's the same story with the Toyota iQ. That looks like an urban runaround, but the new Ka does not. It looks like a normal car; a Fiesta that's shrunk slightly in the wash. Which is why I was expecting it to be able to get up a hill. Which in fifth it often could not. Sometimes, I had a problem in fourth.

Even on level ground things are far from rosy because at anything above fifty the whole car really does start to feel loose and disconnected, a problem that was amplified by a graunching front nearside brake disc. Often I found myself doing forty, at which speed following drivers became impatient and started to overtake in silly places.

Then it went dark and as a result I discovered the new Ka's biggest problem. It's a whopper. A proper full-sized elephant in the wardrobe. A genuine, bona fide reason all on its own for buying something else. The headlights are absolutely useless. For seeing where you are going, a Hallowe'en pumpkin would be better.

I did a test. I drove at the speed at which I could safely stop in the distance visible in the light from those miserable candles in jam jars. And it was 18mph. Any faster and I was having to rely on crossed fingers that there was nothing out there in the gloom.

The only solution was to drive on full beam, which was a) little better and b) just bright enough for oncoming motorists to retaliate, making me even more blind than if I'd stayed on dipped.

Of course, not having been at the press launch, I didn't understand any of this. So I tiptoed along, with my heart beating like broken plumbing, wondering how on earth Ford could possibly have got it all so wrong. Vauxhall? Yes. Kia? For sure. But Ford? No way. Ford makes good cars these days. Some of them border on greatness. So, finding that it's got one this wrong is like going out for dinner at a Marco Pierre White restaurant and being served a plate of sick.

Here's the thing, though. Subsequent investigation revealed that Ford hasn't got the Ka wrong at all because, despite the Ford badge, despite the Ford styling and despite the Ford fixtures and fittings, this car, actually, is a Fiat 500. It has the same basic structure and the same engine. It's even built in the same factory, in Poland.

The fact that it's come out of the joint venture so wrong demonstrates two things. First, that the Fiat 500 must be a fairly bad car as well, but neither I nor anyone else has noticed because it's so lovely to look at and so delightful to own. And, second, that we're all doomed.

Obviously, Ford would have wanted to develop its own

small car. Asking its engineers to reclothe a Fiat rather than asking them to design their own baby from the ground up is like asking Stella McCartney to sew some new buttons on an Ozwald Boateng suit. No one becomes an engineer in a car company so they can spend their life sanding the word 'Fiat' off components and writing 'Ford' on them instead.

The only reason a company would do this is to save money. It gets a new car for a fraction of the cost of designing one itself. The problem is, the new car we are asked to buy simply isn't as good as it could have been. Or good-looking enough to mask the faults.

Worse, because every car company must now save money – great, big, fat lumps of it – almost all automotive development is going to stop. We're already seeing this with new propulsion ideas. Most people accept that in the fullness of time, cars will have to be powered with hydrogen, but developing the fuel cells necessary to make the technology work is fantastically complicated, and this, in an accountant's mind, means ruinously expensive.

As a result, car makers are simply launching much simpler, much cheaper and almost completely useless conventional battery-powered cars instead. Or idiotic hybrids that make owners feel smug and organic but move the human race about three feet in completely the wrong direction.

The upshot is that when the oil does start to run out, we as a species will be completely unprepared.

And that's what's given me an idea. At present, most governments in the world seem to agree that the only way out of the financial hole is to print money and throw this at various state projects. Unfortunately, because we in Britain are governed by fools and madmen, the projects they have in mind are street football outreach co-ordinators and ethnic watchdogs who will ensure the dole queues accurately reflect the nation's ethnic diversity.

You can see this is idiotic. We all can. So why not give the money instead to British engineering firms, which would use it, under close supervision, to make sure they didn't employ any health-and-safety people or ethnicity czars, to get the hydrogen fuel cell working on a practical everyday level?

Maybe we could team up with Iceland, partly because – heaven knows – we owe the Icelanders a favour and partly because they have enough geothermal power to make hydrogen cheaply. I can see no flaws with my idea at all. It pleases the global-warmingists because it spells an end for carbon-based fossil fuels; it pleases me because I get a whole new range of extremely powerful cars to play with; and, best of all, it puts Britain back where it belongs – on the prow of HMS *Progress*.

If we don't do this, we will emerge from the financial crisis only to discover that because of a lack of oil all the lights have gone out. And this is going to be a big problem if you have a Ka. Because you simply won't be able to see where you're going.

25 January 2009

Never mind, Daphne, at least you're pretty

Volkswagen Passat CC GT V6

Stop. Don't turn the page. Look again at the picture of this morning's car. Pretty, isn't it? It might not cause other motorists to swivel round in their seat, nor will it send a frisson through crowds on the pavement. It's not pretty like Abi Clancy or Meg Ryan . . . was.

With its slim side windows and those gently dished alloy wheels, it's quietly pretty, subtly pretty. Pretty like Daphne du Maurier. The sort of pretty you don't really notice until it's pointed out to you. And then you can't get its prettiness out of your head.

There are other cars that pull off a similar trick. The new Renault Laguna Coupé, for instance. But, of course, that is French and, therefore, the sort of car that beckons you in with many sultry promises and then has a massive breakdown.

The car in this morning's picture is unlikely to do that, because it's German. In fact it's the new Volkswagen Passat CC, and that's a bit unfortunate. It's like meeting the girl of your dreams and discovering, at the last moment, that she's called Ermintrude. Or Daphne, for that matter.

Actually, it's worse because 'Volkswagen' smacks of National Socialism and 'Passat' has a whiff of the municipal golf club. That's a really bad image to have in your head. Hitler in Rupert Bear trousers, swinging a nine iron with his mates Rudolf and Martin at the council's eighth tee.

However, you'd put up with the bad name and the horrific imagery for a slice of this pie. Same as you'd put up with Daphne du Maurier's apparent fondness for dining at the Venetian Y. I would too.

I'm a sucker for pillarless doors. One of the reasons I like the Subaru Outback so much is that the windows are frameless. In fact, when I look back at all the cars I've owned over the years, it's a common thread. The CLK Black I have now, the BMW CSL, the Honda CRX, the Ferrari 355, the Gallardo. Some people buy cars for speed; some for practicality or value. It seems I buy on the strength of a frameless window in a pillarless door.

Step inside the CC and, after you've rubbed your head better – you will bang it the first time, because the roofline is lower than you were expecting – you will note that all is well. Better than well. In the base models, everything is a bit dreary, a bit public convenience, only without George Michael to liven things up, but in the car I drove, it was all brushed aluminium and ivory leather and splashes of chrome.

I thought when this car came out that what it would say about you most of all is that you couldn't afford a Mercedes CLS. That still holds true. It is a less expensive rip-off of the Benz original – base model for base model, it's £25,000 cheaper – but you know what? The VW is better.

Certainly, it's better in the back, because even though the Mercedes is the larger car, the Passat offers more room for the two passengers it can carry back there. It really is two, though. The centre of the back seat is suitable only for people who like sitting in cupholders. Or who actually are cans of Coca-Cola.

Further back still, we find a boot that is vast, and as we

slam it we're left scratching our heads. Cavernous, well priced, good looking and nicely trimmed. So where's the catch? Apart from the municipal golf club handle.

Well it's simple, really. You can dress a VW Passat up in whatever you like in the same way that you can dress me up in whatever you like. But underneath I'm still the same clodhopping, fat, wheezing, middle-aged man.

The Passat I drove – a £30,492, 3.6-litre, four-wheel-drive GT – is not bad but it doesn't exactly set your world on fire. The figures suggest it will get to 62mph in 5.6 seconds, which is pretty fast, but at no time did I think, 'Wow. Even my pubic hair is standing on end.'

The figures also suggest it will get to 155mph, but the feel suggests you are never going to get there.

Part of the problem, I suspect, is the DSG gearbox. Usually, this is the best of the flappy paddle systems, but in the CC it felt strangely dimwitted and unwilling to change down fast. And the simple fact of the matter is this: you can have the best four-wheel-drive system in the world, the sharpest handling and the creamiest engine, but if the gearbox is going to behave like a trade union leader in gooey shoes, the whole effect is going to be ruined.

Luckily, there are lots of things to play with as you bumble along. First of all, there's the suspension that can be adjusted with a little button. To begin with, you will put it in 'sport', which makes everything very uncomfortable and therefore at odds with the relaxed gearbox and the discreet styling. So you'll then go for 'normal', which is still too uncomfortable. Which means, after two minutes, I guarantee you'll put it in 'comfort' and leave it there for the rest of time.

Then you have the safety features. One – not fitted to my

car – is an electronic driving instructor who grabs the wheel
if you try to change lane on the motorway without indicating.
I mean this. Apparently, you can feel him pushing you back
where you came from as though you are driving down a kerb.

Is that a good thing? Citroëns wake up the sleeping motorway driver by vibrating the seat. Other cars sound a buzzer.
But Volkswagen has taken this rather more direct approach,
which is fine, in theory. But what happens if you need to
swerve and there isn't time to indicate? The interfering buf-
foon in the dash is going to try to steer you into the obstacle
you were trying to avoid.

The radar-guided cruise control is much better. This system works like a normal cruise control but should a car pull
into your lane, you slow to match his speed until he moves
over, then you automatically speed up again. In some cars –
and I'm thinking of Mercedes here – it doesn't work very well
because it follows the car in front at such a great distance, its
driver doesn't realize you want to get by. In the VW the system
allows you to get right up his bottom and bully the dozy halfwit out of the way.

There are lots of toys, too, some of which are quite good.
The graphics on the sat nav, for instance, are so clear it's as
though they are being transmitted in HD – and that's great.
But what's the point of a big glass sunroof the size of a tennis court if it doesn't open?

It's a funny old swings-and-roundabouts car, this, which is
why, for once, I've spent the whole column writing about it.
On the one hand, it's a Mercedes CLS for half the price. On
the other, while it's comfortable and relaxed to drive, it lacks
sparkle.

I'm therefore going to give it three stars. But they tell only
three-fifths of the story. You see, there's a hotel in San Fran-

cisco called the Golden Gate. It's a three-star sort of place as well and it has a name that is every bit as unimaginative as 'Volkswagen Passat'. Yet I always choose to stay there when I'm in the city because it's pretty. Subtly pretty. Quietly pretty.

1 February 2009

The sinister . . .

BMW 730d SE

Quite rightly, it is no longer acceptable to mock people for being black, homosexual, ginger, deformed or Irish, so let us start this morning by mocking Gerald Ford, George Bush Sr, Bill Clinton, Ross Perot, Al Gore, Obama Barrack and John McCain. People, in other words, who are all left-handed.

At present, this terrible condition affects around 11 per cent of the world's population and yet in certain fields the number is high enough to raise statistical eyebrows. Quite apart from American politics, there is tennis, which is dominated by lefties. McEnroe, Connors, Rusedski, Ivanisevic and that Spanish ape whose name I've forgotten all hold their bats with the wrong hand.

What's more, if you give birth to a leftie, there is a good chance he'll go into space. One in four Apollo astronauts were left-hand-drive. But, conversely, things are not so rosy if he wishes to become a top-flight racing driver. All the big stars in recent years have been normal, apart from Gerhard Berger. He'll also struggle to be a writer because his hand-writing will be all smudged.

We can see from all this that left-handed people are different to you and me. In short, they are what science calls 'weirdos'.

History is less kind. The word 'sinister' is actually derived from the Latin *sinistere*, meaning left. *Gauche* is left. Maladroit is left. Derek Hatton is left. All the things you don't want to be are left. Left has come to mean bad, clumsy, difficult or awkward. And it's easy to see why this happened.

It is, for example, very difficult for a left-handed person to operate a camera or be a woman. Almost all are men and that's sinister for sure. What's more, a left-handed person can adjust more easily to seeing underwater than a right-hooker. There's only one conclusion to be drawn from this – their eyes are not human. Furthermore, they grow more pubic hair more quickly than a normal person, and this would imply that they may be wolves, or bears.

Certainly, we can deduce from this that it's not only the wiring of their arms that is the wrong way round. Their whole body is an electrical mess. I'm surprised they don't sneeze every time they get an erection. Certainly, they have a greater tendency to stutter. And many are slovenly time-keepers.

(Actually, I made that last bit up simply to annoy the producer of *Top Gear*, who is a) left-handed; b) three hours away from where he's supposed to be at any given moment of the day; and c) like all left-handed people, absolutely convinced that he is in some way 'special'.)

People from other minorities never try to claim they are better than the majority. You never get gingers going around saying that because of Simon Heffer and Nicholas Witchell, people with orange hair are cleverer than average. Nor do you get homosexuals pointing at Oscar Wilde with a smug look on their faces. They just want to be seen as 'the same' as everyone else.

But people who need upside-down hands to write their signature on a cheque spend a huge amount of time and effort forming clubs designed to prove that because Leonardo da Vinci was left-hand-drive, they are superior beings.

In this respect, they are a bit like the Freemasons or Mensa, that magnificently strange organization for people who think they're special because they can put some shapes in the right hole while playing chess.

Mind you, left-hookers are worse. They lobby the makers of household appliances to consider their plight when designing computers, cookers and power tools. They even complain about sinks and, I'm sorry, but I fail to see how something that is perfectly symmetrical can possibly favour right-handed people. Maybe they are saying the plughole isn't big enough to handle all their pubic hair.

Frankly, I'd just tell them we right-handers have our problems, too. The sextant, for instance is very difficult for us to operate and, er . . . I'm sure there are other things as well.

What annoys me most of all about southpaws, though, is that these sinister fish-wolves have a point. I have never knowingly met a left-hand-drive bore. For some reason, they tend to be interesting, different, worth having round for dinner. Sniffpetrol.co.uk, for instance, is written by a left-handed person. Angelina Jolie is left-handed. And while I can't say for sure, I bet Stephen Fry is sinistral. A word only he would understand.

And, luckily, all of this brings me neatly to the BMW 730 diesel.

You see, ordinary businessmen who have no problem using scissors have always bought, if they were in the market for a large and well-appointed mobile living room, a Mercedes S-class. The main reason for buying something else is that you're the chairman of a large British company, such as Jaguar, in which case you'd have to get a Jag.

Of course, if you are Bonio, out of U2, you will see a Mercedes as a bit Institute of Directors so you will buy a Maserati. If you are Sir Alan Sugar, you will have a Rolls-Royce Phantom because a Mercedes is too cheap. If you are a Manchester United footballist, you will have a Bentley because you are a frightful show-off. If you are sane, you will have a Range Rover and if you are bonkers, you will have a Maybach.

In short, then, before buying the big ugly Beemer, you would have to say, 'I am not a businessman, sane, Bonio, Alan Sugar, Wayne Rooney, or Theo Pamphlet from *Dragons' Den*.' You'd have to be a bit odd to be none of these things. You'd have to have strange underwater eyes and the hairiest scrotum in the world. To go for the left-field car, you would – and can you see what I've done here – have to be wired up all wrong.

Now, though, there's a ncw BMW 7-series. You wouldn't think so from looking at it, or from studying the engine, which is largely the same as before. But this is a brand new car.

Headlines? Well the cheapest model – the 730 diesel – starts at £53,730 and for that you get a car that produces just 192g/km of carbon dioxide, which is less than comes from the back of some Ford Mondeos or a cow. More importantly, it will achieve 45mpg on the open road, if you are careful with the throttle. And if you are not, 0 to 62mph in a shade over 7 seconds and a top speed of 153.

That's all lovely. Mind you, I'm surprised they didn't make it 2mph faster. Then they could have claimed it was so fast it had to be limited. But there we are. Transparency is what it's all about these days.

Further up the scale, there's the usual range of engine choices, including a twin-turbo V8, and the usual range of what the backroom computer nerds have put on the options list. You can have, for instance, a head-up display that keeps you abreast of the prevailing speed limit, or you can have a thermal imaging camera that spots pedestrians lurking in the shadows, or you can have side-mounted cameras that can spot traffic at blind junctions. That's all lovely, too.

Sadly, though, the 7-series is let down by two things. First of all, BMW makes much noise, quite rightly, about the inherent sportiness of all its cars. But sportiness is all wrong in a car like this. It's like buying a coat when you want a tablecloth. Yes, it has great steering, great reactions and great urgency, but they all come at a price. And the price is comfort and quietness. Put simply, a Mercedes is a more relaxing ride and in a big, very wide, very heavy and completely unsporting package, that's what you want.

Then there's the iDrive system. In essence, one button – think of it as a computer mouse – controls thousands of controls on the car, and I'm sure you can get used to it in the same way that you can get used to having a nasty headache.

Here's the thing, though. In Germany, you operate the button with your right hand. That's fine. But here, it's the other way round, and as any normal person who's tried to operate a computer mouse with their left hand knows, it's nigh-on impossible. In short, then, the right-hand-drive 7-series works only for left-hand-drive people.

8 February 2009

A smart, thrifty choice

Toyota iQ2 1.0 VVT-i

For the past month, I've been on the *Top Gear Live* world tour so the only driving I've done is in a Lamborghini, indoors and sideways. The lights in the arena would go down, a voice of God would announce my name, I'd floor the throttle, kick the tail out, arrive on stage in a flurry of tyre squeal and fireworks and shout, 'Hello, Sydney.' Which was a bit embarrassing if I was in Auckland.

There would then follow an hour and a half of more tyre squeal, explosions and shouting. AA Gill described it as all the headaches he'd ever had in one go – and he had to go through the process only once. We were doing it four times a day, which meant as night fell I was too exhausted and broken to operate anything more complicated than a bottle opener. Which is why I'd be taken back to the hotel by a driver.

This sounds very Elton Johnish but there is one big problem with using chauffeurs. Almost none of them can drive a car.

Let us first of all examine the case of the chap I used in Hong Kong. We'll call him Albert, because that's his name. Albert had a Porsche Cayenne, and what he liked to do was test every one of the speeds it would go. We'd start off with 37 and then we'd do 105, 21, 16, 84, 9, 0, 163, 41, and so on, until he'd established that they were all working properly.

Then he'd start testing the braking distances: 47 to 41, 50

to 5, 16 to 15 and, once, a terrifying 170 to 3. The range of possibilities was enormous and all of them were very bad, especially as Albert had the spectacularly annoying habit of impersonating the engine noise as we lurched along.

Cornering, however, was his speciality. He would make the noise of the tyres screeching as he turned each bend into a series of straight lines interspersed with a series of violent jerks. He was a lovely man. Which is why I felt so guilty, sitting alongside him, imagining what he might look like with a pencil jammed into his throat.

Elsewhere in the world the drivers were far better but each one of them had roadcraft habits every bit as irritating as hawking up phlegm. They'd follow the car in front too closely, sit too near the wheel, brake for no reason on the motorway, steer too vigorously, dawdle or, worst of all, pretend they knew where they were going when plainly they didn't.

Naturally, each would claim he was an above-average driver – we all do, despite the statistical impossibility of it being the case – and it's probably true. They probably were better than most. But the fact is that everyone has their own driving style and it's never quite as good as your own.

For instance. When the lights on a dual carriageway are red and you have a choice of lanes in which to stop, I would never pull up behind a Peugeot. This is because anyone with a Peugeot knows nothing about cars or they'd have bought something else. And because they know nothing about cars, they will know nothing about driving. Which means they'll be sitting there in neutral with the handbrake on, and that means they won't move off smartly – or even at all – when the lights go green. I have a rule at the lights. Always pull up behind the Beemer.

But other drivers don't do this. What's more, they fiddle

with the radio, changing stations whenever they are presented with a song they don't like. Why? Tunes are never more than three minutes long and I can just about handle CeCe Peniston for that long. Leave it. LEAVE IT. But no. Chchch, goes the tuner … 'In parliament today' … chchch … 'nothing but a dreamer' … chchchshshsh … 'on the day that you were born' … chchch … 'Jade Goody' … and then, 'Aaaaaaaaarghgurgle,' as I jam a ballpoint into his epiglottis.

Worse, some drivers think an urban one-way street actually means you can travel on it in only one direction. Rubbish. If nothing is coming, then it's idiotic to drive for miles just to satisfy some residents' committee's over-inflated sense of self-importance.

There is a similar problem with speed limits. Of course, they are a good idea. Absolutely. Definitely. But when it's one in the morning, a driver who puts his licence ahead of your need to get home as quickly as possible is just annoying.

Seriously, being driven by anyone – even Jackie Stewart – is as horrendous as having someone else make love to your wife. 'No. No. No. Not like that, you idiot. You have to be more delicate. What in God's name are you doing now, man? You can't park it there …'

The worst thing about having a driver, though, is the sense of guilt. If you ask him to pick you up at midnight, you should – if you have a heart – feel duty-bound to leave at the appointed hour. Which is a damn nuisance if, at 11.45, you meet Miss Iceland, who announces at 11.55 she's forgotten to put on any pants.

In short, it doesn't matter how tired I am or how convenient it might be to have someone run me home; I always prefer to drive myself.

Unfortunately, this is becoming increasingly fraught with difficulties. Quite apart from the sheer expense, you have the speed cameras, the problems with parking, the sleeping policemen and the wide-awake ones in their vans. Then, in every major city, there are Communists who believe what they hear about the environment and call you a murderer.

I genuinely believe that soon there will be a sea change in our attitude to car ownership. That soon the number of families who own one will start to fall dramatically, and that the few who do continue to plunge along in the wake of Mr Toad will drive and dream about machinery that's far removed from the Ferrari and Range Rovers of today.

And so, the Toyota iQ. First, the good things. It is 2½ inches shorter than the original Mini, but because the differential is mounted in front of the engine the cabin is big enough for four seats.

Then there's the business with carbon dioxide. The three-cylinder 1-litre petrol engine produces just 99 somethings of CO_2 and as a result it falls into the tax-free category; unheard of in a car that runs on unleaded. More important, it should do 70mpg if driven carefully.

Better than all of this, though, is the way it looks. In white, with the tinted windows, it's like a Stormtrooper's helmet. I liked that. And I loved the enormous array of equipment, too. It's hard to think of a single toy fitted to my Mercedes that isn't in the little iQ.

Now for the bad things. Yes, there may be space in the back for two seats. But very few people are small enough to actually sit on them. The boot is pitiful as well.

Then there's the price. The entry-level model costs a whopping £9,495. Add an automatic gearbox and the price shoots up by another thousand. And, finally, there is the performance. Or rather there isn't. To keep those emissions down, the oomph has had to be abandoned, so that it takes a dreary 14 seconds to get from 0 to 60. Quite why it needs traction control I have no idea. And why you would ever need the button that turns it off is even more baffling.

So, some swings and some roundabouts. As a long-distance car, obviously, it's about as much use as a horse, but as a station car or an urban runaround, especially if your children have no legs, it's good. I prefer the cheaper Fiat 500 because I prefer the looks, but, of course, that'll be less reliable. Either way, these cars are the future. Small. Cheap to run. Good-looking. And surprisingly well kitted out with toys. They really do make Mondeos and Volvos, and so on, look awfully wasteful and unnecessary.

It's a brave new world and we have to get used to it. A thousand cc is the new black. No g in the corners is the future, and that's that. I suppose it isn't the end of the world. Certainly, I'd rather drive an iQ than be driven by Albert in his Cayenne.

I should make it plain that none of the observations about drivers in this column refers to Paul Grant, who is brilliant.

8 March 2009

Perfect, the car for all seasons

Range Rover TDV8 Vogue SE

When you stop and think about it, there's no real point to this newspaper's travel section. Or any of the few remaining high street travel agents. Or indeed the BBC's *Holiday* programme – wait a minute, that's already gone. Because, when it comes to taking a vacation, we only really need France.

It has beaches on the Atlantic coast where you can surf, and more on the south coast where you can spend all day pretending not to look at breasts. It has mountains for skiing and hiking. It has the best cheese in the world, the best mustard in the world and the best wine in the world.

I could go on, so I will. It has the best weather in the world, the best scenery in the world and it's even replete with funny-looking little locals who sit outside their houses in baggy clothes. But, unlike poor people in, say, India or Brazil, they don't pester you for money, or try to sell you paper napkins and hot dogs at the traffic lights.

You could go to Arizona to see the Grand Canyon, but what's the point? France has canyons too. You could go to Russia for the culture, but why? The popes never lived in Moscow. There are no Roman viaducts in St Petersburg. You are simply wasting jet fuel.

James May once said that France only exists so we can drive more easily to Italy but this, I'm afraid, proves the man is mad. Because France has everything anyone could ever want from a holiday destination and, of course, it's right next door.

There is a similar answer to the question of food. Every night, someone comes on the television to explain how to make a lemon sauce for your halibut and how jalapeño peppers go very well with pineapple. But I'm afraid Gordon, Ainsley, Jamie, Marco, Raymond, Nigella, Delia and the countless others I've forgotten are wasting their breath, because we all know that what we want is bacon and eggs.

You can have it for breakfast, lunch and supper. It works with ketchup just as well as it works with wine. You can make it in five minutes, even if you are eight. And it's impossible to get the recipe wrong.

Indeed, I have decided there is a simple answer to every choice we face in the world today. Brand of television? Sony. Music? The Stones. Pin-up? Carla Bruni. Religion? Buddhism. Phone? iPhone. Newspaper? The *Sunday Times*.

And that brings us on to sport. Rugby is too complicated. Cricket is too dreary. Golf is for Freemasons from the Order of St Onyx. The fact is that you can't beat football. It's easy to understand. It flows nicely. And there's always a local team you can support. What more do you want?

Sadly, since I'm talking myself out of a job here, it turns out there is an answer to cars as well. Over the past thirty years or so, I have road-tested thousands of models, driven hundreds of thousands of miles and written millions of words on the subject. But all the while, the answer to absolutely everyone's motoring problems has been right under my nose. The Range Rover.

This is the automotive equivalent of France, the Sony Bravia, the *Sunday Times* and Mick Jagger. It is the answer.

Let us imagine for a moment that you would like to have a

Rolls-Royce Phantom because you want to bathe in that glorious art deco cabin full of timber and hide. Well, a Range Rover offers exactly the same sense of wellbeing for a quarter of the price.

Plus, a Range Rover allows you to look down on the chap in a Roller, and over the car in front, which means you have more warning of any impending unpleasantness. Of course, the figures suggest that if you do have an accident, you are no better off in a Range Rover than you are in a Renault Laguna. But if I were to give you the choice of which car you'd most like to be in when you hit a tree . . .

And it's not like you are left wanting for toys either. You can even have something called a VentureCam – a wireless hand-held camera that feeds its picture to the sat nav screen on the dash. The idea is that you hang it out of the window while driving off-road so you can see what the terrain directly ahead of the wheels is like.

However, since its docking port is in the passenger footwell, it can also be used for looking up your wife's skirt. And trust me, you aren't offered that facility in any other car I've driven.

You want to go to a point-to-point? Well, there is nothing to beat a Range Rover, which can not only deal with the muddy entrance but also comes with a handy drop-down tailgate on which you can perch while enjoying a glass of sloe gin and some cake.

Thinking of driving to the slopes for a bit of late skiing this Easter? Well, sure, there are many luxury cars that can eat up those autoroute miles. But none do so more elegantly than a Vogue – providing you avoid the 20-inch wheels, which look good but spoil the ride a bit – and none will be quite so accomplished once you're in the mountains, on the snow and ice.

You might imagine that in Knightsbridge, a Range Rover is as cumbersome as a pair of wellies and that, as a result, it is most definitely not the answer for the city dweller. Wrong, I'm afraid. Other off-road cars are indeed too large and unwieldy to make much sense in urban areas but the Range Rover – dicky throttle response in the diesel aside – never feels like it's too big or unmanageable. And let's be honest, when you put money in a meter, you rent an entire parking bay, so you may as well use all of it.

The Range Rover is often called a dual-purpose vehicle, but it's so much more than that. It has the anatomical properties, and abilities, of Kali, which means it can glide, hurtle, waft or lug depending on your mood. You shoot? Get a green one. You ski? Go for blue. You deal drugs? Make it black and have the Sport. The Range Rover, quite simply, answers every motoring question that's ever been posed.

When the snow came back in February, schools were closed because people couldn't get there. My kids could, though. Because I've just bought a 15,000-mile TDV8 Vogue SE on a 57 plate. It cost a smidgen over £30,000. That's less than half price. And you can halve that again if you go older. Or go petrol. It's almost cheaper than walking.

And it's better for the environment, too. Yes, you could buy a Toyota Prius, but let's be honest, the nickel for its batteries is mined in Canada, and shipped – not on a sailing boat, I might add – to Norway or some other intermediate location where it's processed and then shipped on again to Japan where it is put in the car, along with an electric motor and a normal engine. The finished product is then shipped halfway back round the world again before it arrives in a dealer near you. You may think of it, if you like, as an Israeli strawberry.

A Range Rover, on the other hand, is made in the Midlands, which means, if you buy one, it only has to come down the road. You may think of it, then, as an organic, farm-fresh product, sourced and grown locally. And I know how important that is to shoppers these days.

Without wishing to sound pompous, my heart swells with pride that humankind can make such a wonderful, graceful, dignified and beautiful thing. And while patriotism may be the last refuge of a scoundrel, I'm proud, too, that this car was conceived by the Germans, who are basically British but with a bit less humour.

Often, over the years, I've been asked by passers-by in the street to name the best car in the world. I've never known quite what to say because my mind has swum with all the options. The fact is, though, there aren't any options at all. There's just one island of brilliance in a sea of also-rans.

15 March 2009

Flawed but fun

Alfa MiTo 1.4 TB 155bhp Veloce

I suppose that in the days when your fishmonger knew your name and what sort of cod you liked on a Friday, 'brand loyalty' made sense. Now we live in a world of supermarkets and corporations, it is the most ridiculous thing on all of God's green earth. No matter how many loyalty cards you have in your wallet.

That said, I am the worst offender. Even though I know Virgin is the best airline, I always try to fly BA. Even though I know HSBC is in fairly good shape, I bank at Barclays. Even though I know the new style of Levi's reveals my butt crack when I bend over, I would still never buy a pair of Wranglers.

And this brings me neatly onto the question of watches. For some time now, I've been on the hunt for a new one, but the choice is tricky. I couldn't have a Breitling because I don't own an Audi. I couldn't have a Calvin Klein because they are pants, I couldn't have a Gucci because I'm not a footballist's wife, I couldn't have a TW Steel because my wrist isn't big enough to sport something that can be seen from space, I couldn't have a Tissot because I'm not eight and the only thing in the world worse than a fake Rolex is a real one.

Have you noticed something odd about Rolexes? Especially the modern ones that wind automatically when you move your wrist about? A great many owners wear them on their right hand. I jump to no conclusions here but you can feel free.

Mostly, though, I cannot wear any of these watches because I am an Omega man. I have worn a Seamaster for years, not because James Bond has one and not because Neil Armstrong wore something by the same maker on the moon, but because on the day I went away to school my parents gave me a Genève Dynamic.

The trouble is that for the past few years Omega has been the Pillsbury Dough of Swiss watches. The Terry and June. Omegas were dreary. They were boring to behold. They were Vectras in a world of Ferraris and Lamborghinis. The De Ville Prestige, for example, was plainly designed by someone who had a black-and-white telly.

This filled me with despair. I wanted a watch. For the same reasons that I bank at Barclays and wear Levi's, it had to be an Omega, and it just wasn't coming up with the goods. It was like Leeds United. Once the home of Peter Lorimer and Gary Sprake but now an also-ran bunch of unimaginative clod-hopping no-hopers.

And then one day, in Hong Kong, I saw it. A new Omega. It's called the Railmaster and it is a thing of unparalleled beauty. There is no button that owners think will call for help if they find themselves in a crashing helicopter on Kiliman jaro, it is not waterproof to 8,000 metres, there is no stopwatch, there is no swivelling bezel to tell you how much air you have left in your tanks, and you even have to wind it up every morning or it will stop. Plainly, this is a watch for the seden-tary soul. The man with no hang glider or mini sub in his garage. I bought it in an instant.

And so it goes with Alfa Romeo. My loyalty to the brand began when I had an old GTV6. It let the air out of its tyres most nights. It would weld its twin-plate clutch to the fly-wheel if you didn't drive it for a day or two. And once, it dumped its gear linkage onto the propshaft when I was doing about 60mph. The noise that resulted was extraordinary: a bit like Brian Blessed being raped.

Even the design was silly. It was a hatchback, but the rear seat couldn't be folded down because someone who'd had too much wine had put the petrol tank between the cabin and the boot. And the driving position had to be experienced to be believed. The only way you could get comfortable was if you had arms that were 6 feet long, a compressed spine and feet attached directly to your knees.

You might expect me to say that I forgave it all these trespasses because it was so glorious to drive. But it wasn't. In fact, not since the Alfasud has there been an Alfa which is demonstrably better than the competition. And now, of course, Alfa is just a division of Fiat.

However ... I have argued many times that owning an Alfa is a portal through which all petrolheads must pass if they genuinely want to know what it is that differentiates a car from a toaster or a washing machine.

Because Alfas have flaws, they feel human, as if they have a soul and a temper. Each one – except the Arna, obviously – is like the tortured hero of a Russian novel, a car of extraordinary depths, a car you can never truly fathom, especially when it is four in the morning and it is enveloped in a cloud of steam, yet again, on the North Circular.

They are like cocaine. The unimaginable highs are always matched by immense, brooding lows. Massive electrical storms that inevitably follow a glorious sultry evening.

For years I have longed for the day when Alfa could put all of this humanity in a car that was good to drive as well. And

I really thought the new MiTo might just be the answer; the Railmaster moment, when Alfa stopped being like Leeds United, stopped living on its reputation from the 1970 cup final and put a corker in the back of the net.

It isn't. It may come with a clever electronic package that enables you to choose what sort of response you'd like from the engine, but it doesn't matter which option you select: the whole package is let down by a cunning new electric power-steering system that feels, I imagine, like fondling a pair of silicone breasts. There's no escape from the fact that you are playing with two bags full of jelly.

Then there's the clever new suspension, in which there are coilover springs inside the shock absorbers. Sounds intriguing but so far as I could work out, the main result is a harsh ride.

There are other issues, too. The sloping roof means headroom in the back is poor and the boot is small. The steering wheel is connected to the dash by what looks like a set of Victorian bellows, and the whole horn assembly felt like it was about to come off.

Of course, I loved it. I found myself ignoring the defects and concentrating on the way there's a choice of what material you'd like to surround the headlights. I loved the crackly, almost flat-four exhaust note, I loved the 155bhp turbocharged engine (from a Fiat), I loved the interior, which feels like it belongs in a much more expensive car. But the thing I love most of all about this car is that, at parties, when people ask what you're driving, you can say, 'An Alfa.'

Men will imagine you are a grand-prix racer from the fifties. Women will think that you are a bit like the Daniel Day Lewis character in *A Room with a View*. A bit interesting. Like you might prefer poetry to *Nuts*. It's the only brand in the world of sub-supercar motoring that can do this.

There are better small cars if you want a household appliance – the Mini, for instance. There are better small cars if you want a fun drive. The Mini again. And of course, there are better-looking cars built to a higher standard. Um, the Mini springs to mind. But I'm afraid there are no better small cars if, like me, you are brand loyal and what you want is an Alfa.

22 March 2009

Problem is, I don't think I ever met anyone who would buy a Mazda 6 – and also it's pretty hopeless

Mazda 6 2.2 five-door Sport Diesel

My daughter rang from her boarding school last night in a state of righteous dudgeon and high indignation. Apparently, some pupils had been caught drinking, and as a result all social activities have been banned until the end of term.

'It's so, like, you know, so unfair,' she wailed. And, of course, she's right. It is unfair that the innocent are punished for the sins of the guilty. But it's good training for when she leaves school, joins the real world and finds it's going on there, too.

One man runs amok with a gun and the entire British Olympic shooting team is forced to train in Belgium. One yobbo crashes his Vauxhall Nova into a bus shelter and we all have to pay higher insurance premiums. One man decides to fill his training shoe with explosives and now all of us have to get undressed every time we want to get on a plane.

Of course, the problem is that today, thanks to all sorts of lily-livered nonsense, the range of punishments available to governments and schools is extremely limited. Hanging is banned. So is drawing and quartering. The rack is gone, along with hemlock.

I'm no fan of capital punishment, but surely we can do better than the unimaginative procession of fines, prison and the Asbo ankle bracelet. Why not tattoo something appropriate right across a criminal's face? Or make him walk the streets naked for a period of time? Or get him to see how far he can pull a car with ropes tied to his eyelids?

I even have some ideas for football. When Ronaldo is tapped on the ankle, he falls over clutching his face as though he's tumbled into a vat of acid. This spoils the flow of the game and may result in an unjust free kick being awarded.

What I'd like to suggest is that any player who's in that much pain plainly has no future and should be put down. No, really. I'd have a vet at each match, and anyone writhing around on the floor like a big girl's blouse would be shot in the back of the head with a humane killer. This is not capital punishment. It's kindness.

Unfortunately, it is not possible, for all sorts of reasons, to put schoolchildren to sleep if they misbehave. Or to tattoo 'loser' on their faces. So what do we do instead?

I was punished a very great deal at school, mainly for refusing to play cricket. I couldn't see the point of it. You'd sit around for hours, with terrible hay fever, and then you'd be asked to stand in front of three sticks while an enormous boy called Phil Lovell hurled what is best described as a rock at them.

It was ridiculous, which is why, every week, I took two hours' detention instead. It was indoors, so there was less hay fever, there was no chance of having all your teeth smashed out and it lasted for only two hours. Not two years.

Detention, then, was a pleasure. So what about corporal punishment? Hmmm. Picture the scene. You have a housemaster, who likely as not is a 'bachelor', in a quiet room, behind a locked door, whipping the bottom of an attractive fourteen-year-old boy with a length of cane. It's straight from page one of the Max Mosley Catholic Priest Handbook, for crying out loud.

We all used to be beaten fairly regularly at school until a friend discovered a way of ensuring it would never happen again. Having been caught – oh I don't know – walking across the ruins in home clothes, or some such nonsense, he was summoned to the master's study and ordered to bend over a chair, whereupon he lowered his trousers to reveal he was wearing a pair of black satin girl's knickers. And then, to fluster the poor man still further, after the first thwack he moaned softly for 'more'.

Be assured the next five lashes were more like taps and from then on the beatings stopped. And weren't even reinstated on the occasion when I stole the sixth form's television and put it in the school's annual charity auction . . . while engaged in the unforgivable, heinous act of chewing gum.

So, detention is comfortable, corporal punishment is dodgy and more elaborate punishments will be a no-no with parent groups. What, then, is the modern school supposed to do when a pupil steps out of line? Stern words are an encouragement, public humiliation is cool and everything else is outlawed by wetties.

The worst punishment I can think of for a child is boredom. Make them do something mind-numbingly tedious, something that achieves nothing – the adolescent equivalent of breaking rocks. That's what I'd do with modern-day miscreants. Foist tedium upon their active little heads.

Let me put it this way. The worst punishment I was ever given was being ordered to write 1,000 words on the inside of a ping pong ball. It was hell.

Strangely, however, while it seemed to have absolutely no point at the time, it has come in very handy this week. Because writing 1,000 words on the inside of a table tennis ball means I am well placed to write 1,000 words on the Mazda6 Sport.

In fact, I've written 862 and I haven't even started yet.

It took me even longer, actually, to get into the car. The day it arrived, I settled behind the wheel, encouraged by the 'sport' badge on the back. The clatter from under the bonnet when I turned the key suggested it was in fact a 'diesel'. So I climbed back out again and went to London in my Range Rover.

The next day I was going to drive it but I couldn't be bothered. On day three I didn't have anywhere to go but on day four I had a trip planned to Didcot and I decided I had to be professional. And I was, right up to the moment when I climbed into the Range Rover again. On day five it sat there and then on day six, lo and behold, it sat there some more.

Here's the problem. Normally, when I review a car, I have in my mind the sort of person who might like to buy such a thing. But I don't think I've ever met anyone who would buy a Mazda 6.

I can tell you, having walked past it very many times, that it's not an ugly car, by any means. But it's not a looker either. In the language of the teenage nightclub, 'You would. But you wouldn't cross the road . . .'

I did drive it today and can reveal that it's pretty hopeless. Fitting sporty suspension, hard seats and quick steering in a diesel-powered family hatchback is like trying to sell Farley's Rusks with added vodka. The fact is that it was uncomfortable and it had a gearchange that felt as though the lever was set in a bucket of shingle.

But the worst thing is that it commits the greatest sin of them all: it's boring. It really is like the inside of a ping pong ball. It's 15½ feet of nothing. Driving it felt, therefore, like I was being punished for something I hadn't done.

29 March 2009

Trying to break the speed limit in this car would be like trying to break the speed limit while riding a cow

Fiat Qubo 1.3 16v MultiJet Dynamic

Now that no panty liner company can afford to display its wares in the commercial breaks, the government and various other bodies have stepped in to fill the void with a range of exciting new public information films.

Quite how they arrive at the selected topics, I have absolutely no idea but in recent months we've been told not to sneeze in lifts, to look more carefully for motorbikists and, weirdly, how to determine whether someone is having a stroke. Why a stroke? Why not bird flu or a heart attack or syphilis? And why can't I sneeze in a lift? If that's where I am when the need arises, what am I supposed to do? Keep my mouth closed and pinch my nose? That'd blow my eyes out.

Oh, and if motorcyclists want people to spot them at junctions, here's an idea. Buy a car.

Of course, there is nothing new in any of this hectoring. In my youth, I remember being told by Harold Wilson not to put a rug on a shiny floor, and by Rolf Harris to learn to swim. But the sheer volume of finger-wagging today is incredible.

We are constantly being told not to smoke, not to eat too much salt, not to drink and drive, not to ignore our tax returns, not to play with fireworks, not to stay in third gear and not to spend all day watching television when we could be up in our loft with a mile of lagging.

Then, this morning, while reading the handbook for the new Fiat Qubo, I discovered that behind the scenes, things are even worse.

It's like any normal handbook for a car. Written for tribes in the Amazon, and Martians, there is advice on how to start the engine and what the speedometer does, but buried away in the middle of a fascinating passage on how to use the seats, I discovered a little nugget that said the car is equipped with a 'European On Board Diagnosis' system.

It sounds harmless. A little light comes on to tell owners when an emission-related component is wearing out. But then it goes on to say, casually, that a log of the engine operation is kept . . . and can be 'accessed by traffic police'.

I'm probably worrying unnecessarily but does this mean Dixon of Dock Green can now hook a laptop up to your engine management system and see how fast you have been travelling?

If it does, the good news is that if you have a Fiat Qubo, Jim Bergerac can dig about in the wiring as much as he likes, because he's going to find that since you bought the car you have never broken the speed limit once. This is because it'd be like trying to break the speed limit while riding a cow.

The Qubo is a van. Oh, they've tried to liven it up with fancy green paint and triangular windows and they plainly got a room full of men in polo-necked jumpers to think up the name. But it is still a van.

I have no problem with this. The Citroën Berlingo is a van and as a family car it works rather well.

The Qubo doesn't. It was designed in conjunction with

Citroën, sits on the platform of a Punto and is powered, if you go for the diesel option, by a 1.3-litre engine from Opel.

Needless to say, there are all sorts of silly mistakes. For instance, the boot lid is opened by pressing a little button on the key fob. Great. Except, I guarantee that every time you turn the key to start the engine, you will press the button by mistake. So you will then have to get out and shut it again.

Of course, being able to open the boot with the button is jolly useful if you are coming back from the shops laden with bags and toddlers. But I'm afraid that because the tailgate is so huge, it cannot be opened if anyone has parked within a mile of your rear end. These are the details that turn what could have been a good idea into one that simply doesn't work at all.

In engineering terms, you really can't have 'brilliant, apart from . . .', whether it's a nuclear power station, a motorway crash barrier or a car. I mean, the *Titanic* was brilliant, apart from its crappy rudder.

Of course, you may look at the low price of a Fiat Qubo – it's about the same as a McMeal – and the low running costs and say that you don't mind a wonky tailgate, or a gear lever that feels as sturdy as one of Bugs Bunny's ears, or the fact it has no carpet at all – let me repeat that, 'no carpet at all' – because it provides so much more space than a conventional hatchback.

Well, let's look at that space, shall we. The inside of a five-seater Qubo is not much wider than a normal car and certainly no longer. It is simply taller, which is jolly useful in a van, but unless you are 9 feet tall or you have a massive Afro, it is of absolutely no use at all in a car.

Citroën got round this in the last Berlingo I drove by fitting a series of cubbyholes above your head. The Fiat Qubo I drove just had mile upon mile of useless air.

The space isn't all that versatile either. Yes, the back seats fold down and can even be lifted out altogether. But unless you actually enjoy trapping your fingers, you won't want to put them back in again.

Then there's the speed. I tried the 1.3-litre diesel model, which takes more than 16 seconds to get from 0 to 62. You might not be bothered about this because you are a Porritt. But let me be clear. I am talking here about performance that can only really be measured in geological terms.

Honest to God, the Qubo is so slow that if you climbed into one this morning in Hunstanton and attempted to drive south as fast as possible, coastal erosion would swallow you up by Wednesday evening.

Mount Everest is currently moving northwest at around 5 centimetres a year. That's the sort of speed you'll be going in your Qubo, and be assured, on a road, this kind of pace is not just antisocial. It's dangerous.

I have no problem if you want to recycle your tofu and knit your underwear from hemp, because none of these things affects anyone else. But driving a Qubo affects everyone. It clogs up the system. They should have called it the Imodium.

Yesterday, on the A44, I built up a massive, mile-long tail. I was going to say, I felt like the head of a comet, trailing gas and fury in my wake, but the imagery is wrong. In fact, I felt like a sperm.

One poor woman, in a Citroën C2, became so fed up with my tectonic drift, she attempted to get past in a place that was suicidal. Had I not braked to let her back onto my side of the road, she would have had a head-on.

You might argue that the crash would have been her fault.

But what if her mum had rung to say she thought she'd put too much salt on her lunch and was having a stroke? What if she was about to sneeze and needed to get home as quickly as possible?

The crash would not have been her fault at all. It would have been mine for putting the needs of the polar bear ahead of the needs of everyone else.

5 April 2009

I raised my knife, snarled . . . and fell in love

Jaguar XKR convertible

In the past twenty years, I cannot recall a single bad review in any British publication of any new Jaguar. More than that, I can't recall a single review that wasn't drowning in its own hyperbole. 'Jaguar gets it right'. 'Jaguar kicks Johnny Foreigner's arse'. 'Jaguar pounces on Porsche and smashes its Nazi face in'.

Unfortunately, none of these rave notices made much of an impression on the car-buying public, who read the rave notices, recalled the strikes of the seventies and the woeful unreliability of the eighties and, fearful that the car would smell of Arthur Daley's sheepskin, bought a Mercedes instead. Which is why Mercedes is still owned by Mercedes and Jaguar is owned by some Indians who are currently asking the British government for a bit of money to keep their ailing British operation alive.

None of this matters to Britain's car journos, though, who are at it again with the new XKR. *Autocar* tells us it's better than a 911. *Car* magazine calls it 'brilliant', *Evo* says it's 'great'. And we can be in no doubt that when the *Telegraph* tests the XKR, it will say, 'The spirit of Sir William Lyons lives on in this fine automobile.'

I don't know why the Brit hacks are so blatantly pro-Jag. But I really do get the impression that if one of the company's engineers were to drop in to the offices of a car magazine one day and relieve himself all over its photocopying machine, the reporters would argue that his stream of urine shone out like a shaft of gold, bringing light and warmth and wholesome goodness to everything it touched. Whereas, if a bloke from BMW popped by to pee on the pot plants, they'd call the police.

I'm afraid, however, that the worst Jag apologist among Britain's shrinking band of motoring hacks is me. I'm dreadful. I try my hardest to remain calm and rational. But reviewing a Jaguar is like reviewing the performance of a Wimbledon underdog. They are always brave and plucky and full of spirit and you'll sort of forgive them anything, even when they've served 200 double faults on the trot, vomited on a ball boy and topped off the afternoon by sending round a horrid XJ40 that is held together with duct tape and powered by a stupid and weedy 3.2-litre engine. A car I once described as 'magnificent' – just before I bought another Mercedes.

Well, with the new XKR, I decided it was high time to remove the underdog sympathy gene and explain why it was too little too late. I was going to point at the huge amount of extra brushed aluminium body piercings that have sullied the original – and extremely beautiful – shape and explain in no uncertain terms that there's no point fitting back seats when there is no human being, not even the pygmy tribes of South America, who could ever actually fit in one.

Then, I was going to send in the nuke and explain that no one in their right mind would pay £78,400 for a car that had its light switch on the end of the indicator stalk. This may be acceptable in a £7,800 eco-box from the jungles of Burma, because one switch that does two things saves money. On a car like the XKR, it should be on the dash, as it is in my Mercedes.

And while we're on the subject of the interior. No. Really, no. You cannot have a touchscreen satellite navigation system, because, as anyone who's tried out the new BlackBerry will testify, they do not work.

I was primed. I'd dipped my keyboard in acid. I'd swallowed a handful of honesty pills and I was going to fire a lexicon of invective in the direction of Coventry, but then my XKR test car was delivered by two rather forlorn figures from Jag, who sat at my kitchen table admiring my central heating and drinking coffee like it was exotic. Both said with expressions that I thought had gone west with Sir Clement Freud that they felt so unhappy, because now, at last, they had a range of great cars either on sale or nearing the end of the pipeline and that unless the damn banking crisis ended soon, all their efforts would have been in vain. I felt sorry for them, I'm afraid.

So, the new XKR? What a beaut. Jesus. This thing could rip a 911 clean in half while actually eating a BMW 6-series. And it'd still have enough energy left to pull an SL's spine out. It's the Battle of Britain all over again, and the result's the same. I mean, think about it – this XK is even made in the same factory that produced Spitfires.

The heart of the beast is a new 5-litre supercharged engine that develops 503bhp and enough torque to knock Dresden over again. There's so much it'll get from 50 to 70mph in a mind-blowing 1.9 seconds. Give this car an inch . . . and it'd get past an Aussie road train.

There's more. You get more bucking broncos for your bucks than in any other comparable car and yet, despite the tsunami of grunt, it produces just 292 carbon dioxides, which will put it in the new top tax band that starts next month but is nothing compared with, say, a Lamborghini Murciélago's 495. It is, therefore, a brilliant engine. And it sounds good too. Like it's made of meat.

Underneath, you get an electronic limited-slip differential such as you find on a Ferrari 430, and a new type of adjustable suspension, neither of which will make any difference on a road. But should you be inclined to don a branded jumper and go to a track day, in your ludicrous watch, then you are in for a gay old time. The old XK was good. This one is sensational.

There is, however, a fly in the ointment. Other journalists have glossed over the problem, but I won't. In order to make the car work at track days, the ride, even in comfort mode, is too knobbly and hard. This might be acceptable if the Jag were a sports car, but it isn't. It's supposed to be a long-distance grand tourer. And over even a short distance you quickly tire of the constant pittering and pattering.

In dynamic mode, as Jag calls it, the pittering and the pattering become so bad that you could not possibly hold your finger steady enough to operate the touchscreen interface thingy. You might even accidentally select Radio 1.

The fact is this. If you want a sports car, an edge-of-the-knife, superhighway samurai sword, then you are better off with the Porsche 911 S, which is faster, smaller, lighter, tighter and more responsive. If, however, you want a car a little more tuned to the needs of everyday living, a car which has its boot, let's say, at the back, then the Jag is the natural choice, although the ride is always going to cause your nib to hesitate over the order form.

So, the conclusion then. Honestly. Absolutely honestly. Hand-on-heart, honestly. The XKR is not perfect. It's not even close. The light switch is wrong. The back seats are stupid. Some of the new jewellery is awfully Cheshire and that ride is way, way too firm.

But when I look at the opposition – the chintzy SL, the

overly complicated M6, the vomitously ugly Maserati Coupé and the expensive Aston V8 – I know for sure, and for the first time, that if I were in the market for a car of this type, I would have the Jag.

26 April 2009

The car adds up

Lotus Evora 2+2

Honda announced recently that it's to stop making the drop-head, two-seater S2000. And since this has always been my favourite small sports car, I thought I'd borrow one and go for one last, tearful drive.

God, it was horrible. There wasn't enough room for even small parts of me to get comfortable. The digital instruments looked like they had come straight from a Nik Kershaw video. The plastics would have looked shoddy on an Ethiopian's wheelie bin. It was as sparsely equipped as an Amish barn. And the noise. It was hip-hop horrendous. Conversation was impossible. Thought was impossible. It was the kind of relentless drone that, after a while, can drive a man mad.

So how come I used to love this car so much? It's not like I'm talking here about meeting up with an old girlfriend. The Honda has not become fat and frumpy. It isn't pushing a pram or wearing tweed instead of miniskirts. It's not now married to a golfer called Colin. It's exactly the same now as it was in 2005. And 2005 is not that long ago.

Except, of course, in automotive terms, 2005 is somewhere between the big bang and the Norman conquests. And what was acceptable then – heavy steering, no sat nav, religious persecution and dinosaurs – is not acceptable any more.

Cars are not getting faster or more economical. But in

terms of refinement and comfort, they are a country mile better than the cars you could buy as recently as a week ago last Tuesday. (Unless you have a Peugeot.)

This is great for us, but it's a big problem for Britain's small car makers. Because in the olden days (1994), when all cars exploded every few minutes, you could have a Lotus or a TVR or a Morgan and it wasn't that much different.

Today, though, as the big car companies churn out cars that have no transmission whine and never break down – Peugeot excepted – the offerings from a small car company look as out of date as a ruff. This is because small car companies have no robots. There isn't the money for relentless testing of every component in every corner of the world. The car must be designed on an Amstrad and put together by a man in a brown store-coat. And saying a car is hand-built is just another way of saying the glove box lid won't shut properly.

Take the Lotus Elise. It squeaks. It rattles. It drones. It vibrates. It's hard to get into and impossible to get out of. It's badly equipped and hard to operate. All of this might have been acceptable thirteen years ago when the Elise first came out and it might be acceptable today if it were the last word in zip and vigour.

But it isn't. Compared with even a Golf, it feels old and slow and understeery. It's a twentieth-century car in a twenty-first-century world where last Friday is already last year. And the last new car Lotus made, the Europa, was even worse.

That's why I wasn't looking forward to driving the new Evora. I knew it would smell of glue, give me cramp and fall to pieces, because Lotus, up there in the turnips, simply doesn't have the sort of bang-on, bang-up-to-date production line that makes modern mass-produced cars such engineering marvels (except Peugeots, obviously).

I was in for a bit of a shock. No. I was in for a lot of a shock. I was in for so much of a shock, in fact, I had to have a little lie down.

First of all, the bad news. Because it was designed on an Amstrad in someone's mum's bedroom, there are mistakes. All you can see in the windscreen is a reflection of the dashboard and all you can see on the ancillary dials is a reflection of whatever weather happens to be prevailing at the time.

What's more, the buttons are all carefully placed to ensure you can neither see nor find them. And even if you do, they have plainly been labelled by someone who was mad, or four.

Then you have the Alpine sat nav-cum-multimedia interface wotsit in the dash. Why didn't Lotus develop its own box of tricks instead of fitting one that's designed for youths in Citroën Saxos? Simple. It didn't have the resources.

And so, you get a system that speaks. And what it says is, 'You are breaking the speed limit,' every time you go near the throttle. This is very annoying, but happily there is a solution. Because it speaks only once, at the moment you stray over the limit, you should accelerate as quickly as possible to beyond the speed limit and then stay there all day.

The other solution is to turn it off. Which is impossible. Because I'm forty-nine. And a man. So I won't look things up in instruction books. Or listen to my wife, who said she knew how. Because I know best.

As you can see, then, the Evora features many things to cause much wailing and gnashing of teeth. So the car would have to be very good or very cheap to make those problems worth tolerating. And here's the thing. It's both. The 3.5-litre Toyota V6 is not the most powerful engine in the world but it's smooth – and refined – and the power it produces is delightfully seamless. There's no sudden savagery. No 'Oh my God, I'm going to crash now.' It's brilliant.

So's the packaging. Normally, a mid-engined four-seater car looks all wrong. The Ferrari Mondial springs to mind here. But the Evora is bang on. It really is a genuine surprise when you've studied the nicely proportioned exterior to find there are two seats in the back. And a dribble of legroom, too, provided the driver isn't too tall.

And speaking of tall, the front is a revelation. I could get in easily. I could get out without crawling. Inside, I didn't even need to have the seat fully back. Anyone up to 6 feet 7 inches is going to fit in an Evora and that alone makes it special.

Especially when I tell you the boot, which is at the back, where it should be, is big enough for two sets of golf clubs.

So, the driving. Sadly, I didn't have much chance to really push it – the weather was horrendous and time was tight – but I put in enough miles to know this car has great steering and handles well. Of course it does. It's a Lotus. And because it's a Lotus, it'll crash and jar and lurch from pothole to speed bump.

Wrong. It simply glided over absolutely everything a torrential rainstorm and Britain's B roads could throw at it. There is no other mid-engined supercar that has ever been so compliant. Or refined. Or quiet. It's amazing. It doesn't feel like it was made in a shed in Norfolk. It feels like it was made yesterday, by a machine.

The Evora, then, is not a car you buy because it's a Lotus and you have always fancied one. It's a car you buy because you want a comfortable, practical, mid-engined supercar and no one else makes such a thing. Not Ferrari. Not Lamborghini. Not anyone.

As I wafted from corner to corner, gradually forgetting about the smell of the glue they used to hold the chassis together, and the reflections, and the silly sat nav, I started guessing how much this car might cost. I reckoned on somewhere around £60,000. I was wrong. It's less than fifty.

And that's what makes this the most modern car of them all. It's the first to come to the market with a deflationary price tag.

3 May 2009

No, fatty, you do not give me the horn

Citroën C3 Picasso 1.6HDi 110 Exclusive

In a car, lightness is everything. Too much fat blunts acceleration, ruins the handling, spoils the fuel economy, affects the composition of gases in the planet's upper atmosphere and generally makes everyone miserable.

Everyone from Lewis Hamilton to Jonathon Porritt wants lighter cars but every single year every single new car is a tiny bit heavier than the one it replaces. The family saloons from my youth weighed less than a ton. Today, most tip the scales at nearly twice that. And some cars are now so obese that if you attach a trailer and go a bit bonkers at the garden centre, you need an HGV licence to get them home again.

Mostly, it's your fault. You demand more equipment, which means the dash has to be laden down with stuff even Raymond Baxter failed to see on the horizon. Satellite navigation, parking sensors, rear-view cameras, and so on. You also demand better soundproofing, thicker carpets and more leathery seats.

Then there's the question of safety. In order to achieve the coveted Euro NCAP five-star rating, cars must be made from a latticework of high-tensile cross-members and fitted with airbags for your face, shoulders, knees, ears and in some cars even your testicles. Although, frankly, I'd rather have mine smashed off than have an explosive balloon wallop into them at 250mph.

The upshot is simple. Even a plastic Lotus Elise that is built on the Colin Chapman principles of 'simply add lightness' weighs more than a 1973 Triumph Dolomite, which came at you with a wooden dashboard, squidgy seats, pig-iron wings, a vinyl roof and opening quarterlights.

Obviously, this can't go on. If we are to have cars that sip petrol like Jane Austen sipped tea and accelerate like a scalded cock, something has to be sacrificed.

But what? Now that the government has made it crystal clear that no one should ever die of anything ever, we can't go back to the old days when cars were made from spit, spikes and Kleenex.

So, let us look at the fixtures and fittings. What are you prepared to lose? Air-conditioning? No chance. Nobody wants to go back to the days when you were suffocated by your own armpits. And anyway, on a warm day the only way of staying fresh without air-con is to drive with the window down, which completely negates the advantages of losing the cooling system.

Sat nav? These systems get a lot of bad press but for every dimwit who follows the onboard instructions to drive over a cliff or into a pensioner's bungalow, there are a million people arriving smoothly at their destinations. Lose the guidance and you end up lost, driving around for hours, using all the fuel that's been saved by the hole in the dash. And then, when you sneak a look at the road map, you will crash and be killed.

Yesterday, while negotiating the Oxford ring road, I was thinking quite hard about what could be lost from the modern car when – whoa – a Peugeot full of three overweight teenage girls lunged across all three lanes and I used a feature I'm pretty sure I have not used in the past twenty years of motoring. The horn.

It was not a blast. It was a pip. But nevertheless, the reaction from the fatties was extraordinary. Instead of waving an apologetic hand, the driver and her enormous mates turned round as one and at the next set of lights unleashed a torrent of abuse so vitriolic and so profane that even my headlights blushed.

This, I understand, is quite normal. Because if you blow your horn, what you are saying to the offending motorist is, 'You are not a very good driver.' Which is the same as saying, 'You have an impossibly small penis and all your children are as ugly as they are stupid.' As a result, you will unleash in even the most mild-mannered soul a stream of pure, unadulterated, naked bile. I bet a pip could cause even Ann Widdecombe to use the c-word.

The horn, then, causes more civil unrest than a poll tax riot and, to make matters worse, as a device for avoiding accidents it is completely useless. No, really. When a car pulls out of a side turning into your path, you can do one of many things. You can scream. You can permit a bit of wee to come out. You can freeze. Or you can brake. Who thinks, 'Oh no. A car has pulled out of that side turning and a collision is imminent so I must immediately find the horn button to signal some displeasure at my imminent death'? No one.

The horn, therefore, is only fitted to signal your anger after the collision has been avoided. It is, therefore, a tool for retribution, and retribution, as we know, is the last refuge of the weak.

In other countries a horn is much more than this, of course. I noticed on my recent trip to Barbados that it is used there to suggest you've recognized a driver going the other way. And since everyone on a small Caribbean island knows everyone else, it is a more prolific sound over there than the crickets.

In Rome it is used in traffic jams to alleviate boredom. In large parts of Africa it is used to clear the road of peasants and ducks so that you can blast through the village at full speed. And in France it is used to drown out the awful noises coming from the radio.

That, obviously, is why the Citroën C3 Picasso that I drove recently is fitted with such a thing. But then it's also fitted with all sorts of other stuff that in Britain we don't really need.

Let us start at the front, where we find a bluff nose designed to make any impact with a pedestrian soft and comfortable. The problem with this is that if you have a tall nose the whole car is going to end up being bigger than necessary. Bigger. Heavier. Slower. More wasteful of fuel. And all because under new government regulations no pedestrian is allowed to die, even if they are drunk and stagger into the path of a speeding car.

Whatever, the Picasso is a much bigger car than the C3 on which it is based, and that does mean you get bags of space on the inside. This is filled on expensive models with such things as airline-style seats in the back (think Easyjet rather than Cathay Pacific) and a huge and heavy glass roof that gives you some impression of what it might be like to be a goldfish.

Then there's the perfume dispenser. It's fitted as standard to all models. I can think of nothing to say about this.

Except that the Citroën is heavy. So heavy that the diesel model I drove takes nearly 13 seconds to get from 0 to 60, it uses more fuel than rivals from Nissan and Renault and it's blessed with handling so questionable that the optional traction control can be disengaged only at less than 32mph.

Of course, obesity is a problem that affects all cars, so

now let's move on to a problem that's unique to the Citroën. The driving position. It may work if you are French, or an orang-utan, but for a human being the seat simply doesn't go back far enough.

Frankly, this car is hammered by the Skoda Roomster, which offers more space, as much power and more speed for less money. To buy the Citroën, then, you'd have to be as much of a mentalist as the artist after which it's named.

10 May 2009

It's the eco-nut's roughest, itchiest hair shirt

Honda Insight 1.3 IMA SE Hybrid

Much has been written about the Insight, Honda's new low-priced hybrid. We've been told how much carbon dioxide it produces, how its dashboard encourages frugal driving by glowing green when you're easy on the throttle and how it is the dawn of all things. The beginning of days.

So far, though, you have not been told what it's like as a car; as a tool for moving you, your friends and your things from place to place.

So here goes. It's terrible. Biblically terrible. Possibly the worst new car money can buy. It's the first car I've ever considered crashing into a tree, on purpose, so I didn't have to drive it any more.

The biggest problem, and it's taken me a while to work this out, because all the other problems are so vast and so cancerous, is the gearbox. For reasons known only to itself, Honda has fitted the Insight with something called constantly variable transmission (CVT).

It doesn't work. Put your foot down in a normal car and the revs climb in tandem with the speed. In a CVT car, the revs spool up quickly and then the speed rises to match them. It feels like the clutch is slipping. It feels horrid.

And the sound is worse. The Honda's petrol engine is a much-shaved, built-for-economy, low-friction 1.3 that, at full chat, makes a noise worse than someone else's crying baby on an airliner. It's worse than the sound of your parachute failing to open. Really, to get an idea of how awful it is, you'd have to sit a dog on a ham slicer.

So you're sitting there with the engine screaming its head off, and your ears bleeding, and you're doing only 23mph because that's about the top speed, and you're thinking things can't get any worse, and then they do because you run over a small piece of grit.

Because the Honda has two motors, one that runs on petrol and one that runs on batteries, it is more expensive to make than a car that has one. But, since the whole point of this car is that it could be sold for less than Toyota's Smugmobile, the engineers have plainly peeled the suspension components to the bone. The result is a ride that beggars belief.

There's more. Normally, Hondas feel as though they have been screwed together by eye surgeons. This one, however, feels as if it's been made from steel so thin, you could read through it. And the seats, finished in pleblon, are designed specifically, it seems, to ruin your skeleton. This is hairy-shirted eco-ism at its very worst.

However, as a result of all this, prices start at £15,490 – that's £3,000 or so less than the cost of the Prius. But at least with the Toyota there is no indication that you're driving a car with two motors. In the Insight you are constantly reminded, not only by the idiotic dashboard, which shows leaves growing on a tree when you ease off the throttle (pass the sick bucket), but by the noise and the ride and the seats. And also by the hybrid system Honda has fitted.

In a Prius the electric motor can, though almost never does, power the car on its own. In the Honda the electric motor is designed to 'assist' the petrol engine, providing more get-up-and-go when the need arises. The net result is this: in a Prius the transformation from electricity to petrol is subtle. In the Honda there are all sorts of jerks and clunks.

And for what? For sure, you could get 60 or more mpg if you were careful. And that's not bad for a spacious five-door hatchback. But for the same money you could have a Golf diesel, which will be even more economical. And hasn't been built out of rice paper to keep costs down.

Of course, I am well aware that there are a great many people in the world who believe that the burning of fossil fuels will one day kill all the Dutch and that something must be done.

They will see the poor ride, the woeful performance, the awful noise and the spine-bending seats as a price worth paying. But what about the eco-cost of building the car in the first place?

Honda has produced a graph that seems to suggest that making the Insight is only marginally more energy-hungry than making a normal car. And that the slight difference is more than negated by the resultant fuel savings.

Hmmm. I would not accuse Honda of telling porkies. That would be foolish. But I cannot see how making a car with two motors costs the same in terms of resources as making a car with one.

The nickel for the battery has to come from somewhere. Canada, usually. It has to be shipped to Japan, not on a sailing boat, I presume. And then it must be converted, not in a tree house, into a battery, and then that battery must be transported, not on an ox cart, to the Insight production plant in Suzuka. And then the finished car has to be shipped, not by Thor Heyerdahl, to Britain, where it can be transported, not by wind, to the home of a man with a beard who thinks he's doing the world a favour.

Why doesn't he just buy a Range Rover, which is made from local components, just down the road? No, really – weird-beards buy locally produced meat and vegetables for eco-reasons. So why not apply the same logic to cars?

At this point you will probably dismiss what I'm saying as the rantings of a petrolhead, and think that I have my head in the sand.

That's not true. While I have yet to be convinced that man's 3 per cent contribution to the planet's greenhouse gases affects the climate, I do recognize that oil is a finite resource and that as it becomes more scarce, the political ramifications could well be dire. I therefore absolutely accept the urgent need for alternative fuels.

But let me be clear that hybrid cars are designed solely to milk the guilt genes of the smug and the foolish. And that pure electric cars, such as the G-Wiz and the Tesla, don't work at all because they are just too inconvenient.

Since about 1917 the car industry has not had a techno-logical revolution – unlike, say, the world of communications or film. There has never been a 3G moment at Peugeot, nor a need to embrace DVD at Nissan. There has been no VHS/Betamax battle between Fiat and Renault.

Car makers, then, have had nearly a century to develop and hone the principles of suck, squeeze, bang, blow. And they have become very good at it.

But now comes the need to throw away the heart of the beast, the internal combustion engine, and start again. And, critically, the first of the new cars with their new power systems must be better than the last of the old ones. Or no one will buy them. That's a tall order. That's like dragging Didier Drogba onto a cricket pitch and expecting him to be better than Ian Botham.

And here's the kicker. That's exactly what Honda has done with its other eco-car, the Clarity. Instead of using a petrol engine to charge up the electric motor's batteries, as happens on the Insight, the Clarity uses hydrogen: the most abundant gas in the universe.

The only waste product is water. The car feels like a car. And, best of all, the power it produces is so enormous, it can be used by day to get you to 120mph and by night to run all the electrical appliances in your house. This is not science fiction. There is a fleet of Claritys running around California right now.

There are problems to be overcome. Making hydrogen is a fuel-hungry process, and there is no infrastructure. But Alexander Fleming didn't look at his mould and think, 'Oh dear, no one will put that in their mouth,' and give up.

I would have hoped, therefore, that Honda had diverted every penny it had into making hydrogen work, rather than stopping off on the way to make a half-arsed halfway house for fools and madmen.

The only hope I have is that there are enough fools and madmen out there who will buy an Insight to look sanctimonious outside the school gates. And that the cash this generates can be used to develop something a bit more constructive.

17 May 2009

Enough power to restart a planet

Audi Q7 V12 TDI Quattro

I bring news of a worrying development. People have begun to drive much more slowly. Some will argue that this is because speed cameras are doing their job. And they probably have a point. When you have nine points on your licence you quickly discover a terror of ever going faster than 14mph. And these days almost everyone I know has nine points on their licence. And those who don't will have by Wednesday morning.

There is, however, another reason people are slowing down. It began last year when we thought we were giving all our money to the oil companies. But it's really caught on now it's turned out we were actually giving it all to the banks.

When you are frightened that you will lose your job, you need to look after the pennies. And driving around at forty, rather than seventy, is a good idea. Driving economically – or hypermiling as the Americans call it – will cost you a little time but save you a lot of money. Seriously. If I drive normally, it costs around £50 in fuel to get my Mercedes to London and back. If I drive carefully, it's around £35.

Of course, if you have someone who is on nine points, and is also frightened of losing their job, you end up with a car that is travelling so slowly you would need at least seven fixed points in space to determine that it is moving at all.

And if they happen to have a Hyundai, or a Kia or one of those Rextons, which is made by a company you've never heard of in a country you couldn't place on a map, then their speed will not be measurable at all.

This is because cars made by companies that earn most of their profits from shipping and cutting down forests, and have an automotive division only because it's good for the local economy, are almost always rubbish.

No, really. A car made for someone who just yesterday was going to work on an ox will be of no use to people who were brought up on a diet of Ford Mustangs. Cars made for southeast Asia and Africa are tools. And so are the people in this country who buy them.

Whatever, the nationwide slowdown has met with a great deal of cheering from many quarters. The quarters you wouldn't want to have round for dinner. Indeed, the comedian David Mitchell, writing recently in a newspaper you don't take, said he welcomed it and that soon the petrolheads would just have to get used to the fact.

He's quite wrong. The petrolheads will not get used to it. They will swear and curse and overtake the slowcoaches in dangerous places and there will be many more accidents and the only people who will benefit are transplant surgeons.

The only way you will get everyone to stick to the speed limits is by forcing them to do it. Physically, with satellite guidance. The technology is with us now. It's operational. So all that's missing is a government mad enough to impose the legislation. Which is why we can thank God this lot have only months to run.

I do not believe cars should be slowed down by Westminster's expenses department. Because what's next? Foodies being forced to become vegetarians to stop the climate changing? The Archbishop of Canterbury being forced to switch to Muslimism to stop the bloodshed? Come off it.

The eco-worms really do seem to think that if they ban smoking, force everyone to wear a high-visibility jacket and impose a blanket 40mph speed limit, no one will ever die. But we all will, of something, one day. If you get up in a morning, you must accept that your head may come off in an accident and there's absolutely nothing you, or anyone else, can do about it.

I'm not suggesting that we all have a God-given right to drive as fast as we like. I'm not suggesting we all tear through villages, blowing the horn at peasants and running them down if they don't move out of the way quickly enough. I am not a Toad. But I am suggesting that when you lead a busy life, it is important to get journeys over with as quickly as possible.

Eco-weeds argue that the busy life must be banned, too. They think the world will be a better place if we all get up, have lunch, drive our electric Hyundai very slowly back to the office for a snooze and then go home to make wooden puzzles with our children.

Well, if they want to live like that, fine. But I don't. I like spur-of-the-moment decisions to see friends in London and squeezing in a meeting in Pontefract at three before picking up the kids in Oxford at four. I like the buzz. I like the action. I like to think I have only one life but I'm getting three out of it. And that's why I drive a 500 horsepower Mercedes.

And because I drive it quickly, I pay attention, and because I pay attention, I see speed cameras. And because I see them, I have time to slow down, and because of that I have a clean driving licence. And the people in eco-Hyundais, dawdling about in a dream, don't.

There. That's fate tempted, and now we shall move on to this morning's car. The Audi Q7 V12 diesel.

I am no fan of the Audi Q7. It is bread-bin ugly and despite its enormous size it's so small inside that you are faced with a simple choice. Leave the dogs at home. Or the kids. Unlike a Volvo XC90, it cannot do both. However, to worry about tedious practical issues in this particular model is like worrying about what sort of golf clubs Alan Shepard used when teeing off on the moon.

That's because this is the first road car ever to be fitted with a V12 diesel. It produces 493 horsepowers – more than any other diesel – and 738 torques. That's about 160 more than you get from a McLaren SLR: 738 torques is enough to restart a dead planet.

You would imagine that with such an engine lurking under the bonnet it would be impossible to drive. Nope. The herculean torque is sent quietly and with no fuss to each of the four wheels. All is consequently docile and benign. And you begin to wonder why anyone might spend more than £94,000 on such a thing when for around half as much they could have the V8 petrol version instead. It's not like the diesel is going to elicit any thank-you letters from Johnny Polar Bear. And it's not notably more economical either.

And then . . .

It had been a busy morning. I'd written a newspaper column, dropped in at a friend's house to shoot some magpies and then I had to get to the *Top Gear* test track, ninety miles away in Surrey, to shoot a Ford Focus.

Several miles out, I hooked onto the back of a motorbike. It was a Suzuki Hayabusa GSX1300R and it had such a hideous rear end that I decided I should overtake it as soon as possible. But the rider was having none of that. So off he went.

Except he didn't. No matter what the poor chap did on

that twisting, turning road, he simply could not pull out any notable lead on the big, 2½-ton diesel-powered monster. You might be thinking, if you are a motorcyclist, that the rider must have been useless – and you may have a point since it turned out to be Richard Hammond – but you are missing the point.

Even a fast bike, and few are faster than this ghastly Suzuki when ridden by a normal person or that mad-eyed Italian, cannot pull away from the Q7 diesel. And there is something deeply, gooily satisfying about that.

It is a hysterical car, this. Mad. Bonkers. Stupid. It sits on the road network like a Class-1 powerboat would sit at the Henley regatta. Of course, it is also utterly pointless. No one is going to buy a lumbering Q7 for outright speed.

However, let us not dwell on such things. Let us instead rejoice at the fact that it exists. It's crap. But it's brilliant, too. I don't want one. But I don't want to live in a world where I never had the choice in the first place.

24 May 2009

Ghastly but lovable, the Vauxhall VXR8 Bathurst S is vulgar, terrible but ridiculously exciting

Vauxhall VXR8 Bathurst S

It was late, dark, cold and pouring down. But even though I was soaking wet, I simply couldn't get into the car you see photographed this morning. My wife was screaming at me, saying the rain was ruining her hair and making her dress see-through and would I please stop being so stupid and just unlock the damn doors. But I couldn't because it would have been just too embarrassing.

Had I been at the annual general meeting of the Ray Winstone Appreciation Society, then things would have been fine. I would have been proud of the car's gigantism, and its black bonnet stripes and its flared wheel arches and its own-brand badge. But I was outside the New Theatre in Oxford, and Oxford theatre crowds, with their mad hair and their cycling helmets and their hairy sports jackets, really don't take kindly to cars like this. Or the people who drive them. Especially as it sported the numberplate DE51RED.

Frankly, ATW4T would have been less blushingly awful. So I stood there pretending it wasn't mine until they'd all wobbled off on their stupid foldaway bicycles.

Things were a bit quiet on the way home, and they remained that way until, with just two miles to go, the engine coughed. I thought at first I'd fluffed a gearchange. But then it coughed again. And then it ran out of fuel. And it didn't matter how much I pointed defensively at the gauge, which showed I had a quarter of a tank left; the facts were these. It was the middle of the night. It was the middle of nowhere. And the raindrops were now as big as rabbits.

So the Vauxhall VXR8 Bathurst S did not get off to a good start. It had made me very wet, then it had made me very angry and now it was in the process of making me very divorced. So what is it, then, this tattooed bouncer with a neck like a birthday cake and, you suspect, a pickaxe handle down its trousers?

Well, in short, it's the result of an Australian civil war. In Oz, everyone is either a supporter of Holden, part of General Motors, or a supporter of Ford. Oh sure, there are solicitors and accountants who will claim they are above such nonsense, but when pressed they will say, 'Of course, I'm a GM man by birth and I would never allow a Ford onto my drive because . . .' – and at this point they start to get a bit red in the face – 'they are all raving poofters and . . .' – by this stage they will be banging the table – 'I hate them. I would gladly lay down my life and the lives of my children for Holden and I will kill anyone with a hammer if they disagree.'

At the Bathurst race from which this limited-edition Vauxhall takes its name, there are pitched battles between gangs of Ford and GM fans. Proper bike-chains-and-flamethrower, Hell's Angel-type stuff. And the only time they ever came together was when a chap called Jim Richards won in a Nissan Skyline. Such was the torrent of catcalls as he climbed onto the podium, he leant into the microphone and called the entire crowd 'a pack of arseholes'.

That's the background from which this big Vauxhall comes. A rough, partisan sink estate, where there are no women and even the spiders are frightened. It's a car deliberately built to be uncouth. To stick its face into anything Ford might do by way of response. It's designed to keep those bike chains whirling.

Strangely, however, it's not actually Australian. It's built there but it was engineered by a Scotchman called Tom Walkinshaw. So since he's a neighbour I thought I'd go to see how on earth such a quiet, reserved chap could possibly have come up with something so . . . wilfully ocker.

It's easy to find his house. You go left at Alex James's agreeable cheesery, straight on past David Cameron's delightful wisteria, right by Ben Kingsley's lovely gable ends and through the dry-stone walls that mark the entrance. But I didn't want to go past all those places – and people – in a car with stripes and DE51RED written on the back. So I stayed at home.

The next day I was due for lunch at a friend's house. And I decided that since he lives down a long private drive, it would be okay to turn up in what was essentially a bull-necked version of Crocodile Dundee. But, for no reason, the battery was flat and it wouldn't start. So I went in a Range Rover. As did everyone else.

Eventually, though, when it was dark and the nation was asleep, I did sneak out to see what on earth this car was like. And I found after a very short space of time it was like being in 1978. There is no refinement at all. When you dip the clutch pedal to change gear, you can feel and hear the entire driveline moving around. Something I haven't felt to anything like this degree since the Chevette HS went west.

Then there's the steering wheel. It's made from the cheapest plastic in the world and has a diameter exactly an eighth of an inch bigger than the outer ring round Saturn. You don't steer this car. You flail.

And finally there's the noise. Oh. My. God. There has never been a car that sounds like this. Not ever. Obviously the V8, lifted straight from the latest generation of Corvette, is quite a noisy thing, but when you accelerate you don't hear it at all. What you hear is the supercharger. It's not a whine or a whistle, as you might expect. It's as though someone is feeding a million squirrels into an industrial wood chipper.

It is a deafening sound and it's at a pitch that could shatter Katherine Jenkins' hair. So after a while you can take no more and you lift off, whereupon you are treated to the sound of distant artillery fire as traces of unburnt fuel ignite in the exhaust's tailpipe. It is the most glorious noise in the world.

So you find yourself gritting your teeth through the squirrel-mincing phase and then sitting there, with your foot off the throttle, waiting for the revs to drop to 1800, when the sound of far-off warfare comes.

There are other good things too. For something that produces an almost insane 564 horsepower, it is surprisingly easy to drive. You put your foot down, the squirrels die, and you expect you're going to spend the next five minutes wrestling with the ship's wheel, trying to keep in a straight line.

But no. It just squats and goes. And it's not like it's being held in check by all sorts of clever stability controls. All you get is traction control that is on, or off. And that's it.

Of course, it is a very big car. So massive, in fact, that very often those on the left-hand side are going through quite different weather from those on the right. And the people in the back are still in bed. But as a result of this vastness, there is room to lounge, and space in the boot for several grandfather clocks. It's got a good ride too.

Equipment? Yes, it's got some but not much, and the little there was didn't work.

And you know what? I didn't care. I'm ashamed to admit I loved this car. Yes, it's vulgar and terrible but it's almost ridiculously exciting and there is no other car that offers this much space and this much power for less.

So you go ahead. You buy yourself a BMW M3 instead. In the meantime, I'm going to join the Ray Winstone Appreciation Society. And go to its meetings, in Spain, in what can only be described as the real sexy beast. Ghastly but utterly, utterly lovable.

31 May 2009

Oh please, angel, Daddy wants a go now

Toyota Urban Cruiser 1.33 VVT-i

My daughter has just bought her first car. Ordinarily this would be no big deal. All daughters buy a first car at some point. But the daughter I'm talking about is only ten years old.

She did the right thing: saved her pocket money, pretended to believe in the tooth fairy and hoarded cheques from her grandmother until she had £50. Enough to buy an M-registered Ford Fiesta 1.3 with a radio that doesn't work, no MoT, wind-down windows and the ultimate 1980s luxury – a lift-out sunshine roof.

Of course, when the time comes, she'll be able to part-exchange it and get £2,000 from Cash Gordon but until then she'll be using it in our paddock. Getting all the 'need for speed' out of her system so that when she's old enough to go on the roads, she won't end up in a tree or, like her dad, on television, endlessly going round corners, shouting.

Obviously, the job of teaching her how to drive it fell to me, but before we could actually set off, we had to have a lesson in how to get an M-registered Ford Fiesta going. This involves a lot of looking under the stairs and in all the kitchen cabinets, shouting, 'Where are the bloody jump leads?'

Soon, though, as the poor child's enthusiasm waned, we had the bonnet up and the leads connected and we were treated to the unmistakable sound of a starter motor clicking uselessly. 'This is your first lesson, darling. All jump leads, no matter how much you spend, don't work.'

We were therefore faced with the prospect of a bump start. And there's a dilemma if ever you've seen one. Do you put a ten-year-old child, who has never driven a car, in the driving seat and do the pushing yourself? Or do you get behind the wheel and expect her to push a ton of metal?

In fact, what you do is go back to shouting at the jump leads and making sparks until eventually, usually after about three hours, the little Ford's rusty old 1.3 will cough into life.

And so it begins. 'Right, sweetheart. I want you to let your foot off the clutch pedal very smoothly and very slowly while keeping the revs up with the throttle pedal. Okay. Okay. That's good. Oh, never mind. You've stalled. Doesn't matter, darling. Don't cry. Everyone stalls when they first learn. Just turn the key and let's start again . . .'

But, of course, we couldn't start again because the battery was still flat. Which meant I had to charge it up, which is why I spent an hour last Bank Holiday Monday driving round and round our paddock in a £50 Ford Fiesta.

God, it was fun. I pounded my way round so often that soon a circuit began to form in the long grass, and then, as I pounded some more, I started to experiment with the hand-brake and the apexes . . . and the stopwatch.

My daughter, I'm afraid, learnt nothing at all during this time. She just sat in the passenger seat, bouncing. But I learnt, once again, that anything with an internal combustion engine gives you just the biggest adrenaline rush when you remove it from the clutches of the authorities. Behaving yourself in a Ferrari simply cannot be as much of a laugh as running wild in a small half-broken Ford in a field full of buttercups.

Once, I spent two weeks in an upmarket hotel, dining

three times a day on exotic seafood in unusual sauces. It was great. But by the time the holiday ended, I wanted a cauliflower. I wanted a chicken leg, cold, with some sandwich spread. I would have torn out my own eyes for a poached egg on toast.

What's more, exotic cars, with their flappy paddles and their five-way traction control systems and their switchable throttle responses, have a habit of masking the purity of the simple internal combustion that lies within. I feel this with the 6-series BMW and the Mercedes CL, especially. The basic ingredients might be fresh and superb but all you ever taste is the electronic sauce.

That old Ford Fiesta and the freedom of a paddock rekindled the love I have for cars and the need to get back to basics. So let me introduce you to the subject of this morning's missive: the Toyota Urban Cruiser.

Obviously, this is a very stupid name. Urban Cruiser makes it sound like a predatory homosexual, stalking inner-city lavatories at night in search of some George Michaelism. The test car I drove reinforced this by being purple.

Whatever, it is designed for the city – and that's stupid too. Because, in my experience, urbanites go to work on a bus or the Tube and then use their car to go somewhere far away at the weekend. And, trust me on this, the Urban Cruiser is not going to get you very far at all before you are overcome by a need to step outside and commit suicide.

The problem is the 1.3-litre engine, which develops such a small amount of power that by the time you reach the end of the motorway slip road you are doing only 56mph – the same speed as all the trucks on the inside lane. Which means you are faced with a choice: pull out and be crushed, or brake and spend the rest of your life sitting there waiting for the

200-mile gap this car needs to pull out safely. It's idiotically slow. Dangerously slow.

It also suffers from the same problems that afflicted the Citroën C3 Picasso that I didn't like on these pages a few weeks ago. In short, it's a normal little hatchback with a boxy body dumped on top. What's the point? Unless you have a job delivering hat stands.

You end up with something that has the same number of seats but is worse to drive, more thirsty and slower than the small car on which it's based. The Yaris, in this case.

And here's the clincher. The Urban Cruiser, with no sat nav and pleblon seats, costs £14,500. That makes it more expensive – much more expensive – than a Mini or the normal Yaris, which isn't exactly bargain basement in the first place.

And yet, perhaps because I was in the mood for some broad beans in a parsley sauce, rather than a boned pigeon in a reduction of some kind, I rather enjoyed my time with the Cruiser.

The optional satellite navigation system was easy to use, the trim felt durable and there were seven airbags to help out if I hit a bus shelter. What's more, the bonnet is designed to be soft and comfy if it crashes into a person, and even the wiper bracket is designed to disintegrate if it comes into contact with the skull of someone who had been a pedestrian until he was launched into the air by the duvet draped over the engine.

Mind you, a better and even more comfortable way of not being hurt by this car is simply to stroll out of its way.

From behind the wheel, things are better still. If you join motorways at their source rather than via a slip road and if you avoid built-up areas, where people laugh openly at the name, it is possible to enjoy this car. It steers nicely and bounces like a small dog when pushed.

And in a paddock, it's a hoot. It even has air-conditioning to prevent you from getting hay fever in the long grass.

But is it better, really, than my daughter's Fiesta? The short answer is no. Because when it comes to small cars, what you really want is small bills. And truth be told, they don't come much smaller than fifty quid.

7 June 2009

You'll really stand out – for paying too much

Mini Cooper S Convertible

If you are a television detective, then it makes sense to have a classic car of some sort because you never actually need to drive it anywhere. A production team runner does that, and then you simply drop into the driving seat to pull up stylishly outside the murderer's house.

If you were a real detective, your chief constable would want a word in your ear if you insisted on using a MkII Jaguar or a Triumph with running boards. 'Look, Bergerorse. This is the third murder on the trot where you failed to catch the baddie because your car broke down. Now stop being so stupid and use one of the Astra diesels like everyone else.'

While doing the school run this morning, I saw a chap in a mustard yellow Volvo P1800. Presumably, he was on his way to work. Definitely, he wouldn't get there.

All of the things you take for granted in your Renault or your Ford — brakes that slow the car down, heating that works, electric windows, power steering – none of it is fitted to the Volvo. Plus, you know what happens when a cliff has been exposed to the wind for long enough. So can you imagine what a piston will be like after it's spent twenty-five years headbutting a hundred billion explosions. It'll be like a pebble.

This means there will be no compression, which means you will have a top speed of one. You'd go faster if you got out and pushed. And you'll be doing that a lot with your Volvo because the alternator won't work.

The only good news about this is that by modern standards the P1800 is extremely light. And that's because it has virtually no safety features. A point that will become blindingly obvious should you ever reach two and hit a tree.

Classic cars are all rubbish. My Mercedes Grosser is rubbish. The Ferrari 250 GTO is rubbish. Even a Lancia Stratos is rubbish. They are typewriters in a computerized world. So why would anyone choose to buy such a thing?

Simple. Anyone who has a classic car hates his wife.

Our friend in the Volvo P1800 is almost certainly a branch secretary of the owners' club. He will have written to his old school magazine about the appointment and he will spend many hours at night trawling the internet for interesting Volvo titbits. This means he doesn't have to sit anywhere near his wife of an evening.

When the club meets, he gets to go away for a whole weekend. With a bit of luck, he will break down on the way home and be forced to spend the night in a Travelodge. And that's excellent, too, because it means he doesn't have to sleep with her either.

Furthermore, by driving a 1972 mustard yellow car, he will be seen by other road users as someone a bit unusual. Perhaps someone who writes poetry for a living or is Kevin McCloud from *Grand Designs*. Consequently, women will give him their telephone numbers at the traffic lights. Or stop to help when he is sitting at the side of the road, exhausted from all the pushing, and looking a bit like Mr Darcy as a result.

Well that's what he thinks. But, of course, being a classic car enthusiast, he will be wearing shoes like Cornish pasties

and Rohan trousers and he will have trouble with his aden-
oids. Which means he won't look like Mr Darcy. He'll look
like Man at Millets. And as a result no women will give him
their numbers and soon he will stop typing 'volvo' into his
search engine at night and start typing 'vulva' instead.

This is the sad truth. Show me a man with a classic car,
and I'll show you a hard drive that the police would confis-
cate in a heartbeat.

The trouble is that all of us quite like the idea of owning
a classic. We fancy the idea of having something unusual in
our lives. We just don't want to be tarred with the Millets
brush and we don't want to break down every morning.

That's why I like the idea of limited-edition modern cars.
They used to be ten a penny, especially when dealers would
add some stripes, paint the door mirrors pink and call the
end result – which came with a £1,000 premium – the 'Car-
nival'.

Driving a car like this makes you all gooey because you
know you won't see another; but unlike a classic, it won't
arrive everywhere on the back of a lorry and you won't feel
compelled to join an owners' club.

I wonder sometimes why car makers don't do more limited
specials. The Prius 'Berk', with bark doors and seats made
from moss. The Audi 'Cheshire', with clamshell leatherette
upholstery and an onyx gearknob. The GM 'Bust', which has
no bodywork at all.

In the days of homologation, any manufacturer wishing
to enter rallying or saloon-car racing would be forced by the
rules to sell a small but finite number of that car to the public. As a result we got the Mitsubishi Evo, the Lancia Delta
Integrale and the Ford Sierra Cosworth RS500.

Even the Golf GTI was intended to be a limited edition

car when it first came out. But these days? Er . . . Renault
occasionally fits a hatchback with polythene windows and
sells it as a special but that's about it. Which means that if
you want something different, you are forced into the steamy
bri-nylon world of old Volvo P1800s.

And that brings us on to a small batch of Minis that were
made to commemorate the car's fiftieth birthday.

I can't see that there was much to celebrate, frankly. Yes, it
was a brilliant little car back in 1959, but it should have been
updated in 1964. And because it wasn't, because they were
still making the same damn thing – usually at a loss, in a factory with a picket line – into the twenty-first century, the
company was eventually bought by BMW, who brought out
a new car, which, because it had almost the same wheelbase
as a Land Rover Discovery, was about as much of a Mini as
Julie Andrews' nun frock.

No matter, they've now launched some limited-run specials . . .

There is the Mini 50 Mayfair, which, I presume, comes
with gold teeth, a dishdasha and, instead of a radiator grille,
a nice beard. There's the Mini 50 Camden, which runs on grass
and only goes left, and there's the John Cooper Works World
Championship 50, which has some stripes.

I haven't driven any of those. What I've done is driven the
Mini Cooper S Convertible, which is now available with the
same turbocharged 1.6-litre engine that you get in a Peugeot
207 GTi and, soon, the Ford Fiesta.

It's a fine engine that produces not many carbon dioxides,
absolutely no turbo lag at all, unusually, and 172bhp. It
doesn't feel like that much. It certainly doesn't zing.

And then there's the hood. When it's up, you can detect a
bit of wobble, but when it's down, so the front and the back

are only connected by the floor, there's only one way to describe the feel. It's floppy.

Other problems? Well, visibility when the roof is up is woeful. It's like sitting in a postbox. The only people who can get in the back are those who have stepped on a bomb and the boot is miserable.

And yet, despite all this, it remains a great little car to own. Because the style – and there's tons of it – buries the substance, it doesn't feel, or look, like anything else on the road. You therefore get to stand out without actually being in a lay-by trying to make a fan belt from plaits of pubic hair. The only trouble is that the new Cooper S rag top costs £19,000. The car I tested with something called the Chili pack was £21,205. And I'm sorry, but if all you want to do is stand out while driving something new, it'd be impossible to ignore – or resist – the £13,605 Fiat 500 Abarth.

14 June 2009

The ultimate driving machine, or so I thought

BMW Z4 sDrive35i

As we know, stag nights are terrible things that cause perfectly normal men to be sick and push root vegetables up one another's bottoms. So imagine my delight when a friend announced recently that his stag do would be alcohol-free. 'Yippee,' I thought. 'I shall be able to come home with a full complement of pubic hair.' Then I discovered why there would be no drinking. Because it was a 'driving day'.

One of the other guests, a public-relations man of some repute, couldn't understand why I was so harrumphy. 'Well, dear boy. It would be a bit like inviting you to spend your day off pretending to like journalists. You'd be a bit harrumphy too.'

I'd heard all about these track days, of course, and none of what I'd heard was very encouraging. Rubbish cars on their last legs. Lots of cones. Two hours of safety lectures. Four hours of hanging around. Ten minutes of driving. Undrinkable tea. Wilting biscuits. And a million rules about overtaking, none of which says, 'And if the bastard doesn't move over, ram him.'

Happily, however, we went to Jonathan Palmer's gaff on an old airbase near Bedford, which is about six days away from everywhere else in the British Isles. Jonathan seems to know that people don't like waiting four hours to drive a Maestro. Which is why, five seconds after arriving, I was behind the wheel of a Caterham.

And then, after ten laps, we were whizzed in luggzury 4x4s to another track, where we did 'ten laps in some Renault Clio touring cars, and then it was Porsche 911s and then it was a funny sort of miniature Le Mans racer. And then we were dipped into Nomex, asked to put on some driving slippers and slotted into the single-seaters.

The instructor asked if I'd ever driven such a thing before. 'Of course I have,' I replied indignantly. 'I am a presenter on *Top Gear* and so I have driven everything.' But then I started to think. And realized that I hadn't. That's a bit like Jonathan Ross realizing one day he's never seen *Brief Encounter*.

Obviously, it wasn't a Formula One car, but it wasn't a puny Formula Ford either. It had slick tyres, a 3-litre Jaguar V6, a power-to-weight ratio of 500bhp per ton, a top speed of 170 and easily enough room in the cockpit for anyone up to 6 feet 3 inches. I'm taller than that but I've been cramped before in exotic cars so I wasn't even remotely worried about the drive that lay ahead. I should have been.

You hear motor sports commentators talking about the problems of cold tyres and you see all those mechanics draping the rubberwear with electric blankies to keep them warm and you think, 'Oh, don't be so silly. And stop weaving around like that. Cold tyres can't possibly make any difference.'

That's why I went barrelling into the first corner only to discover I had no grip at all. I'm not talking about the rear end being a bit skittish. Or the front washing out. I'm talking about the steering wheel being completely and utterly redundant. So into the grass I went.

Happily, because the track is in Bedford, you could spin for a thousand miles in any direction and not hit anything, so soon I was off again, imagining that I'd made a mistake of some sort. But no.

I crawled round the second corner because everyone else was facing in the wrong direction and made it all the way to the third, where I braked carefully, came down the sequential box, turned in gingerly and – whoa – spun again.

I simply do not know how those F1 boys get round the first lap at all. And, what's more, I don't really have much of a clue about how they do the second, either.

Because, having slithered and spun round the first lap, you slow right down because you simply don't trust the tyres to work. And that means they don't get hot.

It's catch-22. Go fast enough to warm them up and you spin. Go slow and you have to play the snail until the chequered flag comes down. After several laps, however, of eyebrow-matting concentration, I hit a pigeon. Which was a bit uncomfortable. For it.

Stopping was no easier. Brake at what you think is the right place and you will stop dead about 400 yards before the corner. A car this light has no real mass and, consequently, stops with a panache no road car can match. So you start to get cocky, braking later and later until, eventually, you will lock the fronts. When this happens in a normal car on normal tyres, there is much wailing and screeching. But in the single-seater, on slicks, there is no noise at all. For a while, you sit there, thinking all is well. Then you notice the smoke, and then you realize that you are heading straight for the pit wall at about a million.

Over the years, I have driven many cars, some of them very fast. And in my mind, this had prepared me for life in a proper racing car on proper racing tyres on a proper racing track. It hadn't, though. It's like spending your life hiring out donkeys on a beach and then imagining you could win the Grand National.

And then there's the question of g. F1 racing drivers talk about how they suffer from the effects of this, and I always feel compelled to drive to their houses and punch them in the face. Because the g they are talking about is lateral. And lateral g is for nancy boys.

In essence, the effects of g are felt in the form of blood moving around inside your body. In a fighter plane it moves up to your head in times of negative g – which makes you feel light-headed and sick – and down in times of positive g, which causes you to lose your peripheral vision and then die.

In a racing car it can move only laterally – from side to side. So it's not all in your head or all in your feet. It just sloshes from shoulder to shoulder. Which is no big deal . . . I've always thought.

You see, eventually I did start to push the single-seater, and it was a revelation. Because you can see the front tyres and because they have so much grip when they are warm, you can place the car precisely where you want it to be at speeds you would imagine were simply impossible. All these years, I've scoffed at racing drivers for dismissing all road cars as rubbish, but I began to see their point. I may have even whooped occasionally like an American. And then my neck started to hurt. And then the muscles in it turned to fat. And then, after a couple of laps, I couldn't hold my head up at all. When I got out of the car, it looked as though I'd been hanged. Lateral g, then, is unpleasant.

Which brings me to the BMW Z4. To a racing driver, who is used to slick tyres and fish-sharp reflexes, it's wallowy and slithery and horrid. But, to me, it's brilliant. Mostly, because you can drive for more than ten minutes without your head coming off.

I also liked the styling, the ride – provided you stay out of the sport settings – the engine's urgency, the fluidity of the responses and the elegance of the interior. Though, that said, this is not a car you can drive in cuff links. Because the centre console is set up for left-hand drive, every time you change gear your silver dog turd, or whatever, will hit the iDrive knob, which in extreme circumstances can cause the cabin to be filled with rap noises.

However, I've thought quite hard about this and can confidently say that the Z4, with its folding metal roof and softer feel, is now the best of the medium-sized sports cars. Certainly, I prefer it to the Boxster and the Mercedes SLK.

However, if it's a real driving experience you want, forget the ultimate driving machine. Because, as I now realize, it isn't.

21 June 2009

Strip poker in the . . .

Ford Focus RS

Would the Duke of Edinburgh ever buy a bright orange pair of trousers? Would your fourteen-year-old daughter wear a calf-length tweed skirt and a hand-knitted cardigan? Can you imagine Sir Ranulph Fiennes in a mankini?

The fact is this. A very, very small number of people choose to buy and wear an item of clothing because of the quality of its stitching or the way it hangs, even when hailing a cab. But mostly, people only wear what they think suits them.

People drive what they think suits them as well. A harassed woman, for instance, knows that her bird's-nest hair and nightie go well with a Volvo XC90. A woman with expensive hair on her head and none at all between her legs realizes that she can have nothing but a Range Rover. Red cheeks and overalls work with Mitsubishi's pick-up trucks. Lacy tops look right in a Peugeot. And the Audi and the Montblanc pen fit together as beautifully as the ladder and the Vauxhall Astra.

Naturally, this brings me on to the Ford Focus RS. Who does it suit? What person did Ford's marketing department have in mind when it said, 'Yes. Let's give it a wing the size of Tommy Sopwith's and wheel arches big enough to provide shelter for a herd of cows. And yes, again. Let's sell it with a choice of just three colours: lime green, Rooney blue and toilet white.'

Can you think of anyone who would wish to own such a thing? We know that Rio Ferdinand has a strange taste in shorts and that David Beckham is not averse to going out at night in a skirt. They would probably love a lime-green Ford with a Boeing appendage on the back. But top-flight footballers earn as much as £150,000 a week and will not therefore be interested in a £26,000 Ford.

I am aware, too, that small boys like cars such as this. But when they grow old enough to drive, they are also old enough to know it's a bit onyx; a bit Cheshire, a bit vulgar.

We know that Jonathan Ross has a pair of yellow training shoes. We also know he has a pink Ford Thunderbird. But would he want an RS? No. Nor would Stephen Fry, Susan Boyle, David Attenborough, Konnie Huq, Kirsty Young, Ian Hislop, Brian Ferry, Mick Jagger or Harry Potter.

No one would, because these days we know the rules. In the UK the *Daily Mail* regularly informs us that that anyone who earns more than £40,000 should be made to stand in the street and rub off their own face with a cheese grater.

That's why those who do buy Ferraris increasingly ask for them to be grey, and it's why the ivory-white Mercedes SL is not an everyday sighting. Because this is showing off. And showing off is bad.

There is no question, then, that if you want a smallish, fastish hatchback you are better off with a VW Golf GTI, which looks just like the diesel and, consequently, will not be smeared with dog dirt by the *Mail*'s Paul Dacre every morning. And that normally would be the end of that.

But it isn't, because underneath the vivid paintwork and behind the wall of crackling, sash-window-rattling noise coming out of the Ford's twin exhaust tunnels lie the sort of fun and games that the Golf GTI simply can't deliver. The

Volkswagen is a game of chess. The Focus is a game of strip poker.

Under the bonnet, beneath the snow-shoe heating ducts, there is a 2.5-litre five-cylinder Volvo engine. That does not sound like a particularly enticing starting point but you only have to look at how delightful it became in the Ford Focus ST to know that silk purses can be made from sows' udders.

And for the RS it has been given new pistons, a new management system, a new turbo – a new everything, really, so that the end result is a whopping 300bhp. That's nearly a hundred more than you get from the Golf. And that's before we get to the 325 torques: 119 more than you get from the Golf.

No one has ever put a 300bhp engine in a front-wheel-drive car before. Not that long ago, most car companies argued that 175 was the maximum. Any more and you'd be in a world of lost traction, torque steer, burning rubber, pain, misery and death.

To get round this problem on the last Focus RS, which delivered only 220bhp, a front differential was fitted. This didn't work at all. Put your foot down hard, the steering wheel would lock in your hands and you would spear into the nearest tree.

On the new RS, there's a new type of diff allied to a new type of suspension set-up called the RevoKnuckle. It is extremely boring and it doesn't work properly either. You still get torque steer and the wheel doesn't half feel weird in the bends.

However, there is no doubt that you can go round corners in the RS at a speed that can boggle your mind, and then use g-forces to squeeze it out of your left ear. What's more, you can put one of the driven wheels into a puddle while cornering and the little hatch will still not deviate from the line you've chosen. Around Ford's test track, we are told the RS is actually faster than the 5-litre GT.

Do not imagine, however, that it's some kind of stripped-out racer with all the interior fixtures and fittings removed and replaced with air. Instead of scaffolding in the back and carbon fibre, you get a voice-activated command centre that handles the satellite navigation and the stereo, a sunglasses holder, air-conditioning, a million acres of leather and plenty of dials telling you all the things you don't really need to know.

It is as luxurious in there as it is in a top-flight Mercedes. And about as comfortable. No, really – despite the tyres, which sit on the wheels like a coat of paint, it rides nicely. Which is a good thing because the bucket seats, finished in the same colour as the exterior for added vulgarity, offer lots in the way of lateral support, but not much protection from bumps for the buttocks.

I loved this car in the same way that I love nearly all fast Fords. Once, in the dim and distant past, I even ran an Escort Cosworth, which was no shrinking violet either. But something has changed since then. Maybe it's me, or maybe it's the world. I don't know. But I do know I could not ever drive an RS on a day-to-day basis. It would sit outside my house about as well as a ceramic collie.

You may be different. You may not want the Golf because you want people to see how well the tanning salon business is doing. You may like to signal your arrival at parties with a Colonel Bogey air horn. You may choose to wear your hat back to front, and your trousers in such a way that we can see your pants. You may admire Wayne and Coleen. If so, you will love the RS.

Me, though: I just wish they did a Cotswold version. Exactly the same but in olive green and with seats made from the Duke of Edinburgh.

28 June 2009

Hey, Hans – don't squeeze my bulls

Lamborghini Murciélago LP 670-4 SV

Last weekend, the restored Vulcan bomber, the only one in the world now flying, lumbered slowly and noisily over my house. And I damn nearly wet myself with excitement. I ran around the garden, clutching at my private parts with one hand, pointing with the other and screaming at the top of my lungs for the children to put down their Facebooks so they could see it too.

I bet things were a good deal less exciting in the cockpit, though. I bet it was hot and squashed in there and, if we're honest, a bit frightening as well.

I have never been on the flight deck of a big Brit bomber but I have sat at the pointy end of a Blackbird SR-71 and I imagine it's about the same. Because there are so many dials and knobs, you are constantly reminded that you are in something that's made from about a million different parts. All of which are operating at the very limit of what 1950s technology allowed. But you can't crap yourself, because there simply isn't enough room.

In my own small earthling way, I sort of know what this feels like because I have driven a Lamborghini Countach.

When it came along in the early seventies, your dad was pottering about in a Ford Cortina or maybe a Morris Marina and then, one day, a company he couldn't pronounce unveiled a car the likes of which the world had never seen.

I once wondered, on television, how New Yorkers must have felt when Brunel's propeller-driven liner, the SS *Great Britain*, steamed into their harbour. Because there they were, with their horses and their coracles, when into their midst came a metal ship that had no obvious means of propulsion. They must have felt very backward. Almost as backward as they felt in 1977 when Concorde screamed into JFK for the first time.

Well, that's what I felt like as a fourteen-year-old boy when I first saw a Countach. I couldn't believe any of it. Not the noise. Not the lowness – it was only 42 inches tall. Not the vast rear wing. Not the monstrous size of the tyres. And certainly not the claims that it would do 170mph. At the time, you must remember, the world was a slower place, so 170 was about Mach 6.

It was many years before I actually got to drive one, and, oh my God . . . as disappointments go, this was like getting your girlfriend's kit off for the first time and discovering she had an Adam's apple.

The steering wasn't heavy. An elephant is heavy. A school is heavy. An American is heavy. The Lambo's steering was in another league. Sometimes, you'd try to turn the wheel to go round a corner and, for a fleeting moment, you actually thought the whole system had jammed.

And then there was the clutch. If they'd set the pedal in concrete, it would have been easier to depress. And all the while, you were rammed into a space that was tiny and very, very hot. I'm sure you've all seen *The Bridge on the River Kwai* hundreds of times, which means I'm also sure you remember the box in which Alec Guinness was made to live. Well, imagine being in there, on a sweaty day, while doing a full SAS workout, at 170mph. That's what it was like in a Countach.

Parking, however, was even worse because you could not see out of the back, at all. The window would only wind down an inch. The car was wider than the owner of a Cheshire tanning salon and, to complicate everything even more, you could be assured you would be trying to get kerbside while under the scrutiny of a very sizeable audience.

You might have imagined as you took delivery of your new Lamborghini that you would spend the rest of your life drowning in girls. 'Fraid not. Because you didn't step out of a Countach; you crawled out, sweating, exhausted and dehydrated to the point of death. Sex? It was the absolute last thing on your mind.

In 1990, Lamborghini replaced the Countach with the Diablo. It was much less striking to behold, principally because the Countach had been there and done that. But it was even faster. And that was a bad thing, because now you were in a hot, cramped box, with heavy controls, doing 200mph. Death was always a very real possibility. Often you'd have embraced it.

By the twenty-first century, every other supercar maker had got round this problem. Their cars had light steering, Nissany pedals, air-conditioning and so on. But not Lambo. It was sticking to the original recipe: make it mad and paint it orange. Which is why the Murciélago, which came along in 2001, was as much of a bastard as its predecessors.

I spent some time last week with the latest – and possibly the last – incarnation of this insane raging bull. It's called, rather snappily, the LP (for longitudinally positioned engine) 670-4 (to denote the horsepower in metric terms and the number of driven wheels) SV (meaning SuperVeloce). My, the Italians are a romantic bunch.

In English, what they've done is upped the power from

the 6.5-litre V12 by 30. That's not much. But they've also lightened the car by 220lb. That's a lot. And the result is extraordinary.

When you fire up a modern-day Ferrari, it is almost as though you are stepping into the innards of a PlayStation game. You sense the technology. You feel the wiring working. You can almost hear the electrons monitoring this and covering that. It's a wonderful feeling, even though you can't help wondering if half the stuff is there only for marketing reasons – 'We have an F1 team you know . . .'

In the Murciélago, it's just pure unadulterated violence. The grip from the four-wheel-drive system as you leave the line is so immense that you usually leave half the clutch behind. But you've no time to think about that because you are already doing 100. And by the time you register that, you're doing 150. And still, there's no let-up.

The speed is incredible. Mesmerizing. Intoxicating. Bonkers. And then you get to a corner.

In a Ferrari, you feel an electronic interpretation of what's going on through the magnetized dampers and the five-way traction control. There's none of that in the Lambo. It's the road. And then your arse.

The grip is phenomenal. There is so much g that you can actually feel – and I'm not making this up – your face coming off. But you'd better not be worrying about that, because when, eventually, the laws of physics intervene, you will be doing somewhere in the region of a million. And you will need the reactions of a ninja lightning bolt to stay out of the Armco. This car, in the words of the Stig, is 'a bit fighty'.

And that's it. That's what the Lambo does. It goes very fast in a straight line. It goes very fast in the corners. And that's it. Want heated door mirrors? Forget it.

I'm not saying for a moment that life inside is as bad as it was in a Countach. The air-conditioning works for a kick-off and there's nearly enough room for a human. But it's still pretty basic. You get the impression they got the stereo from the local motorists' discount store and that the factory manager's mum did the stitching on the centre console. Even the seatbelts are the wrong way round.

I like that. Sometimes, I can find a Ferrari a bit up itself. Whereas, you get the sense when you're in a Lambo that it was all built for a bit of a laugh. The company doesn't have a racing team. The managing director looks like a male model. And you get the impression they'd far rather sell a car to Paris Hilton than Michael Schumacher.

Now, though, I'm a bit nervous. You see, in 1998, Lamborghini was rescued from oblivion by Audi and for a while it was a good master, keeping the wolf from the door and nothing else. But today you sense it is about to make Lamborghini a bit more – there's no other word – German.

I don't doubt for a second that this will make the cars easier to drive, easier to live with, less bonkers, less zany and less prone to breaking down. But here's the big one. Is that what we really want?

Let me put it this way. I ran round the garden last weekend pointing at a Vulcan. I would never do such a thing if you flew over in a Gulfstream G500.

5 July 2009

They've blown the saloon's last chance

Mercedes E 500 Sport

There's a curious and extremely ugly styling detail on the rear wings of the new Mercedes E-class. It's a crease that sets off from the back end with much purpose and drive, but when it reaches the door, it sort of gives up and, like the Okavango River, meanders about before giving up on the idea of existing in the first place.

One thing is for sure. It serves no purpose. It will make the car no faster, no more stable at speed and no more economical. And it's not a traditional Mercedes thing either – it's not like the BMW Hofmeister kink in the rear window, which is present on all models.

Mercedes says, apparently, it added the crease as a nod to some model in the company's dim and murky past. Probably the one Hitler drove. But this makes no sense, really. When I buy a new iPod, I don't want it to look even remotely like my grandfather's gramophone player. So, why should I want my new car to have a feature from the days of running boards?

And, anyway, no one is going to say, 'Ah, so. I see you've hinted at the 1942 Doogleburger model with that crease on the flank.' They're just going to do what I did: spend hours wondering if Mercedes has the first idea about form and function.

I dislike conspiracy theories. The smug, self-satisfied, arms-crossed demeanour of those who would have us believe that

Neil Armstrong didn't walk on the moon or, indeed, any-where more exciting than a sound stage in Nevada, invariably fills me with an uncontrollable need to set them on fire.

We see the same sort of thing with *Top Gear* fan sites on the internet.

Every single thing we do is analysed and then dismissed as fake. All the races are staged. Every word is scripted. Every opinion bought and paid for. Recently, a deer ran out while I was belting down the runway in a Mercedes. The shot was included in the film and, immediately, the boys were at their keyboards. 'Aha,' they said, 'the car wasn't moving. Television jiggery-pokery has been used.'

Honestly, chaps. If we were going to spend a fortune CGI-ing something onto the screen, we'd blow Richard Hammond's head off. Or detonate Belgium. Certainly, it'd be something a bit more exciting than a horned rat running about on an airfield.

Nevertheless, despite all this, I don't believe the crease in the E-class was there from the get-go. I may be wrong, of course. But in my mind the stylists did the car and then thought, 'Oh dear. That's a bit boring. Let's put a styling detail on the rear wings to distract people from the tedium.' Think of it, then, as one of Jon Snow's ties.

There are more problems with this car. I tested the E 500, which has a 5.5-litre V8 engine. That means 382 horsepow-ers and 391 torques. It means 0 to 62mph in 5.2 seconds and, you'd think, plenty of excitement. However, there is none. I have experienced more interesting drizzle.

No matter how brutal you may be with the seven-speed gearbox, it is extremely reluctant to put down its paper, extin-guish its pipe, change out of its slippers and actually go. Kick-down provokes a reluctant surge of sorts and if you go right to the bottom of the throttle pedal's travel, right through the carpet and into the firewall itself, the surge becomes a bit more meaty. But if this car could talk, and you did that, it would say, 'Oh, for God's sake.'

Seriously, asking this car to behave like a 5.5-litre V8 super-saloon is like asking a man to empty a dishwasher. It's technically possible but only if you are prepared to put up with a lot of harrumphing. I wouldn't mind, but the engine – the only one in the line-up not changed from the previous model – is either silent or making a strained noise you don't want to hear.

There are other things, too. The steering is inert. The brakes feel as uninterested as the engine, and the ride, on air suspension, is disappointing at low speeds. On the move, it's fine, or even good, but around town, which is where this car will spend most of its time, picking up Cilla Black from func-tions, it's as jittery as the Jag XF I recently tested (of which, more next week).

There is, then, absolutely no point in buying the 500 ver-sion of this car. You may as well have the diesel, which is less powerful but much more economical and, in the real world, every bit as fast. But if you are going to buy a mid-range die-sel saloon, then the E-class simply doesn't hold a candle to the Jag

Normally, with a Mercedes, you feel that everything is there for a reason. With the E-class you have that crease on the rear wing – which isn't – and a lot of things on the options list that border, I suspect, on being a bit gimmicky.

Certainly, if you specified everything, you'd have a car that would buzz and beep and bong more than Apollo 13 after the oxygen tank exploded.

This is a car that can read speed limits and alert you if

you break them, that uses radar to decide how much braking force you should use, that spots pedestrians in the dark, that knows about traffic jams ahead and cars that are overtaking in your blind spot and walls that you are about to reverse into. This is a car that shouts at you if you take your seatbelt off or open the door or leave your key in the ignition. And if you shout back, it will respond without fuss or murmur. Individually, some of these things are interesting. Some might even be worth specifying. But combined, they'd drive you mad.

The upshot is that the new E-class is not as good as the Jaguar XF or the BMW 5-series. It doesn't look good, it's boring and, worse than that, it probably signals that the end of the road for the four-door saloon car is not very far away.

Mercedes has always been the company to which we turn for the next bright idea. It was first with internal combustion and first with anti-lock brakes and first, frankly, with everything in between. But all I see on the E-class is a rounding-off of the edges. A bit of fiddling with an idea that's out of steam.

In the olden days, the four-door saloon was the only real choice for the consumer. It sat in our lives like fish and chips and the Post Office and British Rail tea. What do you mean, you want a skinny latte? Or an Earl Grey? Or a curry? Or O_2? Or a Mac? Choice hadn't been invented. So you had a Cortina.

Now, though, the family man or woman can have an MPV or a mini MPV or an SUV or a drop-top or an estate or a four-seater coupé. And every single one of these alternatives is better than the traditional three-box idea.

It's very difficult, as Porsche has just proved with the Panamera, to make a four-door car sexy. And it's very difficult to think of any new way of making the drive feel different or better than it was in the previous model. Yes, you might find an extra 2mm of legroom here and a slight cut in carbon dioxides there. But, really, the genre is advancing like world records in athletics. A tiny bit at a time towards a moment when going any faster or making things any better will be simply impossible.

Mercedes has always shown us the way forward. But with the new E-class it has shown us that we're at the end of the line. Some day, then, all saloon cars will be this dull.

19 July 2009

The fastest pair of comfy slippers around

Jaguar XF 3.0 Diesel S Portfolio

Back in the late eighties, I was sitting outside a pub in Fulham with my old writing and business partner when someone pulled out of a side turning in a Toyota Supra and accelerated smartly down the road. As the car shifted lumpily into second gear, I remember, even today, that we each looked at the other in an eyc-rolling way and said, 'What a prat.' He'd bought a sports car and then specified it with an automatic gearbox. Which meant he hadn't bought a sports car at all.

When I was a young man, I reserved a special kind of hatred for automatic gearboxes. They made all cars, no matter what they were, into convenience tools. Take away the pleasure of a well-executed downshift and you were taking away everything that mattered to the true petrolhead. Auto cars, even the Ferrari 400, were the automotive equivalent of fast food. Convenient, for sure, but no burger, no matter how easy it is to eat in the street, can possibly be a match for a blood-red fillet steak.

Things, however, have changed. There are all sorts of moments in a man's life when he can truly say he has become 'old'. The moment his first child is born. The moment he buys his first pair of slippers. The moment he starts to think the world is getting worse. But, actually, the real moment is when you say to a car salesman, 'Can I have it with an automatic gearbox?'

Graham Norton summed it all up the other day when he appeared on a television programme. He said that changing gear in a car is like having a remote-controlled television and getting up to change the channel yourself. It's stupid. And, of course, he's right.

I like to kid myself these days that I prefer an auto because I'm busy and having something change gear on my behalf allows me to do other things while driving. Speaking on the telephone, for instance, is almost impossible if you have to steer and shift cogs as well, especially now you need to keep at least one eye out for the Stasi. But the main reason is that I simply can't be bothered to do it myself.

So what about flappy paddles, which give you the manual gearbox without the tiresome need to press a clutch pedal down or move a stick? Well, yes, they can change gear very quickly, but speed is not the issue – off a race track, why would you ever want to go from third to fourth in 60 milliseconds? It's the 'feel' you want from a gearbox, the sense that you are controlling the machine.

And with a flappy paddle box, that control is gone. Try to change down when the resultant revs would be too high and the system simply won't allow it. Forget to change up and when you hit the red line, the silicon nanny will step in and do it for you. It's like having a driving instructor along for the ride, with dual controls. It is terrible. The most pointless invention since procon-ten.

I have a similar problem with diesel engines. Time was when I hated them. I said diesel was the fuel of Satan and that anyone who chose a car with no spark plugs had, in effect, given up on life. Choosing such a thing would be like choosing a pair of trousers with an elasticated waist simply because they were easy to clean.

Now, though, I simply cannot understand why anyone would buy an ordinary car with anything but a diesel engine. Of course, those with petrol flowing through the injectors can rev so much more freely, but when was the last time – honestly – you went anywhere near the red line?

The trouble is that second gear in a lot of cars these days can take you to beyond the motorway speed limit. So, in a run-of-the-mill saloon, you simply don't need the engine, ever, to spin up to six, seven or even eight thousand revs per minute. You may as well, therefore, have a diesel, which is all out of ideas at 4500rpm.

I can't believe I'm saying any of this. I remember the launch of the first diesel automatic car – a Citroën BX, if you could care less – and I remember thinking that life couldn't possibly get worse. Canal-boat noises. No go. No need to change gear. It was, I reckoned, the end of days.

Of course, it's not just me that's changed in the intervening period. Diesel engines have, too. Time was when they rattled the windows in your house, gave your children cancer, made the Houses of Parliament black and had all the power of Belgium.

Today, with the notable exception of the diesel in a Volvo XC90, which is laughably awful, they are completely different. BMW's diesels may not be the most economical but they are unbelievably quiet and possessed of so much power, you would swear to God they were running on lightning bolts.

And they pale into insignificance alongside the diesels now being made by Land Rover and Jaguar. The diesel in my Range Rover is unbelievably good. You'd have to be clinically insane to choose the 5-litre V8 instead. And now there's a new 3-litre twin-turbo V6 diesel that you can specify for your XF.

Let me put the figures on it for you. In the top-spec S model I tried, you get 275 horsepowers and an astonishing 442 torques, which means you can get from 0 to 60 in around 6 seconds and onwards to a top speed of 155.

These are the figures you might expect from a petrol car. But now look at the ones you wouldn't – a mere 179 carbon dioxides and the promise of 40 or so mpg. It really is a case of: here's your cake. Now tuck in.

But the best thing about Jag's engine is the silence. It is astonishingly quiet, even when you start it up first thing in the morning. There are no vibrations, either, which means it feels exactly like it's running on petrol. Except for when you put your foot down and that second turbo unleashes the monstrous torque. Then it feels like it's running on a gallon of bloody mary.

There is just one tiny problem, and, weirdly, it affects the Range Rover diesel, too. When you pull away from a stand-still, it feels like the throttle cable has snapped. So you give the pedal a hefty shove, which means that you lunge onto the roundabout at the precise moment you decide the gap's not big enough. Apparently, this is a software problem that can be cured. I wish it would be.

I also wish the ride were better. I think the low-profile tyres are to blame, but, whatever it is, the car pitter-patters at low speeds and such a feel is completely at odds with the torquey diesel engine, the automatic gearbox and the sense that Jags aren't supposed to be this way.

I must also criticize the seats. There is so little side support that in every corner you end up on your passenger, which is fine if your passenger is Lily Allen. But I ended up on James May, and that was horrid. For me.

That, however, is it. A hesitancy to the throttle, a seating problem that's an issue only if you drive fast and a small but important ride flaw that could almost certainly be solved with smaller wheels and taller tyres.

The rest of the car is brilliant. I wasn't sold on the XF when it came out. It simply didn't look as sharp as the concept we'd been shown earlier. But with memories of that concept fading, we are left with a genuine looker that manages to be practical and spacious as well. Plus, you can get one of these cars, albeit not the variant I drove, for £2,500 less than the cheapest BMW 535d.

I apologize for the rather boring, dry review this morning but, having taken this diesel car with an automatic gearbox to a friend's fiftieth birthday party last weekend, it's how I feel. Boring, dry and possibly in need of some slippers.

26 July 2009

Oops, this drunken driver is off to Brazil

Argo Avenger 700 8x8

Not that long ago, some racing drivers were asked to take part in an experiment to see what effect drinking would have on their lap times. The results were never published, since they showed that after five pints the chaps were much faster. And after eight, they were sensational.

It's not hard to see why. Alcohol gives us confidence to be witty at dinner parties, confidence to chat up girls and confidence to take Stowe corner at Silverstone flat in fourth, while laughing.

The people who compiled the report could have explained this. But, since it was being done for television and, since the average viewer is reckoned by most television executives to be unable to grapple with anything more complex than 'Halfwit is in the kitchen', they simply ditched the whole thing.

Certainly, in a soundbite world, there wouldn't have been the time to explain that while alcohol gives you the confidence to take risks you wouldn't normally take, it also slows down your reactions should something go wrong. That's why it's so lethal when combined with driving.

Think about it. If you can't organize your mouth to be able to say, 'Peter Piper picked a red lorry on the seashore,' what possible chance do you have of being able to control a ton of speeding metal?

I am not suggesting for a moment that the government cuts the drink-drive limit. That would be barbaric and stupid. Which is why it probably will. I merely offer it up as an observation. And a bit of an excuse for what comes next.

Yesterday, and I have no idea how this happened, I became extremely drunk. I started with a cheeky beer at midday and ended up on a beach, eight hours later, asking out loud if my lawyer had ever tried lesbianism. That drunk. So drunk, in fact, that as the sun started to go down, I decided that I could drive. So I did. Into the sea.

Before you all write to the *Daily Mail*, again, suggesting that I be sacked, again, I should explain that I wasn't on a road, no pedestrians were present to run over, and that the vehicle I was driving was an Argo – widely known as an Argocat. I've written about this amazing little vehicle before, but only in passing. Today, I am giving it the main picture. The whole caboodle. The full test.

First made in Canada forty-two years ago, the Argocat is currently available with either six- or eight-wheel drive. It skid-steers like a tank, which means that when you turn the handlebars, the wheels on one side are braked, allowing the vehicle to 'skid' round in its own length.

Many engines have been available over the years. Today you get an air-cooled unit from Briggs & Stratton. The motor in mine is a 26-horsepower liquid-cooled affair from Kohler. And I do mean mine. As in, I own it.

I first experienced an Argocat about five years ago and was astonished at what it would climb. So astonished that I rang the British importer and bought one to use for litter-clearing duties at my holiday cottage on the Isle of Man.

Over the years, it has never been anything other than astonishing. We talk glibly about the off-road abilities of a

Land Rover. But no Defender could hope to make progress over seaweed-strewn boulders that often are twice as tall as it is. The Argocat can.

Nor would a Land Rover be much use if your lobster pot was stuck under a rock. In an Argocat you simply drive into the sea, and using the tyres as crude propellers, waddle over to the rope and pull the pot free. Then drive back to the beach, climb over the boulders, and go home via the samphire beds to get some accompanying veg.

Yes, there are drawbacks. First of all, it costs more than a Fiat 500 Abarth, which is a lot when you consider it has no windows, carpets, cruise control, sat nav or air-conditioning. All you get is a bilge pump and a cigarette lighter.

And then there's the complexity. If you lift up the floor, which can be achieved only with minor cuts and a splash of light bruising, it is like peering into a Victorian bicycle factory. Because each of the eight wheels is driven by a chain that takes its drive from the wheel in front, there are more chains in there than you'd find in a fight between two rival gangs of Hell's Angels. All of which, if you go in the sea a lot, are corroded to hell.

Happily, because it's based on the Isle of Man, where there are many motorcycling enthusiasts, it's not hard to find a man who can keep these chains working. But if you live in, say, the rest of the world, where motorcycling is reserved for a handful of homosexuals and lunatics, servicing would be a nightmare.

The only good thing is that the Argocat is one of those prehistoric mechanical beasts that can mend itself. One day it is making a terrible graunching noise in gentle left turns. The next it's fine. Modern, electronically controlled vehicles don't do this. They go wrong and they stay wrong until a man with a laptop comes round and charges you £8m a minute to get them going again.

Fortunately, yesterday, when I was very drunk and filled with a sudden need to drive very far out to sea, all was well with my Argocat. So brrrrm went the engine and splash went the tyres. And we were off.

It's funny but when you actually own something, you are never prepared to test it to the limits because, of course, you will be without a car while it's being mended. But when you are paralytic, all those worries just seem to melt away, which is why I was halfway to Belfast before I decided that what I'd like most of all was some more wine. So I killed the engine, poured myself a glass and just sort of bobbed about admiring the view with that stupid smile people have when their arteries are full of Chablis.

I have no idea what happened to the time but a lot of it must have passed, because the next thing I knew, the water had all gone somewhere else and I was on a rock, about five miles from the beach. That's five miles of sea bed. Five miles of seaweed and boulders. Five miles of terrain so inhospitable you wouldn't even attempt to cross it on foot.

I had some more wine while thinking what to do and calculated that by the time the tide came in again, it'd be dark. And the wind was picking up. And at sea, an Argocat has a top speed of one, which is not much use if you're trying to head-butt a strong northeasterly and a nine-knot tide. What happens is that after about a month, you end up reversing into Brazil.

I therefore concluded, after some more wine, that I would have to drive over the sea bed. I wish you could have seen the scale of the challenge. Because the fact that the Argocat made it without even so much as a moment of wheelspin would leave you as dumbfounded as it did me.

The thing is that so long as one wheel has grip, you have drive. And with eight squidgy balloon tyres tentacling out there for a foothold, there's a good chance one of them will meet with some success. All you have to do is use the bike-style twist grip to keep the tyres fed with a dribble of power.

I look often at farmers and rock stars who have quad bikes for tootling about on their estates and I'm a bit confused. Because they must know that eventually they will end up in hospital with a fractured skull. With an Argocat, there's no danger of that. It only does about 20mph. And only then if you are lucky. You couldn't roll it over if you had a crane.

Sure, a quad bike is very good at cross-country travel. In the same way that a horse is a fine way of getting across a desert. It's just not as good as a camel.

2 August 2009

Cheer yourself up in a . . .

Mazda MX-5 2.0i Sport Tech

There's a farm shop near where I live. Actually, it isn't really a farm shop at all, because the floor is made from oak rather than fertilizer bags and all of the staff look like supermodels instead of burst walnut trees.

Inside, you can buy jumpers made from exotic goats, bread that would make a Frenchman faint and apples so shiny, they could double up as disco balls. It's called Daylesford and it's the subject of much mockery, principally because everything is so bleeding expensive. As a friend of mine said recently, 'I went to Daylesford to get some cheese this morning. But I only had £162 on me.'

The thing is, though, it is excellent value for money. When I go there on a Saturday morning, I always meet someone who invites me round for dinner that night. This means I don't have to buy supper, or cook it.

What's more, without Daylesford I'd have to go to London to buy my groceries, which would cost £50 in petrol, £8 for the congestion charge and £100 to get my car back from the pound. So, all of a sudden, twenty-five quid seems the bargain of the century. Especially when you consider that Daylesford has started to affect house prices. People will pay considerably more to live near it, which means that every time someone buys a loaf of bread, I'm earning about £500,000.

And on top of all this, without Daylesford I'd have to go to a local supermarket to buy my ham. Yes, the ham there is only 4p, but it's Barbie pink and about as nutritional as the plastic bag it's sold in.

We see the same sort of thing with cars. I recently drove something called a Perodua Myvi, which sells for £7,600. That's cheap when you consider it has the same number of wheels and glove boxes as a Rolls-Royce Phantom. But it is extremely expensive when you work out how miserable and dreary it makes you feel. It's a car built utterly without joy. Buying one of these would be like buying a nylon dog simply because it's cheaper to keep.

There are lots of cheap cars on the market, but only a very small number offer truly excellent value for money. The Fiat 500 is one, for sure, because just seeing it makes you happy. And the Skoda Roomster is another, provided you avoid the three-cylinder diesel version. Yes, you will save money when you buy it, but the savings will be offset by the cost of the funeral you'll need shortly after you first try to build up enough speed to join a motorway.

The Jaguar X-type is perhaps the best example of cost having nothing to do with value. Yes, it was very cheap for a Jaguar. But since it was nothing more than a Mondeo in a rented suit, it was extremely poor value for money. That's why it never sold well. And that's why 300 poor souls at the Halewood plant are now facing the dole queue.

And then there's the new Vauxhall Insignia VXR. On the face of it, this looks excellent value. The Insignia is a good-looking car and the hot version is even better. What's more, it has a long list of standard kit, a 321bhp twin-turbo engine and four-wheel drive and, since prices start at a whisker over £30,000, it is way less than its rivals from Audi and BMW.

Yes, but the money you save in no way compensates for the fact that you must spend the next year or so telling your friends that you have a Vauxhall. Which is a bit like saying you have genital warts. People will raise their eyebrows and edge away.

Buying a Vauxhall to save money is like going on holiday to Northampton to save money. You will, for sure, but you will not be as happy as if you went to France.

And all of this brings me naturally to the Mazda MX-5, which I think represents better value for money than any other car on sale in Britain today. A 1.8-litre soft-top version, as opposed to the one that comes with a folding metal roof, is £16,345, and for that you get almost exactly the same amount of fun you would get from a Ferrari 430 Spider. This is the thing with convertibles. When the roof is down, the buffeting and the racket mean that any speed above about eighty is unpleasant. So you really don't need a million horse-power or a gearbox that can swap cogs in a billionth of a blink.

With the Mazda you get the engine at the front, rear-wheel drive and skinny tyres. This, then, is a car designed to thrill and excite and put a massive smile on your face at the sort of speed that won't mess up your girlfriend's hair.

My old mate Tiff Needell, from commercial television, is perfectly capable of power-sliding a space shuttle, but argues to this day that the most fun he's ever had is in a Morris Minor, because it can be provoked into some tail-out action at about 2mph. So it goes with the Mazda. In short, you don't need to be an astronaut with titanium hair follicles to get the best out of it.

Put simply, an MX-5 feels more alive at 30mph than most other cars feel at 100.

So, every time Mazda changes something on its little sports car, I'm worried the end result will be a bit more serious, a bit more 'driver-oriented', a bit more anal. And that the original recipe will have been ruined.

I realize, of course, that an original can be improved, no matter how good it may have been. You have only to listen to the Hothouse Flowers' version of 'I Can See Clearly Now' to understand this. But, for every original that's improved, there are a thousand that are ruined.

That's why I approached the recently facelifted version of the MX-5 with a heavy heart and a sense of foreboding.

Let me give you an example. Mazda has fitted the engine with a forged crankshaft, floating pistons and new valve gear. It all sounds like the wet dream of a diehard, adenoidal car bore. But don't worry. Despite all the work, the amount of power the engine produces remains exactly as it was before. And it's the same story with the torque. The only real change is that you can now rev to 7500rpm before you need to change gear. And it all sounds a bit more sporty.

The company has changed the front suspension, too, and that worried me as well. There was absolutely nothing wrong with the set-up in the old car, so why fiddle? Plainly, it was simply to keep the engineers out of Hiroshima's love hotels, because it is just as sparkling and brilliant as it was before. Maybe it's a bit more focused, a bit sharper. But only if you concentrate, and that's the thing about the MX-5. You don't concentrate: you're way too busy having a nice time.

Inside, you now get Recaro seats and higher-quality switches, but I didn't notice these either.

I said recently that the BMW Z4 is the best of the open sports cars, but after a couple of days with the Mazda I realize I was talking nonsense. The BMW is excellent but the

MX-5 demonstrates that its extra speed, extra grip and extra size are all a bit wasteful. In the little Japanese car you get exactly what you need, and exactly the space you need, and nothing more.

I realize that the hairy-chested among you will be scoffing and tutting and heading straight for this column on the internet so you can speak your mind. You will say 'girl's car' and 'gay' and all sorts of other things.

Well, that's fine. You waste your money on a Mustang or a Ferrari. The fact is that, if you want a sports car, the MX-5 is perfect. Nothing on the road will give you better value. Nothing will give you so much fun. The only reason I'm giving it five stars is because I can't give it fourteen.

16 August 2009

The perfect supercar

Lamborghini Gallardo LP560-4 Spyder

I can always spot those of a *Guardian* disposition. No matter how well disguised as a normal person they may be, they always reveal their true colours at some point by asking, scoffingly, why on earth we feature such expensive fast cars on *Top Gear* when the roads are so congested.

Sometimes, I just roll my eyes, and sometimes, I set them on fire. But, occasionally, I adopt my special calm voice and explain that while the road from Islington to the headquarters of *Channel 4 News* may be a bit jammed up on a Tuesday morning, the road from Thwaite to Hawes in North Yorkshire usually isn't.

Nor is the road past my house. And nor were any of the roads we featured in the final and much misunderstood item in the last *Top Gear* show. In what was supposed to be a lament to the possible passing of the fast, petrol-powered car, an Aston Martin V12 Vantage was seen thundering along on mile after mile of completely deserted blacktop.

This was filmed partly in Wales, partly in the Cotswolds and partly in Hertfordshire. You see my point. Even in the southeast of England, even in a home county, you can still find a road, lots of roads, in fact, where you can enjoy your 500-horsepower sports car.

I found another last weekend. Though it was undoubtedly paid for by you and me, it's in Spain, linking the crime-caper coast with the charming hilltop town of Ronda thirty-five miles away. Sadly, I'd had rather too many wines to drive the Lamborghini Gallardo LP 560-4 Spyder that was parked outside. Indeed, had it not been painted metallic pea green, I might not have been able to find it. But, happily, I had a chauffeur, a man who has no concept of alcohol. Or why ducks float. Or Tuesday.

Strangely, even though I work with him all the time, I had never been in a car with the Stig. And had I not been a bit tipsy, I might not have got into a car with him that night either. Sober, you'd think about the road that lay ahead, with its cliff faces and its precipitous drops and Ronnie Biggs coming the other way, and you'd elect to crawl on your hands and knees rather than get into a car with a man who has two speeds: stationary and absolutely flat out. I'm glad I did, though, because Jesus, his driving is sublime.

Not once did the car pitch or lurch. There was never a shimmy from the rear or a squeal from the tyres. We just went up that brilliant road with the roof down and me looking at the stars flying by as though we were on the Starship *Enterprise*'s observation deck. It was, I think, the most enjoyable drive of my life: to be in a car that good, with its V10 bark echoing off the limestone and a bit of Steely Dan on the stereo, doing about a million with a man who truly knows what he's doing at the wheel.

This is what those of a *Guardian* disposition don't understand: that a car can be a tool but it can also be so much more. It can be a heart-starter, it can be a drug, it can be a piece of art, it can stir your soul and it can get you from Marbella to Ronda before the bar closes.

The new Lamborghini Gallardo does all of those things at least as well as any other car money can buy.

I am aware, of course, that soon Ferrari will launch its new 458, the first truly pretty car it has made since the 355. But even this is only a match for the sheer aesthetic rightness of the Gallardo, one of the most perfectly proportioned super-cars the world has ever seen.

And boy, the Ferrari will have to be good – very, very good – to be a better driving experience. I spent several days at the remarkable Ascari track with it, and it is fantastic. You can turn into any corner at pretty well any speed you like and the grip from the four-wheel-drive system beggars belief. Floor the throttle mid-bend and all you ever seem to get is more and more grip.

The downside is that you have a less flamboyant time than you would in a car with rear-wheel drive. The upside is that when you are in public, overtaking another Dozy Dutchman in a Datsun, you know that you can floor it, use the mon-strous power to get past and not worry too much about braking for the next bend because you will get round.

Then there's the new 5.2-litre engine. It's magnificent and even that doesn't do it justice. The power is immediate, the torque immense and the speed it delivers mesmerizing. I par-ticularly like the way the exhaust makes a derisory snorting noise when you lift off. It's as if it's saying, 'Why are you slowing down?'

There's more. In the past, a Lamborghini was more brittle than a pressed wild flower. One gust of wind and it'd turn to dust. Not any more. I pounded that Gallardo, and its big sister, the Murciélago SV, round that track in blazing forty-degree heat for day after day and neither of them made even a mur-mur of complaint. They felt as robust as Audis. Which, of course, is only right and proper, since, technically, that's what they are.

In the past, you'd look at the whole engine cover sliding upwards to let the roof fold away and you'd think, 'Well, that's going to break.' But now, the whole mechanism feels like it's made from bronze. It's the same story with the system that allows you to connect your iPod to the central command centre and select playlists as you drive along. Yes, it's all wired up by an Italian. But a German was looking over his shoulder, so it works.

The only real technical problem – apart from the minor fact that a lot of Gallardos seem to catch fire – is the gearbox. If you order a manual, the clutch pedal is so close to the transmission tunnel there is nowhere to put your left foot when you are driving. This is extremely boring. So you must select the flappy paddles. However, because the rest of the car's so good, this is a price worth paying.

But . . . here we go. I've owned supercars in the past, a Ferrari 355, the old 5-litre Gallardo Spyder and a Ford GT. But, and this will bring a smile to the Guardianistas' endlessly thin lips, they really don't work on a day-to-day basis.

You quickly grow tired of being looked at when you are stationary. You can't see what's coming at oblique junctions. Your hands are always dirty from lifting the bonnet, under which there's a boot that's never quite big enough for the things you've bought. And while the noise is sublime when you are in the mood, it is annoying when you are not.

Running a supercar as your day-to-day transport is like hacking out on Desert Orchid, or moving to one of those all-glass modern houses, or being married to Jordan, or living entirely on haute cuisine. They aren't really designed for real life. They're designed for dreaming, and that's why I wrote that Aston Martin piece for *Top Gear*. It's why I selected Brian Eno's track 'An Ending' as the score. It's why the director,

Nigel Simpkiss, spent so much time and effort on the pictures. We wanted to highlight the dangers of what the anti-speed lobby and the pressure groups and the government's eco fools are doing. It's one thing removing our freedom to live the life we want to live. But now they are waging war on our freedom to dream.

I've said this before and I'll say it again here. I don't really want a Lamborghini Gallardo. But I don't want to live in a world where it doesn't exist.

23 August 2009

Oh dear, it thinks it's going to save the world

Lexus RX 450h SE-L

You know what it's like when a party breaks up at two in the morning. Chaos reigns. The drunks are trying to find someone who still knows what a steering wheel does, half a dozen chatty souls are inviting you back to their places for more drinks and you have a devil on your shoulder telling you that, yes, it'd be a brilliant idea to go with them.

Amid all the doorstep mayhem that ensued after a party last week, I ended up in my holiday rental car with a French supermodel. And neither of us had the first idea where anyone else had gone. So we drove around for a bit until we became thirsty.

And that's why, last Thursday, at four in the morning, I was in a bar in Corfu with a teenage cover girl when the paparazzi rocked up. Eager for them to go away empty-handed, I left my new best friend and dashed outside, desperately trying to remember what sort of car I'd used to get there and where on earth I might have left it.

It turned out to be a grey Volvo in rental spec, which meant it had no satellite navigation. As a result, I had absolutely no idea where I was, which was bad enough. And to make matters worse, I also had no idea where I was going. Neither did my wife. When I called to say I'd been with a French supermodel for the past two hours, she said – I thought rather curtly – that she didn't know where I was either, and that she had more important things to worry about because she was at another party and her friend Caroline had just fallen into a swimming pool.

And so that was that. I couldn't ask a local because a) the only Greek I know is the Duke of Edinburgh and b) I genuinely did not know the name of the villa I'd rented or the village in which it was situated. All I could recall was that it was near a hotel with a stupid name, and at the top of the very long drive to it there was a wheelie bin.

So, with slumped shoulders and a heavy heart, I simply set off. And here's the really funny thing. Twenty minutes later, having driven past about 60,000 wheelie bins, on a succession of roads that curled as though they'd been made from Michael Jackson's Thriller wig, I found the entrance to my drive and made it home without making a single wrong turn. As a result, I think I may be a pigeon.

This raises an interesting question. We know we all have a sense of smell, a sense of touch and a sense of taste, except in certain parts of Cheshire, obviously. We know, too, that most of us have a sense of what's right and what's wrong. But do we have an in-built sense of direction? Are we salmon?

James May isn't. In a large hotel, it can take him several hours to get from his room to reception. In a city, he can be lost for days. This is a man who claims that in London there are two Albert Halls; Britain, in his mind, is upside down, with Scotland next to France.

There are many other examples of this in the newspapers every week: people who go round and round the M25 until they run out of petrol, truckers who drive into rivers, and then there was that taxi driver who programmed Stamford Bridge into his car's sat nav and kept right on going to

Stamford Bridge in Yorkshire. How could he not have known he was going north? Did the word 'Sheffield' not give him a clue that he was going in the wrong direction?

Perhaps we are losing our homing powers because, in a world of maps and TomTom guidance from outer space, there is no need to employ them any more. Is James May where the world is headed? If so, God help us.

And God help us, too, if the car we will all be driving when we become long-haired pedants is the Lexus RX 450h SE-L. The old version of this car was a big success, especially in London, because its hybrid drive system made it immune from the congestion charge. The exemption for hybrids is now being reviewed; if it is withdrawn it means you will need another reason for buying this £50,000 Alan Partridge-mobile on stilts.

I doubt it will be looks. The wheels appear to have come from underneath a Steinway, so the car has the stance of an elephant on a unicycle. And ease of use is not a big plus point either.

Of particular note is the sat nav, which is controlled, like the computer you use at home, with a mouse. Unfortunately, it is nearly impossible to get the cursor where you want it to be while driving along because there are too many lurches and bounces from a suspension system that appears to have come from Steinway as well.

Then you have the eco-drive system. During each journey, you are shown by symbols that could be leaves, or windmills, how economically you are driving. And then, when you get home, you are given a score that you can compare with your past three journeys.

What's more, the entire dash display changes colour to

give you an at-a-glance clue as to how you're doing. Dark blue and you are being heavy-footed. Light blue and it's a pass. Green and you're given a job at the *Guardian*.

I have no doubt all this would help pass the time on a long journey. But, of course, the result is that the journey will be longer still. That's why I prefer the readout in my Mercedes, which gives a constant update of my average speed.

And, anyway, if you are so bothered about achieving maximum economy from your car, why would you buy a 2.2-ton, 295-horsepower, 124mph off-roader? Wouldn't you be better off with, say, a Mini?

Obviously, the Lexus can handle more stuff, but it can't handle anything like as much as you might expect. Put a fridge-freezer in the boot, close the tailgate and that stupidly sloping rear window is going to end up in a million pieces all over the road.

I've just been on a family holiday and our Range Rover was barely able to handle the requirements of five people. In a Lexus 450, you'd have to leave one of the suitcases, or children, at home. Or go to a nudist camp.

To drive, I have to say the 450 is pretty awful. Quite apart from the ride, which is part pillow, part oak, there is an electric power steering system that is as vague as an Indian railway timetable.

If you have your head screwed on the right way round, then, this car makes very little sense at all. However, I must say the hybrid drive system does, apparently, produce some astonishing results.

There are three motors. Up front you have a 3.5-litre V6, which is helped along when you need some more power by a 165-horsepower electric motor. At the back there's a smaller electric motor that drives the rear wheels, making it four-wheel drive when things get sticky. As a piece of engineering, it's fabulous, and the results, if they are to be believed, are fairly amazing, too. Because here is a large, five-seat car that has the power of a Ford Focus RS, but the fuel economy of a 1.4-litre Fiesta. Seriously. They claim it will do 44mpg. And all the while, somehow, it produces very few carbon dioxides.

And that's really it. That's the nub. To buy this car you have to believe in man-made global warming. You have to honestly believe that by buying a hybrid and driving it home as slowly as possible, you will put out all the world's forest fires.

If, however, you just want a big, comfy car, then take those fuel-economy claims with a pinch of salt and buy something else.

6 September 2009

. . . a great car, but who will buy it?

Ferrari California

Not that long ago, Ferrari named one of its cars after the town in which it was made. So we ended up with the Ferrari Maranello. And now, the company has announced its new entry-level model will be called the Italia.

These are good names. But then Ferrari is lucky because the founder of the company had a cool name and he lived in a cool country where even football chants sound like poetry. Say, 'You're going to get your effing head kicked in,' in Italian and it sounds as though you are lamenting the untimely demise of your much-loved mother.

In Britain we have no such luxury. Let us imagine, for a moment, that the founder of Lotus had adopted a similar model-naming policy to Ferrari. Would you drive a car called the Chapman Norwich? No. Neither would I. Or a Lyons Coventry. Or a Henry East Midlands. Or a Herbert Birmingham. Mind you, I wouldn't want a Gottlieb Stuttgart either. Or an Adolf Wolfsburg.

Occasionally, Ferrari names its cars after the people who've styled them. Recently we had the Scaglietti, and that makes me go all weak at the knees, but again, it wouldn't work here. Or the newest Range Rover would be called the Gerry. And Aston's DB9 would be the Ian.

Sometimes, though, Ferrari names its cars after other places in the world. We had the Superamerica and the Daytona and now we've got the California. California is a brilliant name. Elsewhere in the world, all the leaves are brown and the sky is grey. But in California the sun always shines. You can check out any time you like, but you can never leave. I like California. I got engaged there.

I can't understand why more car firms don't use evocative place names when dreaming up handles for their cars. Ford did it with the Cortina, of course, but actually it wasn't named after the ski resort. It was named after a cafe on the King's Road in London.

It's not as if we're short. I'd drive a Vancouver or a London. I'd drive a Calcutta or a Buenos Aires. I was going to say I'd drive a Wellington but, much though I love the place, I actually wouldn't. Or a Nice.

Strangely, however, when a car is named after a famous place, it's always bloody Monte Carlo. We've had the Lancia Montecarlo, the Chevrolet Monte Carlo, the Ford Comète Monte Carlo, the Dodge Monaco and the Renault 5 Monaco. Why? Seriously, why name your car after a dreary, boring, rain-sodden tax haven full of prostitutes and arms dealers? Get an atlas, all of you, and let's have a Chevy Buttermere.

Or, better still, let's get back to the California. We're often told that a car looks better in the flesh than it does in pictures and I've always scoffed at this. I look horrible in pictures because I look horrible in the flesh. It's not Nikon that gives me yellow teeth and a beach-ball belly. However, I can report that when it comes to the California, the camera really does lie. The images you're looking at this morning in no way do the car justice. Roof up or down, it is absolutely beautiful.

Now for the tricky bit. Ferrari says that this, its first-ever front-engined V8, has been aimed at women.

Aaaaaaaaaaaaaaaaaaargh. And then aaaaaaaaaaaaaaaargh some more.

How can you possibly target half the world's population? Are the people at Ferrari saying they've made it soft and cuddly? Because if they have, my wife will hate it. Or have they given it pink seats and a tampon dispenser, in which case the other half of the population will run a mile?

You can design a film for women. It'll have Hugh Grant in it. And you can design knickers for women. But a car? You might as well design a car for homosexuals. What sort? A big bull dyke or Graham Norton?

So far as I can tell, the only big difference between the California and all the supposedly male Ferraris is the traction control, which comes with three settings rather than five. This is a good thing. It's still not a perfect thing, though, or there'd be only two: on and off.

No matter. The California feels like a Ferrari. It feels digital rather than analogue. It feel dizzyingly light and agile. It feels like no other car made today. Comparing it to a Lambo or an Audi R8 is like comparing lightning to soil.

The steering is incredibly light. American light. And yet there is a feel there, and a fluency that you will find in no other road-going car.

The engine may be the same size as the unit found in the middle of an F430, but the bore is wider and the stroke is shorter. It sounds like the recipe for a screamer, but it isn't. It feels lazy and torquey. The speed's still there, though. It gets from 0 to 60 just as quickly as the 430.

There is, however, a fly in the silicone. It comes with a flappy-paddle gearbox. Now this may be a double-clutch affair such as you get in a VW Golf, but it's still not right. I'd rather have a conventional automatic.

This aside, though, the California is an amazing car to drive. Quiet and comfortable when you want it to be. Vicious and snarling when you don't. But there are some warts.

First, as you drive along, you can't help but notice the bonnet flaps about in the wind. The last time I saw this from the driver's seat of a car, I was in a Montego. Then, at the back, you have a boot lid that weighs nine million tons. If this car really is aimed at women, I dread to think who they had in mind. Fatima Whitbread, perhaps.

And then we have the electronics. It is possible to connect your telephone via Bluetooth to the onboard computer, but every time you try to make a call, the voice-activated system will ignore your instructions and ring Steve Curtis, the powerboat champion. I do not know why.

Then there are the speedometers. For reasons that are unclear, there are two – one dial and one digital – which give different readouts. This makes life particularly worrying when you are going past a Gatso camera. But, then, this is the price you must pay if you decide to buy a car from the bespoke tailors of the motoring world. Ferrari does not employ an army whose job for four years is to calibrate the speedos. It probably doesn't employ anyone who realizes they've fitted two by mistake.

Of course, a specialist car, such as the 599 or F430, will spend most of its life in a pair of woolly pyjamas in your heated garage, so who cares if the phone will ring only Steve Curtis. But the California is designed to be used. And I fear that if you come to it from a Mercedes SL, its little Italian ways will drive you a bit mad.

There's another problem, too. It's a biggie. Would I really buy the Ferrari and not the Aston Martin DBS convertible? That's as tough as decisions get. The Aston has a stupid

Volvo sat nav, a price tag from the Comedy Store, buttons that could be operated only by Edward Scissorhands and a fly-off handbrake that won't. But, amazingly, it is slightly better to drive than the Ferrari, and, staggeringly, even better-looking.

I think that if I were in the market for a comfortable two-plus-two GT car, I would buy the Aston. But I just know I'd spend my entire time with it wishing I'd gone for the Ferrari. And, to make matters worse, if I bought the Ferrari, I'd wish I had the Aston.

And all the time, in either, as you endlessly got lost, got caught speeding and rang various powerboat champions, you'd have this nagging doubt that looks, style and soaring exhaust notes were not, in the real world, a match for the ruthless efficiency of a Gottlieb Stuttgart Sporty Light.

13 September 2009

Excuse me while I park my aircraft carrier

Ford Flex 3.5L EcoBoost AWD

As we know, there is absolutely nothing you ever encounter on holiday that works very well as a part of your everyday life. The sunshine, for instance. If we had an uninterrupted blue dome sitting over Britain 365 days a year, we'd spend all day at the beach and never do any work. This would turn us all into Australians, and pretty soon we'd only be known on the world stage for our large prawns.

Buying a foreign holiday home won't work either because, as Daisy Waugh pointed out recently in this paper, it doesn't really matter how well you speak the local lingo; one day, just after your swimming pool has exploded, you will be in the local hardware store when you realize you don't know the word for pliers.

Do you know how to say 'jump leads' in French? A friend of mine once spent a good half-hour in a chandler's in Cannes pretending to be a dog by barking. Then he pointed to an imaginary lead around his neck and jumped up and down, which was very imaginative but wrong. The words he needed were '*batterie connecteur*'. You didn't know that, did you? You would have gone round to a neighbour's house and pretended to be a dog as well, and then your neighbours would have clocked you as mad.

Beer's another problem. Back in 1984, I spent some time wandering around China, where, so far as I could tell, it was always 120°F and raining. This made me very thirsty so I spent most days drinking gallons of the local brew, which is called Tsingtao. It was delicious. I loved it. And then I tried some when I got home and I decided that actually it was exactly the same as drinking watered-down mouse pee.

And then there's the hire car. This isn't a problem in Europe, where, at best, you'll get a diesel-powered Renault Scénic that won't have enough power to get up the drive to your villa and will smell of sick.

No one ever harbours a desire to buy a version of what they rented in Spain or France. But America's different. I once rented a Corvette in Vegas and spent the whole time wondering why I didn't have such a thing at home. Then you have the Mustang. I know it has a live rear axle and that its massive 5-litre V8 has less power than Luxembourg's milk marketing board. But that doesn't stop me coming home and pressing my nose every night against the plate-glass windows of that American car dealership in Barnes.

This year, though, I didn't rent a Mustang. On my recent trip to Canada, I got myself a Ford Flex, and it's got me thinking.

As is usual for an American car, it came with a half-timbered steering wheel so that drivers are made to feel like they are in Anne Hathaway's cottage. Americans like it in Anne Hathaway's cottage. It gives them a sense of being. There was also some wood – well, I say wood but it was more like Fablon – on the dash. And the seats were quilted. By someone who has ten thumbs. And is blind.

Then you have the doors. They are huge, and they open right down to a point below the sills. That means they won't open at all if you park alongside any sort of kerb.

There's a similar problem with the four-wheel-drive system. The Flex is designed to be a bit of a low rider so that

Obama Barrack doesn't find it threatening. Good. That's fine. But it means the undersides drag along the ground if you attempt to drive down a rutted track.

Furthermore, the dials are awful. Like the dials on nearly all American cars, they look like they came as a job lot for £2.50. All in all, then, it's a terrible place to be, furnished and equipped with all the care you'd find in a North Dakota motel. And while you can connect an iPod, you can't control what tracks or playlists it selects.

However, you tend to overlook all this because of the headrests, which, like the headrests in a 1990s Aston Martin Vantage, are just that. Not some safety device to keep your hair on in a crash. But a place where you can actually rest your head as the miles glide by.

They do glide, too. Apparently, the Flex I drove has firmed-up sporty suspension. You wouldn't know it as you cruise along in great comfort, napping occasionally. The only time you can tell that Ford of America's ham-fisted chassis men have been getting all racy is when you drive over a small pothole. Then, it feels like the Flex has snapped. It always woke me up, and that was annoying.

Technically, then, the Flex is completely backward, and don't be fooled by the badge on the back that says 'Eco-Boost'. That suggests it's a hybrid of some kind or that it runs on soil. But no. What it signifies is that instead of the V8 iron lung you might expect, it's propelled by a 3.5-litre twin-turbocharged V6 that produces 355bhp and will get you and your passengers from rest to 60mph in 7 seconds. 'EcoBoost', then, is a badge on the back. Nothing more.

So why, then, did I think, albeit fleetingly, that such a car might be exactly what you and I would need for the school run here in England?

Simple. Because this is a car that can accommodate seven people and their luggage and some dogs, even if the dogs in question have just won the 2009 Biggest Wolfhounds in the World competition. And all the shopping a family of forty-three could conceivably need for a century.

It doesn't look big from the outside and it doesn't feel big when you get behind the wheel, but there is no car made with quite so much room for seven to lounge. This is extremely good news if you have children who fight when they are forced within 6 inches of one another. Or, to put it another way, if you have children.

The Flex looks like a Mini. It has the same cheeky stance, the same white roof and the same plethora of styling details that sit in the mix like a nice watch sits on Uma Thurman. And yet, inside, it can swallow everything you own.

It's hard to understand how this is possible. But I've worked it out. America, and I'm including Canada in this, messes with perspective. The roads appear to be the same width as they are here but they're not. They're wider. And it's the same story with parking spaces at Wal-Mart.

You can put your Flex, easily, between the white lines, and so you imagine it will fit between the white lines back home at the Co-op. You imagine that because supermarkets are global and standardized, the parking spaces are too. But they're not. Parking a Flex in Chipping Norton, I suspect, would be like parking a Nimitz class aircraft carrier in Buckler's Hard. The fact is this: it can accommodate more than a Volvo XC90 because it is more than a foot longer.

This would drive you mad. There is nothing – nothing, d'you hear – that is quite so annoying as finding a parking space and then having to hand it over to some smug git in a G-Wiz because your car is too big to fit.

So I won't be importing a Flex any time soon. In much the same way that girls shouldn't think too seriously about importing the Tunisian waiter they slept with while on holiday this year, either.

20 September 2009

We have ways of being a killjoy

BMW 135i M Sport convertible

You may have noticed that all actors smile constantly while driving in a car commercial. This is ridiculous. No one smiles while driving, unless Clement Freud is on the radio, and he isn't any more, because he died.

I urge you all to look next time you're on the road. Anyone driving alone is pulling exactly the same face. It's a zombie face. The face of someone who's medically alive but is actually dead. It's a face I imagine prisoners pull when in solitary confinement.

Out of a car, Stephen Fry appears to be interested, intelligent and alert. In a car, he looks as gormless as a scolded dog. We all do. You never see this in commercials, though. Because in a commercial the actor's whole being is 90 per cent teeth, and his eyes are sparkling like a rippled sea at sunset. He is delirious with pleasure, not because he's just thought of something funny or seen a hippopotamus in dungarees going the other way. No. Rather preposterously, he's delirious because he is enjoying the act of driving so much.

There's a lot of smiling in the new BMW advert. It's all sunny skies and wind in the hair and happy shiny people going round corners. It's absurd in every way. Except one. The final words that accompany this uplifting festival of happiness, spoken by Captain Jean-Luc Picard, sum up exactly what motoring is all about.

Here's what he says: 'We realized a long time ago that what you make people feel is just as important as what you make.'

Bang on. You can buy a cheap car that takes you to work economically and you may be pleased with the savings you've made. But saving money is never joyful. It is mean-spirited and demonstrates that you have a heart of coal. If you wish to lead a joyous life, you should always spend 10 per cent more than you earn.

Joy in a car can come from many quarters. It can come from the 'feel' of a button on the dashboard. It can come, such as it does in a Porsche Boxster, from that spine-tingling noise the exhaust makes at precisely 5200rpm. It can come from the way a car turns into a corner or, as you will find in a Nissan 370Z, from the way the engine blips on down changes. Joy can come from a nicely flared wheel arch, from good graphics on a sat nav screen, from the surge you feel when you accelerate. Sometimes, as is the case with the Aston Martin DBS, it can come from so many places, all at once, you are left feeling a little bit light-headed. Even the stitching on the seats made my heart feel all gooey and warm.

I've never been able to put my finger on quite why I don't like cars made by Proton, and so on. But now I do. They are not joyous. They are built purely to shore up an emerging nation's balance of trade, and you will never find any joy in anything where every single part has come from the lowest bidder.

Joy, contrary to what BMW would have us believe, does not make us smile. Even in the aforementioned DBS, I do not gurn like a mad person as I drive along. But joy does make us happy and content and satisfied. In a car, joy is more important than an airbag.

Strangely, however, the one car company that rarely gives me any joy is BMW. It's why I would never buy one of its cars.

That's not to say its cars are no good. The new Z4 is marvellous and the M3 is one of the most perfectly balanced machines ever created by man. It makes an F-16 fighter jet look ungainly and lumpen.

However, you always get the sense with a BMW that science has ruled the roost throughout the entire design process; that anything with a bit of flair or panache has been ditched to make way for another equation. And as for the line, 'We realized a long time ago that what you make people feel is just as important as what you make'?

Hmmm. What BMW made people feel in its early days was not 'joyous', but 'frightened', as those Munich-engined warplanes swooped out of the sky, machine guns blazing.

It's much the same story with the Beethoven/Schiller 'Ode to Joy'. It isn't. It's a stirring piece of music, for sure, but even before the European Union got hold of it, it was never quite as happy-making as, say, the Carpenters' 'Please Mr Postman'.

Joy's not really a German thing, I suppose. We do joy. The Americans do joy. The Italians do joy, even though they never laugh. Germans, though? They're rather better at precision and accuracy and following orders. Which is why I can't quite understand what went wrong with the new convertible version of the 135i.

It is featured right at the start of the 'joy' commercial. The driver is an old man in a hat who is smiling enormously, presumably because he's just caught a glimpse in the rear-view mirror of his comedy moustache. Certainly, it's not because of the car.

I like the hard-top 135 very much. In a road test on these pages, I said it harked back to the big engine/small car philosophy that crystalized the BMW range back in the early eighties. I even gave it five stars, and so I was looking forward to driving its convertible sister.

The 3-litre engine's unchanged and it's still great. You have one little turbo that gets you going and then another enormous turbo that kicks in if you really need some clout to overtake. The result is better economy allied to a seamless, relentless, muscular stream of power that's never exciting or zingy, but always there, ready to arm wrestle its way into your consciousness.

However, the convertible is 254lb heavier than the coupé and that iron lard makes its presence felt every time you put your foot down. This car is as zesty as Stonehenge.

Of course, you'd imagine that with 254lb of strengthening material, it would at least be rigid and strong. But no. All the time the steering wheel is wobbling and vibrating, and sometimes, you can actually feel the flex that is sort of inevitable when the front and the back are joined together by only the floor and a bit of Millets canvas.

I don't doubt that, *in extremis*, the 135 will handle nicely. And we know it's quite fast. But there is no excitement here. Not even a crumb of joy.

As a practical proposition, it's not much cop, either. The boot is tiny and the rear seats are suitable only for people with no legs. I should also mention that with the electric roof up, you cannot see what's coming at oblique road junctions and that getting it down takes a yawning 22 seconds.

In theory, this car should be very good; a modern-day incarnation of the old 2002 or the 323i. I like the manually adjustable seats and the lack of styling. I like the fact the roof is canvas rather than metal. It feels like the sort of car in which the need for driving pleasure has been put above the need for gimmicks and gadgets. But what results is neither an ode to joy, nor a very good car.

27 September 2009

Love is blind, thunder thighs

Audi TT RS Coupé

About a hundred years ago I used to spend a very great deal of time with my nose pressed against the plate-glass window of an exotic car dealership in Chiswick, wondering if there was anything in life quite so perfect as a Lancia Montecarlo.

So, when I drove one this week, I couldn't quite believe there was one rather notable feature that I had somehow overlooked. I had spent days taking in every last detail of this twin-cam mid-engined sports car that in effect bridged the gap between the frankly rather weedy Fiat X1/9 and the frankly rather expensive Ferrari 308. You would imagine, then, that I might have noticed it was about as big as my left shoe.

I suspect the reason is simple. Back then, all cars were tiny, even big ones. That's just how it was. So, the Montecarlo is 5½ inches shorter than the current Ford Fiesta and narrower, too. Technically, that makes it a motorcycle.

There are more examples, too. The BMW 1-series is wider and taller than the 3-series you had in the 1980s. And today's Range Rover is nearly 20 inches longer than the 1970s original.

All of this raises a question. Why?

If you have been fortunate enough to look around the SS *Great Britain*, which is now a museum piece in Bristol, you will undoubtedly have been shocked by the size of the beds.

They are tiny, more like cots, and there's a good reason for that. Back in the nineteenth century, when the ship was built, people were little.

But we have not become that much bigger in the past twenty to thirty years. So why the sudden need for vast cars?

Some would cite safety, suggesting that the crash protection needed to get a car onto the market these days means the car itself must be enormous. But that's not true. A Renault Twingo is not big and that's very safe. A Renault Formula One car is unbelievably tiny and that's safe enough, we're told, to be rammed, on purpose, into a wall.

I think market researchers are to blame. They go out onto the street with their clipboards and their winning smiles and they say, 'Would you like your next car to be bigger?' And since everyone associates a big car with success and prosperity, everyone says, 'Yes.' The car companies are simply responding to that.

The fact is, though, it's nonsense, and it's about time the trend was reversed, because I drove that Montecarlo through a Welsh town with a name I can neither remember nor spell, and it was a joy. Gaps that would have thwarted even a Mini could be dealt with without a problem. Parking spaces that would have beaten a Citroën driver were a doddle. And, most important, small cars are not seen as threatening by pedestrians. They smile at you and that makes the world a happier place.

I can think of no reason cars need be any bigger than that little Lancia. There is room inside for two people, an engine, some wheels and, unless you are Nicholas Soames, the weekly shop. Everything else in your car is just wasted air.

It's much the same story with the little Austin Healey Sprite I drove around Mallorca on *Top Gear* recently. Among modern sports cars it looks as preposterous as a ballet shoe on a building site. But, actually, it's the other way around. It's the modern sports cars that are too big.

And that causes problems because their big, heavy bodies have to be suspended in such a way that they don't roll and wallow in the corners. That means the suspension has to be firm. So firm that it will break your spine every time you run over a catseye. They will also break the bank every time you fill up. And your mind when you can't find a big enough parking space without going to Lincolnshire.

There's another thing I've noticed, too, about cars from not that long ago. The pillars that supported the roof were elegant, spidery little things. This meant there was a bigger glass area, and that made life inside better, especially if you were a tomato. It meant visibility was good, too. Inside a Lancia Fulvia or an old BMW CSL, you really could see all four corners of the car from the driver's seat.

Not any more. I saw a Seat yesterday with such thick A-pillars, they came with their own windows. It's ridiculous and ungainly and demonstrates that we are going backwards. But it does bring me nicely onto the Audi TT RS.

Naturally, this suffers from the problems that affect all modern cars, insomuch as it's supposed to be a small, sleek, agile two-door sports car but is, in fact, about the size of Wales. Or is it the Albert Hall? Or a jumbo jet?

Whatever, it's much bigger than it should be and it comes with pillars big enough to make its blind spots so massive, you might as well actually be blind. Sitting in a TT is like sitting in a postbox. And I banged my head every single time I climbed inside.

There are other issues, too. There is no conventional button to open the boot, so you must either get into the car, where there is a release catch. Or use a remote opener on the key fob, which doesn't work. Worse, though, it has a little read-out on the dash that orders you to change gear as you drive along.

'You should be in sixth,' it says, Germanically. But how does it know? Sure, I should be in sixth if I was interested in achieving better fuel economy. But I wasn't. I was interested in pouncing past the car in front, which is why I was in second. If I'd tried to do this, as instructed, in sixth, I would have been killed.

Then there's the biggest problem of them all – the problem of being in an Audi TT when you are not called Angela. I do not know why it can be driven by only people named Angela, but that's a fact and there's nothing we can do about it. If you have a TT and you aren't called Angela, you have the wrong car.

The news from here on in, however, is good, because the new version – the RS – is an absolute star.

On the surface it looks like a normal TT, except for an optional rear spoiler, a more chiselled chin and brushed-aluminium door mirrors. Which look like silver ears.

Underneath, it has a 2.5-litre turbo engine, which, because it has five cylinders, harks back to the glory days of the original Quattro. It's a corker of an engine. Muscular and zingy in equal measure, it endows the car with a grown-up turn of speed while sipping the fuel. And on top of all this, there's that marvellously offbeat, though surprisingly muted, five-cylinder backdrop.

The rest of the car is either just as good or a bit better. The seats are wonderful, the ride is much more supple than you might imagine, the grip from the four-wheel-drive system is magnificent, the handling is a delight, the stereo is a joy and the boot is huge.

Yes, the car should be smaller, but, accepting that enormousness is the norm these days, I have to say the RS is epic. If you can live with the stupid boot-release arrangement and a sat nav system that accepts only the first piece of a postcode, it's worth changing your name to Angela and getting one.

4 October 2009

Comfort for all the family in a . . .

Skoda Octavia Scout 1.8 TSI

It's hard to identify one single thing that finished Rover. Some say it was the Phoenix Four who bought the company for some beads, grew amazing moustaches and waltzed off into the half-timbered world of Warwickshire with their lumps of cash.

Others suggest that the problems started way before Rover boss Kevin Howe and his mustachioed mates rolled into town. They blame Lord Stokes, who was possibly the nicest man in the whole world. He was so nice, in fact, that he actually believed all the promises made by various trade union officials.

And then, of course, there was Red Robbo, who arranged for various bits of the workforce to come out on strike more than 350 times in a single year. And Michael Edwardes, appointed as boss by Jim Callaghan at a time when production levels had fallen to four cars per man per year.

Others, of course, point their fingers at the cars themselves; the woeful Morris Marina and its bastard son, the Ital, the Austin All Aggro, which was usually supplied to customers with bits of the workers' sandwiches still in the doors, the hideous Triumph TR7 and the Austin Landcrab, a car that had to be driven from one side of the Longbridge works to the other, outside, in all weathers . . . before it was painted.

Most were rusty before they were blue or, more usually, beige.

For me, though, I reckon the end of Rover came about early in 2003 when it launched a car called the Streetwise.

Based on the Rover 25, which was already rubbish, it was jacked up on stilts and came with ostentatious rubber bumpers and side strips that were supposed to make it look tough and rugged but actually made it look like a pensioner in Doc Martens. And they called this engineered-on-a-shoestring mishmash an 'urban on-roader'. Which, when translated, means 'a car that you can drive on the road in a town'. Like every other car in the world, then. But it wasn't. It was worse.

Of course, this sort of thing had been tried before, by a French company called Matra with the Rancho. It was a front-wheel-drive but it was made from polyester and it sported chunky panels on the side, roof bars and various other accoutrements to make it look like it had just driven off the set of *Daktari*. Was it a success? Er, no.

A car needs to look like what it does. A Ferrari needs to be low and sleek. A Volvo has to fit outside an antiques shop. A Rolls-Royce has to look right with Suralan Sugar in the back. It's no good making a car look like a Lamborghini if the engine is made by Atco. And I'm sorry, but a normal two-wheel-drive car, such as the Streetwise or the Rancho, dressed up in off-road gear, looks as stupid as those massive watches that dissolve if they fall in the sink.

Which brings me on to the Skoda Roomster Scout. What were they thinking of? I like the normal Roomster. I think that if you avoid the three-cylinder diesel version, which doesn't move unless you blow it up, it is a brilliant little car. But now Skoda has launched a version that has more ground clearance and various Streetwise styling cues . . . but no four-wheel-drive system. This means that if you take it into a field, it will remain there until June.

I decided, therefore, to not bother reviewing what would be a stupid car and take a look instead at its bigger brother – the Octavia Scout.

Like the Rancho and the Rover and the Roomster, this is also front-wheel drive. But when you go into a field, some of the engine's power is automatically sent aft, making it four-wheel drive.

I went for a drive in the countryside this morning and was very impressed with its ability to make progress over the sort of terrain that would cause the driver of a Range Rover to think seriously about turning round. It may be the same four-wheel-drive system that's fitted to a sporty Audi TT but it really does work. What's more, in a stubble field, the vicious little stalks were prevented from scratching the paint by those chunky plastic skirts, and the raised ride height meant the sump guard was only needed twice.

Of course, you might think you have no need for all this. But you do, because on the road, the taller suspension makes the Scout waterbed comfortable. It's as relaxing as being asleep. On the M40 between junctions eight and nine, the road surface is bad enough to reduce even a Rolls-Royce to its component parts. But the Scout just glides.

Of course, there is a downside. The Scout will not handle quite as well on a racetrack as its standard front-wheel-drive, low-riding sister. But this doesn't matter because it is a Skoda and not since the fifties has any such thing been asked to go round Stowe corner as though it were being chased by the Borg.

Truth be told, it handles and steers perfectly well, and it's much the same story with the performance. I tried the new 1.8-litre petrol version – the only other option is a diesel – and when I pressed the accelerator, it produced the sort of shove that was neither too slow nor alarmingly fast. At motorway cruising speeds it was quiet and entirely fuss-free, but on steeper inclines, you do perhaps need to drop down into fifth. Flat out, it will do 131mph.

It's much the same story on the inside. There was no satellite navigation and no buttons on the steering wheel. There was no hand stitching, nor any kind of frivolity. It was absolutely straightforward. Spacious, too, and as well made as you'd expect from what is, in effect, a Volkswagen.

I have argued in the past that if we all bought cars using nothing but our heads, we'd all have VW Golfs. You are a family man with two children? You need a Golf. You are a wealthy young playboy from Dubai? You need a Golf. You are a school-run mum? You need a Golf. A student? A second-hand Golf. You are a gamekeeper? An astronaut? A golfer? It's the same answer.

But the Skoda Octavia Scout is even more rounded and capable, especially when you look at the price. Volvo will sell you a normal estate car that can be used off-road. And Audi too. But the cheapest A4 allroad is just shy of £30,000. Then you have the Subaru Outback, which, providing you avoid the hopeless diesel, is a fantastic car; one of my favourites. But the cheapest version of this is £26,295. The Scout I drove was priced at just £18,750. You can't even buy a 2-litre Golf GT diesel for that. Just £18,750 for a comfortable, spacious, well made four-wheel-drive estate car is truly extraordinary value for money.

There is no feature of the Octavia Scout that makes your heart melt with desire and lust. You will never fall in love with it and you will, of course, be subjected to much derision from badge snobs who still think Berlin is split in two. But if you apply the cold steel of logic to your choice of car, it is absolutely impossible to come up with anything better.

11 October 2009

A car even its mother couldn't love

Porsche Panamera 4.8 V8 Turbo

As we know, walking is stupid. It is dirty, difficult, tiring and fraught with many dangers. You could have a heart attack, you could be struck by lightning, you could be run over or, and this happens a lot, you could be attacked by a cow.

Look at it this way. No motorist has ever had to be rescued by a helicopter, but from now till the spring we will be bombarded with an endless stream of news stories about walkists who've had to be snatched from the jaws of death by the RAF after they fell over or got lost in a cloud.

I understand, of course, that we need the ability to walk, so that we can get to the fridge. But the idea of 'going for a walk' seems completely ridiculous. Because one of two things will happen. You will either end up back at home again – and what's the point of going out in the first place if that's your goal? – or you will be killed.

Some pooh-pooh this, saying that when you are walking in the British countryside you will see all sorts of animals and plants that you would not see if you simply stayed at home playing Call of Duty 4 on the PlayStation.

Really? The last time I looked, Britain was not even remotely like Botswana. There are no brown hyenas, for instance, in Welwyn Garden City. Nor are there lions in Scotland. As we know from Kate Humble's charming *Autumnwatch* series on the BBC, you need to be extremely patient if you want to see anything at all. And even if you are extremely patient, all you'll ever see is a field mouse. Or maybe a barnacle goose. These are dull. Indeed, the total number of interesting animals in Britain is none.

However, if you are in a car, things are very different. Last weekend, I woke on Sunday morning with a catastrophic hangover, which my wife said would be cured with some fresh air. I tried explaining that the air in the sitting room near the PlayStation machine was just as fresh as the air in the garden but she was having none of it.

So children were roused, horses were tacked and arrangements were made to meet with the friends we'd been drinking with the night before . . . for a morning in the countryside.

Some were in the saddle, some were on foot and a girlfriend and I were in a Range Rover, trying not to be sick. 'This is walking, isn't it?' she said, as we bumped over the field and down a precipitous slope into a wood.

She was wrong. It was better than walking. The noise of the diesel V8 was startling all sorts of animals that would have remained hidden and unseen to the tiptoeing rambler. Deer shot out of every bush, badgers scampered out of their holes and, with eyes blinking, rushed off to alert their mates. Hares leapt, rabbits snouted and foxes looked on slyly, wondering if there was perhaps a baby in the back of the car they could eat.

This is the thing about wildlife. As beaters know, a pheasant will simply sit still when a man walks by. But if the man starts making a noise, it will take off. The same goes for everything. Present an animal with a bearded biped in a cagoule and it will remain *in situ*, holding its breath until the fool has gone away. Present it with a twin-turbocharged Range Rover and it'll leap out of its burrow, or nest, or sett, to reveal itself in what passes in Britain for full glory.

A blast of the horn roused, even managed to scare, a family of barn owls, and normally you'd need a night-vision lens, a night without sleep and several months in hospital recovering from hypothermia to see one of those. I love barn owls, and seeing a whole herd of them, during the day, from the leather-lined, air-conditioned comfort of a Range Rover was sensational.

Later, we met up with the riders, who looked terrified and drained, and the walkers, who were covered in mud. Neither group had seen a single thing of any interest. And, what's more, their hangovers were still just as bad as ours.

This, then, is my message to the producers of *Autumnwatch*. Instead of showing us Kate Humble sitting still for two days in the hope we get to see a stoat, and finding geese with satellites and building elaborate traps to catch shrews, simply drive about as fast as possible in a wood and there'll be such a blizzard of fur and feathers, the viewers will get coochy-coo overload.

This is the joy of the motor car. It has so many uses. A commuter device, a means whereby others can assess your wealth, a crow-scarer, a thrill machine, a beater, a tool, a thing of exquisite beauty, a stereo, an air-conditioned respite from the sun and shelter in the rain. It is something you can love, cherish, abuse, polish and, if you are Stephen Ireland, that Manchester City player with the blinged-up Bentley, ruin.

And this brings me on to the Porsche Panacea, which sits in the mix like an apple core on a birthday cake. It seems to have no purpose at all.

I understand, of course, why Porsche chose to build a four-door saloon. It's the same reason Lamborghini started work on such a thing, and Aston Martin too. These are small companies and it makes economic sense to squeeze as many models as possible from every component. You have the engine. You have the chassis. And you have a lot of people who won't buy anything you make because they want four doors.

The trouble is, while Lamborghini and Aston Martin clearly employ talented stylists to ensure an elongated, widened four-seat variation on a two-seater theme does not end up looking like a supermodel who's gone to fat, Porsche plainly gave the job to a janitor.

I actually wonder sometimes whether Porsche employs a stylist at all. Plainly, it had some bloke back in the thirties, when Hitler created the ancestor of the 911, and it had someone else in the seventies and eighties, when it was making the wondrous 928 (the 944 wasn't bad either), but today, God knows who's in charge. Someone who, I suspect, has never been to art school.

The original design for the Boxster was exquisite, but then someone obviously said, 'Instead of making this, why don't we make the actual car we sell look like that pushmi-pullyu thing from *Doctor Dolittle*?'

Then there's the Gayman, which is simply hideous, and don't even get me started on the Cayenne. No, do get me started. What were they thinking of? I understand the reasoning behind that 911-style nose, but did no one stop and think, 'Hang on. Putting a 911's face on the front of a truck is the same as putting Keira Knightley's phizog on the front of Brian Blessed. The end result is going to look absurd'? And it does.

The Cayenne is one of the few cars that look better when a footballer has added 39-inch wheels, spoilers and wings. Because the bling detracts from the hopeless starting point.

The Panamera, though, is worse. People have tried to be kind, saying that it's challenging and that it's unusual. But the simple fact of the matter is this: it's as ugly as an inside-out monkey. It's dreadful. Part-Austin Maxi, it looks like someone with no talent at all was trying to describe what they wanted to a blind person, over the phone.

I tried one on a recent trip to Romania and I thought it was a very good car. But that's like saying Ann Widdecombe has a heart of gold. It's possibly true but it's completely irrelevant. You still wouldn't.

18 October 2009

Turnip boy has softened its black heart

Mercedes-Benz CLK Black

I was driving home the other night in great pain. Some fool had gaffer-taped my arms to a chair, and in the course of struggling free I had removed several hairs and a great deal of skin, which had been badly burnt just two days earlier, on a volcano in Chile. Mine is not really a conventional job.

Anyway, I was in a bit of a hurry. Not only did I desperately need some cream to soothe the impromptu Brazilian on my arms, but also it was the first night in about a hundred years when my entire family would be all together under the same roof at the same time.

I wanted to hear about my eldest daughter's school trip to Auschwitz and how my son had got on in his rugby match. As a result, I decided I wasn't really very interested in Mr Brown's speed limits. The man's a fool anyway. On the one hand, he tells us about the importance of family values, but on the other he insists that we drive home so slowly that our family will be fast asleep in bed by the time we get there.

However, because the half-term traffic would be light, and because I was driving my own very fast Mercedes CLK Black limited edition, I was confident I'd do the journey from Guildford to Chipping Norton in no more than seventy-five minutes. But alas, it was not to be.

I don't think I've ever seen the snarl-up symbols on my satellite navigation screen look quite so colourful. Every single road was either closed or jammed. And the Chris Evans radio show was nothing more than an endless stream of misery from Sally Traffic.

Roadworks on the M25 forced me onto the M4. The A404 past Marlow was solid, so I took a lane through villages that haven't appeared on any map since Dick Turpin was knocking about. Even the road from Oxford to my house was a non-stop stream of temporary traffic lights, because some idiot at the council had decided that a pavement should be constructed.

A pavement? In the middle of nowhere? In the Cotswolds? Have you ever heard of anything so stupid in your entire life? Ramblers are entitled by law to come and sit by your fire and have sex with your wife whenever the mood takes them. They are allowed to walk wherever they please without let or hindrance, and now I am denied the chance to get home and see my family because someone with a beard and a warped mind has decided they should be allowed to walk in the road as well.

We are talking about a madman, someone who cannot pass a shop window without being overcome by a need to lick it. Someone who may well be extremely dangerous. I think it is important we find him and kill him as soon as possible.

Because of him, and the traffic, and the roadworks on the M25, which are due to end after I'm dead, and the average-speed cameras and the Highway Wombles pretending to be policemen, it was one of the longest and most miserable journeys of my life.

But it could have been so much worse if my Mercedes hadn't just come back from hospital in Norfolk.

When I first tested the 6.2-litre CLK Black, only 300 of which were built, I was overawed by its massive range of abilities. It was not just the thunderous 507 horsepower or the insane wheel arch extensions, though these two things on their own were probably enough. It was the knife-edge handling, the constant sense that you were driving something that was actually designed to kill you. It was called the Black, I suspected, because that was the colour of its heart.

I signed off my review by saying that no one's life was complete without one, and shortly afterwards put my money where my pen was. Yup. I bought one.

If I'm honest, it hasn't been an entirely happy relationship. The seats are so hip-hugging that I am unable to offer lifts to fat girls. To make matters worse, I am also unable to explain why. 'Because your arse is too big to fit in the seat' tends to make women cry.

It is also extremely difficult to fasten the seatbelts and impossible if you are wearing a coat. And then there's the question of range. Like the standard CLK it has a 62-litre (13½-gallon) fuel tank, which is fine if the engine up front is a parsimonious diesel. But when it's a massive V8, 62 litres does not get you to the end of the road.

Worse than this, though, was the ride. On a normal British road that has been dug up by slovenly apes and repaired by companies with both eyes fixed firmly on the bottom line, it was intolerable. I do mean that. Intolerable. So bad that I actually looked forward to it running out of fuel so I could get out and have a respite from the battering.

I knew what had happened, of course. I'd been so seduced by the power and the styling and the Grim Reaper handling that I'd overlooked the bad bits. Buying one had been a bit like choosing a wife based entirely on the size of her breasts.

Honestly, I was thinking of getting rid. But then I read something interesting. The Black comes with adjustable suspension. Lots of cars do, these days. And ordinarily, my advice on this matter would be plain and simple. Leave it alone. A big car maker such as Mercedes-Benz knows an awful lot more about chassis dynamics than you do. If it thought the car could be improved by fiddling with the damper settings, it would have done so at the factory.

Adjustable suspension is nothing more than a sop to the ego of the terminally stupid. And something a salesman can talk about on a test drive, 'Sir can tailor it to sir's bespoke requirements, sir . . .'

But, I'm sorry, Mercedes has test tracks and millions of laptops. It employs thousands of doctors who have no sense of humour, just an insatiable thirst to do the best they can. So, the notion that you, in a shed, can improve on their work with nothing but a screwdriver is as absurd as trying to improve on a Gordon Ramsay soufflé using nothing but what you have in your pocket.

I was chatting about this to a chap called Gavan Kershaw a few weeks ago. Gavan is the top chassis boffin at Lotus. He is responsible for the Elise, the extraordinarily balanced Evora and, I'm told, the marvellously supple new Jaguar XFR. Most of all, though, he is the chap who designed *Top Gear*'s test track.

He's a very clever boy and I trust him, so when he said he would have a look at the Black, I agreed. Mainly because, no matter what he did, he couldn't possibly make it worse.

He didn't. It's still not comfy. It's not even halfway to a nod in the general direction of comfiness. The tyres are too low-profile and the chassis-strengthening beams too vigorous for that. But his twiddles do now mean that, for short periods behind the wheel, it is possible to think of something other than the pain.

And here's the really good bit. By making it a bit softer, he has ensured it is now nearly two seconds faster on a lap round the *Top Gear* test track.

And the steering, already very good, is now sublime.

Normally, I don't really care whether car bosses read my columns. But I do hope the people at Mercedes are reading this, partly because it might cause them to think that maybe a hard ride isn't necessarily the way forward. But mostly because a fat bloke from Turnipshire (Gavan is a bit porky) has managed to improve what they presumably thought was perfect.

I know that sort of thing makes a German very unhappy. And achieving that once in a while compensates for the less savoury parts of my job.

8 November 2009

Jack of all trades

Toyota RAV4 SR 2.2 D-4D

Sometimes, I wonder how the human race has risen to the top of the evolutionary pile when almost every single decision we ever make is bonkers. You do not see blackbirds smoking cigarettes or beavers riding motorcycles. You don't see pigeons ignoring non-organic seeds or bison at the shops buying something they know they can't afford. You do, of course, see elephants on unicycles, but only because we think it is funny.

Let's look at the simple decisions I've made today. First of all, I hit the snooze button on the alarm clock even though I knew full well that I had to get up and go to work or I wouldn't be finished till midnight. Then I went downstairs and had a cup of coffee, which I know will make my teeth all brown. And then I read the *Guardian*, which always makes me angry.

And then, instead of going to work, I put my new cabinet for drinks and guns in the back of the Range Rover. It's an exquisite piece of furniture, this: hand-made in Yorkshire from American walnut, with brushed aluminium handles, it takes sixteen shot glasses and sixteen flutes, and there are cutaway compartments for champagne, sloe gin, soup, whisky, 500 cartridges and two Beretta shotguns.

I will use it probably twice a year and the rest of the time it will render the car bootless and consequently unable to take dogs, wellies or even light shopping. So it's mad. So's my new quad bike. And so is everything I've ever bought. I look at all the things on my desk and I wonder: what on earth was going on in my head when I chose them? The paperweight with the globe inside, the catapult, the Bugatti Veyron cufflinks, the Insanity chilli sauce and the Sony Rolly, which so far as I can tell is specifically designed to do absolutely nothing at all.

I must have said to someone in a shop, 'What does this do?', and he must have said, 'Absolutely nothing at all,' and then I must have said, 'Oh good. Here's my credit card.' How mad's that?

What makes this state of affairs so alarming is that stupidity isn't simply restricted to the dull masses. Those in power can't make a sensible decision either.

You have had very senior politicians standing up and telling us that they know Iraq has weapons of mass destruction. And now you have Bob Ainsworth, who has deliberately chosen to grow that moustache.

You may remember a few years ago when Britain's transport secretary was very fat and had no 11-plus. He made the mistake of digging up the outside lane of the M4 and turning it into a bus lane. This made not just him but the whole government a laughing stock, so you'd imagine no one would make the same mistake again . . .

But they have. Only more so. For the past two years my journeys to and from London have been fraught by roadworks near where the A40 crosses the North Circular. It's been hell and has wasted many hours of my life. But I figured it would be worthwhile because, plainly, those in charge had decided to widen the road.

They have, too. But, amazingly, the new lanes – in both

directions – are for bicycles only. I am not making this up. All that time. All that expense. And all for the benefit of a few idiots who can't afford a car.

To make matters worse, no provision is made for bicycles at either end of the new lanes. It's highway, then bike lane, then highway. So you can't try them out without being killed on the way.

When you look at something like this you stop wondering how the human being has climbed to the top of the evolutionary pile. And wonder, instead, how it's survived at all. Bicycle lanes on the main road from Oxford to London. Whoever came up with that sits on the Darwinian waterfall of change alongside the housefly. Seriously, my dishwasher has a bigger brain.

Of course, this collective stupidity is particularly noticeable when it comes to buying cars because only a tiny minority ever buys anything even remotely sensible. For sure, some people try. They read *What Car?* And they study the findings in *Which?* And they take test drives and they haggle with salesmen. And then, as often as not, they end up with a Peugeot. Which is like studying all the travel brochures and going on holiday to Latvia.

Style is the main problem. It gets in the way of clear thinking. We know we should have a Golf. We know it does everything we want at a reasonable price but we think it's a bit boring to look at. So we buy a Mazda MX-5 instead.

What possible reason is there for buying a convertible? We get extra noise, a small boot, generally less safety, and for what? So that on one or two days of the year we can screw up our hairdos.

Why buy a sports car? It'll just be uncomfortable. Why buy a big car? You won't be able to park it. Why buy an exotic car? You know you're only paying for the badge. Why buy an

SUV? It's only going to make bicyclists bang on your roof and be angry. And why buy something made in France? Or Italy? Or Britain? Or America? You know it's going to explode sooner or later.

This brings me on to the Toyota RAV4 that's been sitting in my drive for the past week.

When the RAV4 first came onto the scene, it was, for sure, a pretty little thing – a slightly more grown-up Suzuki jeep – but it made very little sense at all. I mean, it was a four-wheel-drive car for the town. Graham Norton bought one, and that says it all.

I've probably driven lots of RAV4s over the years, but none sticks in my mind. And that's why I kept ignoring the new one, even though I knew it was the first RAV4 to be available with a diesel engine and an automatic gearbox. Wow.

Eventually, I did take it for a drive, and overall, I have to say, it was pretty nasty. The seats were a bit hard. The diesel engine was a bit unrefined, and while the little television screen in the rear-view mirror that lights up when you are reversing was novel, it was too small to be of any use.

However, while it may not be a particularly inspiring car to drive, or look at, it is a remarkably competent tool to own.

While the rear door opens sideways rather than upwards, which might be a nuisance in tight parking spaces, there's no denying there are many treats in store for the dull and the practical. Instead of fiddling about for hours to get the back seats down and ending up with broken fingernails, and them still in place, you simply pull two levers and, plop, they fold down flat. Then you have a van.

Up front, you get leather upholstery, Bluetooth, air-conditioning, automatic wipers and headlights and heated front seats. About what you'd expect for £25,000.

Yes, you can have more style and panache from a Ford Kuga or a Honda CR-V but they aren't really designed to go off-road and, these days, the RAV4 is. It has a device that stops you rolling back down hills – for when you can't be bothered to use the handbrake – and another that keeps your speed down on steep descents. There's even a locking differential.

In other words, this is a car that can be used on the farm and on the road and on the school run and for trips to the megastore. It does what a small off-road car is supposed to do, and it was made in Japan, so it will last ages.

In short, it is the sort of car you would buy with your head. Which is why no one will buy it at all.

15 November 2009

Land Rover leaves behind the murderers

Land Rover Discovery 4 3.0 TDV6 HSE

I don't understand the Land Rover Discovery. It's like torque and electricity and Peter Mandelson. We know it exists and we know what it does. But we can't explain it very easily. In the olden days, it made sense. There was a big hole between the utilitarian, bring-your-own-earplugs Defender and the Range Rover, which had gone all Surrey, with fancy carpets and seats smothered in cow peelings. In other words, there was no car in the Land Rover line-up for the true country-man, who wanted one car to take his cows to market and his family to the pub. The Discovery filled that hole nicely and, as a result, became very popular with murderers.

Occasionally, the Disco was bought by a farmer's wife but mostly it was bought by people who like complicated guns and camouflage trousers. These people label themselves 'off-road enthusiasts' and 'green-laners' but it's all just a front for murdering.

Why does anyone need camouflage trousers? It's because they want to hide from the police in the woods. And why do they have a Discovery? Because a Discovery can get very far into those woods, which means bodies can be buried in places where they won't be found by pesky dog-walkers.

You may wonder why they chose a Discovery rather than, say, a Toyota Land Cruiser, but that's because you're not paying attention. Like murderers in hillbilly America, 'off-road enthusiasts' are practical people who enjoy mending engines and gearboxes. A Land Cruiser never goes wrong and, as a result, provides no opportunity for tinkering.

And, again, like the American backwoodsman, the British rural murderer is a fiercely patriotic soul who shoots squirrels and badgers simply to prepare for the day when he is called upon to kill Communists and immigrants. Furthermore, if he had a Toyota he wouldn't be able to get as far into the woods, so his bodies would be discovered and there'd be much unpleasantness.

You think this is nonsense? Really? Well, next time you are in the British countryside, look carefully at the person driving along in an old Land Rover Discovery and ask yourself a simple question. Would you let him take your daughter for a picnic?

Anyway, after Ken Noye was sent to prison, Land Rover stopped making a car for murderers and brought out a new Discovery. And, frankly, I couldn't work out who it was for at all.

First of all, it had an extremely odd chassis arrangement. I shan't bore you with the details here but the upshot of this peculiar decision was simple: the car weighed 2.7 tons. That is a lot. And that meant the fuel economy was dreadful.

There were other problems, too. Yes, it had seven seats, but raising and lowering those seats was extremely complicated and required the use of two hands. Which was a bit of a nuisance for the sort of person who needs a seven-seater car – school-run mums. Who usually have to get the seats up and down while carrying a toddler or shopping. This, you knew, was a car designed by men in wellies who had no concept of children. But that's gone now and we have an even more puzzling Discovery to try to fathom.

Apart from some fancier headlamps, it looks pretty much the same as the last version, but inside it's even more upmarket, with lots of soft-touch this and electronic that.

Underneath, they've fiddled with the suspension set-up to make the steering more precise, they've lost some weight, and now you can specify the 3-litre twin-turbo diesel engine that first saw the light of day in the Jaguar XF.

Retuned for the Disco so that it produces 241bhp, it's epic. Yes, it sounds a bit coarse and diesely when you fire it up, but thereafter, it's sewing-machine smooth, nicely zingy and almost unbelievably economical. Drive carefully and you'll get 30mpg.

I liked driving the new Disco very much. It was smooth, quiet and extremely comfortable; the steering was good, the driving position was excellent and, while you still needed two hands to move the seats about, the seven-seat practicality was a bonus as well.

Then there's the price to think about. The range starts – with the old 2.7-litre version – at £32,000, while the car I tested is £47,695. I'm not going to pretend that this is cheap but it is £17,000 less than a diesel-powered Range Rover TDV8 Vogue.

And what exactly does the Range Rover have that the new Discovery does not? They have the same off-road gubbins, and the Disco has – for an extra 600 quid – the same brilliant command system, which means five exterior cameras feed images of what they see to the screen on the dash. You can choose which feed you want to look at, and even zoom in on things you find interesting.

The idea is that you can spot obstacles as you drive off-road, but it's huge fun to switch between the images as you drive on-road, making your own movie. It gets better. It's possible, through mind-boggling technology, for the passenger to watch a DVD while the driver – looking at the same screen – sees the sat nav map. How brilliant is that?

Yes, the Range Rover has a V8 engine, but the Disco, with its new V6, is only 0.4 seconds slower to 60. And that doesn't seem like £17,000-worth of lost oomph to me.

It used to be that the Range Rover felt more of a luxurious car. Not any more. With its hand-stitched leather and 'mood' lighting, the Disco is just as palatial, and you have exactly the same imperious driving position. The conclusion, then, is simple. If you want a go-anywhere luxury car, buy the Discovery 4.

Except you can't, because when you drive along in your new car, no one will think, 'Ah, there's a canny chap. He's saved £17,000.' They will think, 'Oh dear. Poor man. He can't afford a Range Rover.' This is known, in my head, as the Porsche Boxster syndrome – you buy one if you can't afford a 911.

In the same way, it's impossible to drive a Discovery without thinking of the Range Rover. I'm not talking about the (ghastly) Range Rover Sport but what I call the 'proper' Range Rover – aka the best car in the world. There is something about a Range Rover that makes you feel better even though the Discovery feels similar to drive. I can't explain this any more than Faraday could explain electricity. It's just a fact.

All you ever think in a Disco is, 'God. I wish I had a Range Rover.' It's like being on holiday in Port Grimaud. You're in the same country as St Tropez. You're on the same bay. You have the same weather and the same food. And you've paid less. But you're not actually in St Tropez and that makes you feel constantly disappointed with your lot.

Of course, you can argue that you bought the Discovery

because you need seven seats. But if you need seven seats, the Volvo XC90 is a more sensible, more practical, easier-to-use and less expensive solution.

So there we are. The Land Rover Discovery 4. It's excellent. Don't buy one.

22 November 2009

Ye gods, it's smashed through the apple cart

Audi A4 Allroad 3.0 TDI Quattro

As we now know, there are one or two flaws in the concept of global capitalism. For example, if you have a suit and a side parting, you can use money that doesn't exist to create money that does, in your own bank account. And you can keep on doing this until the whole world goes completely bankrupt.

At the other end of the scale there are problems, too. For instance, if you are very fat and lazy and you cannot be bothered to get a job, the system will only really care about your plight when you die and you have to be hosed out of your front room because the neighbours are complaining about the smell. 'And who's going to pay for that hosing?' the men with side partings will say.

Still, I believe that the upsides for those of us who are not very lazy but do not have side partings far outweigh the downsides. Let me give you an example. It is now almost impossible to buy a washing machine that is anything less than brilliant.

Or a burger. Because McDonald's and Burger King offer tasty snacks in every town in the world, anyone selling inferior burgers made from stale bread and dead horses will go out of business extremely quickly. So, even at three in the morning, on the outskirts of Leicester or Wakefield, you know for sure that the meal you've just bought will be delicious and nutritious.

Of course, small retailers whine and complain when Tesco moves into the area, because Tesco will nick all their business. Yes, it will, if what you are selling is expensive and rubbish.

That's the core of capitalism. 'Better' will always win the day. And it doesn't matter what form 'better' takes. Better can mean cheaper, more convenient, nicer, prettier, more tasty, more healthy. In some way, you have to be better than the other guy, or your kids will soon be presented with a bill for hosing you out of your sitting room.

Because the bosses of the giant corporations know this, they strive constantly to make what they sell better, and that's brilliant for you and me. It's why we don't get punctures any more – because the tyre makers are constantly striving to be the best. It's why your car never overheats any more – because the people who make radiator hoses are no longer stuck in the seventies, believing they have a God-given right to keep on making radiator hoses, irrespective of how quickly they dissolve.

When was the last time you had a faulty cigarette? When was the last time your plane crashed? When did you last take a strawberry back to the supermarket because it was all covered in slime? It's not governments or best-before dates or health and safety that is doing this; it's capitalism.

And nowhere is the improvement seen more vividly than in the world of motoring.

In the olden days, car makers thought local, and that was a disaster. They really did think at British Leyland that the sun was still shining brightly on the empire and that people in Britain would always buy Rovers and Austins because they were British. We saw the same thing going on in Italy with

Fiat. So what if the workforce had left its sandwiches in one of the doors and wired up the horn to the starter motor by mistake? The customer would be back. And the government would hand over a fat cheque if he wasn't. But then capitalism went global and, all of a sudden, Terry and June could buy a car from Japan that didn't explode every time there was a 'y' in the day. So they did.

Then it got better. BMW worked out that if it made the X5 in America, the car could be sold more cheaply. Volkswagen thought the same about Mexico, and as Britain slithered further into the mire, we started to benefit from this as well. Toyota, Honda and Nissan didn't come here because their executives liked our weather or the golf courses. They came because they were drawn here by capitalism, the need to be cheaper.

We've reached a point where there are only thirteen or so car firms left in the entire world. Nissan is part of Renault. Lamborghinis are Audis. Jags are Indian and a Lotus is a Proton. The competition is savage. Failure is not an option. One bad car can upset the apple cart. Everyone knows this.

So how come the Audi A4 Allroad has slipped though the net?

Audi has been offering a high-riding A6 for many years and it is popular with people who have double-barrelled surnames to match their double-barrelled Purdeys. I can see why. It's as well made as a normal A6 and as luxurious, but you can raise it up on its air springs to reach your shooting peg and cross that tricky little ford at Fuddlecombe End.

Think of it as a Range Rover for people who really don't want a Range Rover.

I was expecting more of the same from the A4. Yes, it sits on springs made from steel rather than air, so the ride height cannot be adjusted. But that's okay, really, and in any case, it's got lots of plastic padding on the underside and around the wheel arches to protect the paintwork if things get tricky.

There is nothing agricultural about the interior, though. It's all standard Audi and bombproof and there's nothing wrong with that. There's nothing wrong with the performance either. The car I drove had a 3-litre turbodiesel engine that could get it from rest to 62mph in 6.4 seconds. That's properly fast for any car, leave alone one on stilts.

But the A4 Allroad does have a couple of problems. First, it doesn't ride well. I recently tried the excellent Skoda Octavia Scout, which also has a raised ride height, and that was smoother and better than its low-riding cousin.

To make matters worse, the steering is diabolical. It feels digital rather than analogue or, to put it another way, sticky. Like the steering column is shaped like a 50p piece.

It was so bad I lent the car to a fellow motoring hack so that he could have a go, and he confirmed it was dreadful. As he left, I noticed a Biro had burst in his back pocket, leaving an inky stain all over the light grey Valcona leather – a £1,605 option. There are other options, too, none of which you'd expect on a car that costs, as standard, a biggish £34,565. I mean, £540 for pearl paint and £735 for electric seats? Do me a favour.

If you have your heart set on a four-wheel-drive Audi and you can't run to a Q7 or an A6 Allroad, do not be tempted by the A4. The small Q5 is much better. But better still is the Skoda Scout. It's hard to think of a single thing the Audi can do that the Scout cannot. And don't worry about the Skoda badge, because this is a capitalistic world and Skoda belongs to Volkswagen these days. Just like Audi.

29 November 2009

It's fresh, it's funky – and it freaks my kids out

Kia Soul 1.6 CRDi Shaker

While we weren't looking, someone with a Saab and a pair of extremely thin spectacles decided that modern houses should be white, made mostly from glass and heated by burning wood chippings or children or anything so they can be sold with that all-important eco tag.

Of course, because most of the walls are glass, they are see-through, which means you must be very careful when walking around in the nude. Not that you will be walking round in the nude much because the modern house, with its lack of soft furnishings – including curtains – can feel rather cold, especially when you run out of children to put in the eco-boiler.

Despite these small drawbacks, I must say that they do look rather good. I have a seaside property and I think often of asking someone with a Saab 9-5 to build a white-pillared, mostly glass extension so that I can sit and look right back at the ramblers and the endlessly shifting sea beyond. I think it would be peaceful.

However, there is a problem. Although many of us deny it, we all think of our houses as investments and we all know that there are only a very few people out there who would wish to live in a see-through house that echoes even if you whisper. This makes the resale tricky.

We also know that while these houses may look good now, they will probably look as out of date as a Randall and

Hopkirk set by the time we are ready to move on. And that won't make the resale tricky; it'll make it impossible.

As a result, we tend to shy away from being too adventurous. We stick with the bricks and the pitched roofs and the carpets because we know that when we start to dribble and the house has to be sold to pay for our lengthy stay in a home, it will be worth that bit more. In short, then, we're building now pretty much what we've been building for the past hundred years or so.

It's a shame. It means that in years to come, historians will have very few examples of modern eco-houses to examine as they try to unravel the mysteries of why the human race suddenly decided that burning children to save the polar bear was somehow the right thing to do.

There's a similar problem with cars. Citroën recently unveiled its DS3, prompting many to wonder what happened to the DS2, and me to wonder why no one will buy such a thing.

It looks fantastic – and that's the problem. It looks fantastic because it looks fresh and exciting and modern, and nothing like anything that has gone before. And that means the nation's dreary people will think, 'Oooh, no. I'd better not buy one of those because it'll be hard to sell and may look dated in a couple of years' time.'

Better to buy a Mini, which harks back to the fifties, or a Fiat 500, which harks back to girls in short skirts and big glasses jumping up and down on Mick Jagger in Carnaby Street in the sixties. Old works. Traditional works. Fresh doesn't. Fresh is scary.

And that brings me very nicely to the door of the Kia Soul, which is extremely fresh and extremely modern and a little bit eco. And, as a result, my children refused to go to school in it.

They said it looked ridiculous and I said it didn't and there was a row and I won and now they are not speaking to me.

I think it looks brilliant, especially if you order it in ivory white because then it looks like the eco-house I dream about building but never will.

First things first, though. It appears in the pictures to be a small urban runaround but in fact it's quite big. That's why you may be disappointed when you open the tailgate and find a boot that is about the same size as a mouse's matchbox. However, this is a boot with a massive basement into which you can put all your things, no matter what those things might be.

Further forward, it's like being in a big 4x4. There's lots of space in the front and the back and you have a high driving position so that you can look down on other motorists in their dreary, wheeled Edwardian semis.

Prices start at £10,775, which is exceptional value for a car this size, but you can spend upwards of £15,000, which is too much. And, anyway, you need to have some money left in the kitty to spend on some of the bewildering but often rather appealing options. Racing stripes. A red gearknob. Plastic wheel arch extensions. A chrome petrol filler cap. Honestly, everything you can think of and a million things you can't are all available, and if I were buying a car like this, I'd have the lot. Except perhaps the 18-inch wheels. Yes, they look good – bigger wheels always do – but they do make the ride a bit choppy. And now we are straying to parts of the Kia Soul that are not so good.

Underneath the funky exterior, you will find the running gear of a Hyundai i20. And that's fine. There is nothing fundamentally wrong with the i20. But, crucially, there is nothing fundamentally right either. It's just some car. And I'm not sure that 'some car' is good enough when you have a red gearknob, racing stripes and a special-edition model called Tempest. Or Shaker. Or Burner. To paraphrase our friends in the 'hood: 'The Soul is writing cheques its underpinnings can't cash.'

And this is especially true if you go for the diesel engine. It's a 1.6 and on paper it all sounds fine. It sounds better than the petrol equivalent, in fact. But, in practice, it is woefully slow. It's one of those cars that is doing only 50mph when you reach the very end of the motorway slip road, which means you have to take your life in your hands when joining the traffic flow.

Worse, on a normal A road there is rarely a straight long enough to get past the lorry, bus or Peugeot that is holding you up. This means you drive along at the speed of the slowest. And that means you will arrive at school after lessons have begun. This made my daughter very happy because no one saw her getting out of it.

It would also make your bank manager very happy because, by being forced to travel at Peugeot speeds, the engine is hardly using any fuel at all. After seventy-two miles, the needle was still reading 'above full'. Only after a motorway run to Birmingham airport did it shift down to just 'full'.

And, sadly, that's the end of my test. I flew to Newcastle and then drove home, which means the poor little Soul is still in the long-term car park at Birmingham, feeling rather unloved and unwanted.

It isn't. I miss it. And that is remarkable, because that makes it the first car from the Pacific rim that is more than 1.2 tons of metal, glass and plastic. The Soul is that as well, but it has a personality. It wormed its way into my heart.

6 December 2009

Just one trip and I was a mellow fellow

Saab 9-3X 2.0 Turbo XWD

As we know, there is a general trend in the echelons of power to push for lower urban speed limits. And, as a result, woolly-headed researchers are delivering all sorts of evidence – or tricks – to suggest that such a move would save 30,000 children's lives, end the war in Afghanistan and cure the common cold.

It is all nonsense. I have tried driving through urban areas at the suggested new limit of 20mph and it is impossible. Gradients, gear ratios and the need to look up from the speedo from time to time mean that often you look back down again to see you've crept up to a jailable twenty-six.

It is, of course, a fact that if you hit a pedestrian while travelling at 20mph, they will be more likely to survive than if you hit them at forty. But what the woolly-headed fools don't seem to realize is that you rarely hit a pedestrian while travelling at the posted limit because most cars have steel discs attached to the wheels: these are called brakes.

You may well be doing forty when you first see the drunk weaving out from behind a bus. But because of these so-called 'brakes', by the time you actually hit him, you will be doing twenty. Which means he will emerge from the experience pretty much undamaged. Especially if he is really drunk and therefore all flobbery.

The fact is that almost everyone who is old enough to drive a car is sufficiently intelligent to work out the best speed for the prevailing conditions. Of course, there are idiots who charge through town centres at ninety, but do you really think they'll slow down just because the limit goes down a bit? I don't.

It's much the same argument with the drink-drive limit. Cutting it by a few milligrams doesn't make drunken drivers more sober. It just makes them more illegal. And that achieves nothing.

As usual, then, my suggestion to those in power is to let people make up their own minds. But this will never happen. Governments cannot accept that we know anything at all. Which is why I've come up with another plan. Gordon Brown should buy Saab – the brand of choice for any Hollywood hero who wishes to look a bit alternative and interesting.

The Swedish car maker is in a spot of bother. It was bought nine years ago by General Motors, which underwent a major restructuring this year because of bankruptcy. Saab, therefore, is very much for sale. Back in the summer it looked like Koenigsegg would be the knight in shining armour, but the deal went wrong. Perhaps because Koenigsegg makes just eighteen cars a year and employs forty-five people and is, therefore, not ideally placed to run a company that employs about 4,500 and makes 93,000 cars a year.

Then Spyker, the Dutch supercar maker, showed a keen interest but that didn't work out either. Now GM is set to begin an orderly shutdown of the plants, though if you buy a Saab from showroom stocks the company will still honour the warranty. After that, no more Saabs. And that could cause 93,000 more accidents every year.

I am not a particularly aggressive driver, but on the way from London to the *Top Gear* test track in Surrey, a journey I make often, there are certain little manoeuvres that can shave valuable minutes off the journey. Hammersmith roundabout, for instance. It's best to hog the inside, which usually moves better, and then cut across to the Barnes exit at the last moment.

And then at the Guildford exit on the A3, I simply go down the empty right-hand side of the otherwise clogged slip road and turn left at the bottom, where it says 'No left turn'. I'm amazed and delighted no one else does this. It saves a lot of time.

In Guildford itself there are special lanes reserved for 'goods vehicles', but if you squint a bit you can convince yourself that what the sign actually says is 'good vehicles'. Which means they can certainly be used by anyone in an AMG Mercedes – i.e., me.

Last week, however, I made the journey in a Saab, and while it is a good vehicle, I decided against using the special lanes. I also queued with everyone else on the slip road. And for Hammersmith, I got into the correct lane before I'd even left Notting Hill.

And when I was stuck behind a 35mph Peugeot, I didn't dream, as I usually do, of putting its driver in an acid bath or beheading him on the internet; I just smiled the smile of a man at peace with himself.

I am not making any of this up. The Saab genuinely changed my whole attitude to driving. It made me calmer. Who knows – if I'd been in an Audi or a BMW that morning, I might have killed someone. It is, therefore, possible that the Saab saved a life, and that is why I urge the British government, if it is really serious about cutting the carnage on Britain's roads, to step in and save the brand from extinction.*

---

* It won't, because it isn't interested in saving lives; just in raising money from speed cameras.

Of course, the strangest thing is that until recently Saab was still banging on about how its cars were based on jet fighters, but this was rubbish. The car I was driving – the 9-3X XWD – is actually based on a Vauxhall Vectra.

Happily, however, the underpinnings are as lost in the mix as a rat in the bottom of a jalfrezi. It, therefore, doesn't feel like a Vauxhall at all.

XWD stands for cross-wheel drive (four-wheel drive to you and me) and that's funny because it's not that long ago that Saab was saying four-wheel drive was nonsense. It once took me to a frozen lake to prove that its front-wheel-drive cars were just as good as Audi's 'pointless' new Quattro.

But, then, this is not a performance-derived system. The 9-3X is a slightly raised estate car in the mould of the excellent Skoda Octavia Scout or the Audi A4 Allroad. This means it can be called upon to do light chores on the farm, which is why it's fitted with an electronic limited-slip diff.

What it can't be called upon to do is provide any excitement, whatsoever. In the olden days, a 2-litre Saab turbo had a bit of pizzazz. This doesn't. It is woefully slow. Amazingly slow. They say it does 0 to 60 in 8.2 seconds, and that's probably true, but to achieve such a thing you'd have to wring its neck, and that flies in the face of what this car's all about.

Part of the problem is the complete lack of any low-down torque. You cruise up to a junction in second, see there's nothing coming and pull out. Then you stall. At anything up to about 15mph, you need to be in first, or you will judder and die. In a normal car this would have driven me nuts. Because it was a Saab, though, I simply smiled and remembered to be in first all the time.

Toys? There aren't any really, apart from a button that turns all the lights on the dashboard off at night. Yes, this is jet fighterish. No, it's not sensible. The rest of the car is, though. There's room for four and a big boot, and the ride is good. But not as good as it is in the much cheaper Skoda.

At £26,000, the 9-3X just about makes sense. It's handsome, with a bit of badge prestige, and if you drive it in thin-framed spectacles and a black polo neck, people will think you are an architect. But fit it with sat nav, electric seats and electric mirrors and that jumps up to nearly £30,000. That's way, way too much.

A conclusion is needed, then. Hmmm. I won't miss driving Saabs very much. But I will miss the idea that other people are driving them when my children are cycling into town and crossing the road.

20 December 2009

Oh yes, this is why Wakefield trumps Dubai

Aston Martin DBS Volante

With its combination of V10 Lamborghini power, German quality, sublime handling and ease of use, the Audi R8 V10 is an extraordinarily good car. I drove one back in the summer and reckoned that in every measurable way, it was the best car in the world.

It's not as complete, obviously, as a Bugatti Veyron, and it's not as hot-headed as a Lamborghini Gallardo. But if you take price, quality, fire, speed, looks, economy, grip and handling into account, it scores an almost consistent row of tens.

There's a problem, though. When reviewing a car I look for Jedward rather than that toothy midget that ultimately won *The X Factor*. I look for the certain special something that makes oysters wonderful and prawns less so. And that's what the Audi's missing; something you can't imagine or explain. I suppose, in human terms, what it's missing is a soul

It's a bit like Dubai. Yes, there is a sea and sand, and providing you don't play hide the sausage with someone's else's wife, you will have a nice time. And yet I'd rather go on holiday in Wakefield. Why? Dunno. Can't explain it. Call it chemistry, if you like, but I just would.

And this brings me on to an interesting question. Can you truly score a row of perfect tens and emerge from the effort with any personality at all? I give you, by way of reference

points, Steve 'interesting' Davis and Michael Schumacher. I
give you, too, Roger Federer. I like the look of the guy and I
like his style, but can you imagine him climbing under the
dinner table and tying someone's shoelaces together? Can
you imagine him drunk? In short, then, to be good, do you
have to be boring? The answer, of course, is no. John McEnroe wasn't boring. James Hunt wasn't boring. And yes, I could
imagine George Best drunk, easily.

This is because they had a gift. Sure, they worked hard to
reach the top of their game, but plainly they didn't have to
exorcise every human trait in order to get there.

And that's what's gone wrong with the R8. It was designed
by people who are not naturally given to making supercars.
They had to work harder than those who are. They had to
have more meetings, set up more committees, and work
longer into the night to overcome their natural tendency to
give it a diesel engine and two back seats.

You do not see this with a Rolls-Royce Phantom. This
scores just as many perfect tens as the R8, and yet it has a
soul as well. It feels like it was born good, not nurtured over
a billion cups of committee-room coffee to be that way.

I'm not sure we will see such effortlessness from the
new Rolls-Royce Ghost, which I fear is a BMW trying to be
English – a bit like Michael Caine in *The Eagle has Landed*. I'm
frightened it will all end badly, but I will reserve judgement
until I have driven one. Or, more properly, been driven in
one to the ballet.

We do see it, however, in the Mazda MX-5, the new Ford
Fiesta, the BMW M3, the Range Rover TDV8 and the Ferrari 430. All of these cars do what they are supposed to do
perfectly. But they have that certain something as well. They
have a soul.

But the car that pulls off the trick better than all the others is the Aston Martin DBS Volante.

When I first encountered the hard-top version of this car, I was a bit disappointed. Aston Martin was maintaining that it had made an all-new car, but you didn't need an X-ray machine to see it had done no such thing. The DBS, as plain as day, was a DB9 with some sill extensions and a bit more power.

Certainly, I could see no reason for the huge price differential between a 6-litre V10 DB9, which today costs £116,908, and a DBS, which looked exactly the same and had exactly the same engine, and today costs £166,872.

But then I drove it and everything became clear. The DBS was, in fact, a DB9 where every little detail was about 10 per cent better. The brakes, the responses, the steering, everything. They were sharpened up. Shaved. Improved. This was a Taste the Difference Aston Martin.

And then they cut the roof off. Normally, this spells disaster because any car designed to be a coupé and then converted to be a convertible goes all flobbery and soft. So, you're buying something that was designed to be a driver's machine. And then ruined. It's why I always laugh at people in drop-top Porsche 911s.

However, if there is any weakening of the structure in a DBS Volante, I'm damned if I can find it. I've driven this car a lot. From Oxfordshire to London. Around the Earls Court arena. Through Romania. Over mountain passes. And round Silverstone. And not once did it ever shimmy or shake. It's a soft-top rock.

In terms of outright speed, it's epic. But as I discovered in a flat-out charge down the motorway in Romania, a Ferrari

California is faster. This is because it has a seamless flappy paddle gearshifter. It was irritating to reach the Aston's red line and know I'd lose a yard or two while swapping cogs. But frankly, I'd trade that yard or two for the feel of power and control you get from a stick shift allied to a big V12.

And, anyway, put the two cars on a track or a mountain pass and there is no way in hell the Ferrari can pull away. The heavier, thumping Aston just clings on to its rear end until eventually the California has to pull in for new tyres. Weirdly, the Aston, which sits on exactly the same sort of rubber, can go much, much further between trips to Kwik-Fit.

What really settles it, though, is not the Ferrari's appetite for rubber. It's the looks. The California is nice. But the Aston is a sensation. A drop-head DB9 looks like it's got a slipped disc, like it's snapped in the middle, but the DBS, with its raised rump, is just perfect. I know of no better-looking car in production today.

Inside, I could gripe a bit if I wanted to. The sat nav is terrible, the buttons are hard to read and, oh, how I wish it didn't say 'Power. Beauty. Soul' every time you turn it on.

Mind you, at least this is all true. There is power. There is beauty. And there is soul. When you switch on the new four-door Rapide it says 'Pure Aston Martin'. Which is, of course, nonsense. Because it's made in Austria.

Before we leave the interior, I suppose we should pause to laugh at the microscopic rear seats, fitted only so the car can be sold in America as a four-seater – it isn't – but then really we have to get back to the way this thing drives.

What's most astonishing of all is the way it's so utterly sublime on a track – both the Stig and Tiff Needell say it's the best driver's car of them all – but when you are just driving along, it is so docile and quiet. It really is, then, the absolutely perfect grand tourer.

And yet, it's so much more than that. It's the absolutely perfect car.

27 December 2009